Essay Index

The Frontier Re-examined

The Frontier

UNIVERSITY OF ILLINOIS PRESS, URBANA • CHICAGO • LONDON, 1967

Re-examined

edited by John Francis McDermott

Essay Index

Foreword

Who settled the frontier? Who opened and developed the western wilderness? Why did these people leave the civilization into which they had been born? What was their background? Under what conditions did they remove to the frontier? How did they live? What did they do? What did they think?

These are ever interesting questions, the answers to which are not yet satisfactory. Historians have worked out the diplomatic and military history of the movement westward from the Atlantic. They have outlined the political growth of the expanding nation. They have provided a framework, but is the picture they have drawn a sketch of the real frontier world?

History is the story of a nation, that is, of people. It is more than broad outlines, it is more than the search for governing principles, it is more than intriguing theories, it is more than alluring generalizations and abstract conclusions. One cannot rightly come to conclusions about the frontier until one knows imtimately the kind of people found there, until he has examined closely their conditions of life and modes of living and thought, until he has investigated all the aspects of social and cultural history. One is tempted to look for patterns of development, for the discovery of a pattern will simplify one's whole approach—and does often simplify it to the point where he is led to form a hypothesis which "explains" the whole process and may presently so appeal to others as to become recognized as a "law" of historical development. And here lies danger, for the fascinating pursuit of a theory leads to distortion even when no distortion was intended. The theorist finds what he looks for and ceases to see that which does not confirm his theory.

The great example of this process in twentieth-century studies of American history is Frederick Turner Jackson, perhaps the most influential historian of the frontier we have produced. His accomplishment in print was small—after more than thirty years of active professional life he was able in 1920 to gather up for a book only thirteen essays, which had first been delivered as addresses at learned meetings. In 1927 he went out to the Henry E. Huntington Library in California as a research associate to write the book he had long been talking about, but he died a few years later before he had completed more than three or four chapters. Yet though he left few written works, he had a tremendous influence. Enthusiastic scholars were stirred by his grand generalizations and his exciting conclusions, and from his stimulating concepts sprang such extensive, varied, and vigorously pursued research into many phases of frontier history that he has thus tremendously enriched our knowledge of early days.

Ironically, but not unexpectedly, in a reverse manner he accomplished much more, for there were historians who found him too sweeping in his generalizations, too inclined to see only what he looked for, too absolute in denying other evidence and influences that might contradict his vision of the American as a European remade into a new man by the magic of the frontier. From this opposition, which was certainly rising at the time of Turner's death, came new research into the continuity of old ideas and old culture, into local records and foreign archives, which has resulted in a fuller knowledge and a more reasonably balanced view of the character of the frontier.

I hope that some of my associates in this volume will forgive me for expressing in the foreword an attitude toward a notable scholar which they do not share. It was not our intention at the conference on the frontier at which these papers were presented to attack Turner. Rather, it was to look once again at the frontier, but with our own eyes, not Turner's. For some of us this has led to a re-examination of Turner's statements, for others to investigate aspects of life on the frontier which had not been considered by Turner. In this small group we have not undertaken a complete survey of the subject, we have not thought of ourselves as members of a symposium who must arrive at some generally accepted conclusions, we are not laying down laws or establishing general principles.

We have adopted no thesis. We have simply each contributed a study of some phase of frontier history which had particularly interested the individual investigator. We write neither as Turnerians nor anti-Turnerians but as students continuing to be curious about the world of the frontier, and we hope that statements of value will emerge from these papers that will contribute to a fuller understanding of frontier life and will lead still others to further research.

In the papers of this volume, then, we have undertaken a number of tasks. I myself have chosen to emphasize two points which Turner waved aside. In my reading of the evidence the earliest settlers of the middle western frontier did carry their culture with them. So, too, we owe the economic and social development of that frontier not to a trickle or a flood of backwoodsmen but to the men of enterprise who went out in the first wave and established the urban centers on which development was necessarily based.

Donald Jackson has been interested in Spanish reactions to American intrusion in the Southwest resulting from the Louisiana Purchase. Merrill J. Mattes has examined the Missouri River towns as jumping-off places for the movement farther west. Oscar O. Winther has written about transportation as a factor in frontier development. Herman Friis has concerned himself with the cartographic image of the trans-Mississippi West resulting from the

U.S. government's scientific explorations. Ralph E. Morrow has analyzed the role of religion in the West following the Great Revival in the early 1800's. John C. Ewers has studied pictorial truth and falsehood in the documentary art of the frontier, particularly in the depiction of the Indian. Oliver W. Holmes has written of the significance of territorial records.

Two aspects of the fur trade have been scrutinized by Richard E. Oglesby and Preston Holder: the first, in a study of the fur trader as businessman, concentrated on the fur trade in St. Louis between 1820 and 1823; the second describes the effect of the fur trade on the Indian's way of life. Finally, three papers deal with literary treatments of the frontier: Jules Zanger discusses the development of frontiersman into hero in nineteenth-century fiction; George R. Brooks reports on the popularity of frontier fiction in Germany; and Joe B. Frantz reviews the literature of the American cowboy in an attempt to discover a declaration of his philosophy.

These papers were first presented at a conference on the frontier sponsored by Southern Illinois University and held on the Edwardsville campus November 11-12, 1965.

I wish to thank my colleagues John C. Abbott, Head Librarian, Gerald J. T. Runkle, Head (now Dean) of the Humanities Division, Gordon R. Wood, then Chairman of the English Faculty, and Allan J. McCurry, Chairman of the History Faculty, who served as chairmen of the four sessions meeting on campus. Robert William MacVicar, Vice President for Academic Affairs, was kind enough to preside at the dinner and evening session which closed the conference. My colleagues and I are grateful to Southern Illinois University not merely for being host to the conference but for making possible the publication of the papers. My wife, Mary Stephanie McDermott, was, as always, very helpful indeed in many details of the arrangements for the conference.

Finally, a word of warm thanks to my friends who shared this round-table and to Donald Jackson and Mrs. Elizabeth Dulany, Editor and Assistant Editor of the University of Illinois Press, for their patience and forbearance while this volume has been in press.

JOHN FRANCIS MCDERMOTT

Southern Illinois University, Edwardsville
St. Louis   15 April 1966

Contents

The
Frontier
Re-examined

JOHN FRANCIS MC DERMOTT

SOUTHERN ILLINOIS UNIVERSITY, EDWARDSVILLE

More than seventy years ago Frederick Jackson Turner focused the attention of American historians on the character and the significance of the frontier—and today we are still asking for an adequate account of the opening of the West and a true report of life on the frontier.

To read Turner and his followers is to picture a phalanx of ax bearers advancing into the wilderness, pushing back the forest boundary, opening the way for civilization. "These slashers of the forest, these self-sufficing pioneers," wrote Turner, "living scattered and apart, had at first small interest in town life or a share in the markets." Because they had turned their "attention to the great task of subduing [the lands of the West] to the purposes of civilization . . . art, literature, refinement, scientific administration all had to give way to this Titanic labor." Being "remote from the opportunity for systematic education, substituting a log hut in the forest-clearing for the social comforts of the town," the pioneers "suffered hardships and privations and reverted in many ways to primitive conditions of life" until the moment came when they created a new world" in a large degree free from European precedents and forces."[1]

Turner saw the wilderness overmastering the colonist.

It finds him a European in dress, industries, tools, modes of travel, and thought. . . . It strips off the garments of civilization and arrays him in the hunting shirt and the moccasin. It puts him in the log cabin of the Cherokee and Iroquois and runs an Indian palisade around him. Before long he has gone to planting Indian corn and plowing with a sharp stick; he shouts the war cry and takes the scalp in orthodox Indian fashion. In short, at the

[1] Frederick Jackson Turner, *The Frontier in American History* (New York, 1920), 342, 211, 209-210.

frontier the environment is at first too strong for the man. He must accept the conditions which it furnishes, or perish, and so he fits himself into the Indian clearings and follows the Indian trails. Little by little he transforms the wilderness. . . .[2]

The Mississippi River region Turner offered as a "scene of typical frontier settlements." The flow of population "in all the western settlements" (Turner quoted John Mason Peck's *New Guide to the West*, published in 1837) had been in three waves. First comes the pioneer who with "a horse, cow, and one or two breeders of swine . . . strikes into the woods with his family, and becomes the founder of a new county, or perhaps state. He builds his cabin, gathers around him a few other families of similar tastes and habits, and occupies until the range is somewhat subdued . . . and he lacks elbow room. . . . [Then] he 'breaks for the high timber,' 'clears out for the New Purchase,' or migrates to Arkansas or Texas, to work the same process over." Emigrants of the succeeding class develop farms, build more substantial houses, "occasionally plant orchards, build mills, school-houses, court-houses, etc., and exhibit the picture and forms of plain, frugal, civilized life." In the third wave come the "men of capital and enterprise. . . . The small village rises to a spacious town or city. . . . Broadcloths, silks, leghorns, crapes, and all the refinements, luxuries, elegancies, frivolities, and fashions are in vogue."[3]

Actually, in the Ohio valley and in the central Mississippi valley this was not so. It was the men of capital and enterprise who came first. The cities arose before the phalanx of ax bearers spread over the land. That these settlements at Marietta, Cincinnati, Louisville, Frankfort, Lexington, St. Louis were very small is beside the point: from the beginning they functioned as cities. The focus was on business. Daniel Boone was not the restless, romantic hero pictured so graphically by Timothy Flint "on foot and alone, with no companion but his dog, and no friend but his rifle, making his way over trackless and unnamed mountains and immeasurable forests until he explores the flowering wilderness of Kentucky"[4]—he was the agent of a land company planning a real estate development. He did not eventually leave Kentucky because he lacked elbow room but because through business ignorance he lost the stake in life he had acquired as land agent. Undeniably important as the rural

[2] *Ibid.,* 4.
[3] *Ibid.,* 7, 19-21.
[4] Timothy Flint, *The First White Man of the West, or, The Life and Exploits of Col. Dan'l Boone* (Cincinnati, 1854), 8-9.

development of the West was, Richard C. Wade has concluded in *The Urban Frontier,* "the cities represented the more aggressive and dynamic force. By spreading their economic power over the entire section, by bringing the fruits of civilization across the mountains, and by insinuating their ways over the countryside, they speeded up the transformation of the West from a gloomy wilderness to a richly diversified region."[5] This is far from the picture that Turner painted.

In the present brief reconsideration of the midwestern frontier I wish to stress four basic matters of which Turner was ignorant or which he ignored: (1) the prime importance of business (which by that very fact is itself a denial of the isolation that Turner declared characteristic of the frontier), (2) the enjoyment of the amenities of life on the very threshold of the savage world, (3) the dominating types of men on the frontier, and (4) the existence of class distinction. All of these warrant detailed study.

In the beginning were the cities. They were the "spearheads of the frontier," the "centers of economic activity for the whole region, the focusses of cultural life, and the scenes of great social change."[6] If the frontier is to be defined as the line where savagery and civilization meet,[7] the towns of the early West were advance posts set up far beyond the front line of population. They were islands of civilization deep in the wilderness on which all the country around depended, and they must be viewed as frontier phenomena until the line of settlement has caught up with and passed them. St. Louis, for instance, must be held a frontier town at least until, in the decade following the War of 1812, its back country (the central counties of Missouri) was rapidly filling up around *its* spearheading towns.

Let me use St. Louis for an example. Though not the first town to be established in the central portion of the Mississippi valley, it quickly came to be the most significant—the control point for the fur trade and the lead trade, the emporium and jobbing and credit center for all the country to the north and the west, the central terminal for transportation in the vast valley. St. Louis was no accident; it was not a chance accumulation of restless souls pushing on just a bit farther into the wilderness, hoping to find a freedom or a security as yet undiscovered. The establishment of St. Louis was the result of specific commercial enterprise. Merchants of New Orleans, expecting to exploit a rich, undevel-

[5] Richard C. Wade, *The Urban Frontier* (Cambridge, Mass., 1959), 341-342.
[6] *Ibid.,* 1.
[7] Turner, *The Frontier in American History,* 3.

oped fur trade, formed a company, obtained a monopoly grant on the upper Mississippi and Missouri rivers, and dispatched one of the partners to build a trading post at the proper control point.

This project was no little operation. Pierre de Laclède took upriver a cargo so large that in Ste. Genevieve he could not find a house big enough to store one quarter of it for the winter. Although his immediate business was to build his station and to open trade in his territory through the outfitting of *marchands voyageurs,* he was fully aware that the location he picked had "all the advantages that one could desire to found a settlement which might become very considerable hereafter." Returning to Fort Chartres after choosing the site of St. Louis in December, 1764, he told the French officers of the garrison "that he had found a situation where he was going to found a settlement, which might become, hereafter, one of the finest cities of America—so many advantages were embraced in its site, by its locality and its central position, for forming settlements." His young assistant, Auguste Chouteau, was sent ahead in February, 1764, to supervise the clearing of the spot and to prepare for building. In April Laclède went over from Fort Chartres and "occupied himself with his settlement, fixed the place where he wished to build his house, laid out a plan of the village he wished to found (and he named it Saint Louis, in honor of Louis XV . . .) and ordered me [Chouteau] to follow the plan exactly. . . ."[8]

Laclède knew what he was doing. Within a year forty families were settled in his village. In November, 1765, Captain St. Ange, after surrendering Fort Chartres to the British, took his troops to St. Louis and made it the seat of government for the western part of the Illinois country (later to be known as Upper Louisiana) as well as the military headquarters. The town was thus the political, military, and commercial capital, the transportation center of a region stretching along the west bank of the Mississippi from Arkansas to Canada and reaching westward to the Rockies. And though at the time of the transfer of Louisiana to the United States four decades later it still had fewer than 700 white inhabitants—men, women, and children—it was in every sense the cultural and business center of a vast countryside. The comfort and well-being of all Upper Louisiana depended on its commercial enterprise.

I have used large terms for a very small place but let us look more

[8] Quotations in this paragraph are from Auguste Chouteau's "Narrative of the Settlement of St. Louis," in John Francis McDermott, ed., *The Early Histories of St. Louis* (St. Louis, 1952), 48, 49.

closely. Here is an outpost deep in the wilderness—by river (the only road) 1,200 miles from town, as the people of St. Louis called New Orleans. It takes three months of poling and rowing and sailing and cordelling to get a boatload of supplies up the river. The villagers live in log houses; they sometimes wear deerskin clothing. Painted Indians stalk through the dusty streets. Little patches of farm lie exposed on the prairie. Laborious trips must be made a thousand miles farther up the rivers to the north and west to earn a living in hazardous trade with the savages of the forest and the plain. To live in such a rough, hard frontier settlement must be to grub for life cut off from all the comforts and the culture of civilization, a very illustration of the Turner theory of the "return to primitive conditions on a continually advancing frontier line."

But St. Louis did not fill the Turnerian bill. Its log houses were not the hastily thrown-up shelters of squatters but substantial buildings of timbers hewn eight or ten inches square with the spaces between the uprights solidly filled with plaster and the whole neatly whitewashed so that from a distance the town looked like a hillside of stone dwellings. Most of the houses were two- or three- or four-room structures of this sort, but more than thirty of them were of stone. The "rude hut," as some writer once referred to it, built for Pierre de Laclède at the founding of the town, was a stone building of only five rooms, but it measured twenty-three by sixty feet and had both full cellar and garret. Bought by Auguste Chouteau in 1789, a decade after Laclède's death, it was almost entirely rebuilt into a two-and-a-half-story house with stone walls thirty inches thick, a wide portico or gallery surrounding it, and the black walnut floors of the rooms "polished so finely that they reflected like a mirror," as one visitor to the house recalled. The home of Auguste's younger brother Pierre measured forty-five by sixty-five feet, stood two and a half stories high, had storehouses, summer kitchen, slave quarters, and stables of stone, all within a block of ground. When his house and its contents were destroyed by fire in 1805, Pierre Chouteau estimated his loss at $30,000. And the Chouteau brothers were not the only St. Louisans to have residences like these in the colonial days.

In such houses dinners were given and balls were held that sometimes cost from $400 to $600. Considering the low cost of living and the absence of income taxes these were appreciable sums of money. There were silks and satins aplenty for suitable occasions and some tables could be well set even in this wilderness. Silvestre Labbadie, a brother-in-law of the Chouteaus, at his death in 1794 left silver service worth nearly 4,000 livres; some idea of its extent may be formed when we note that twenty-nine place settings accounted for only one-fifth of the total value, candlesticks, bowls, a chocolate pot, and other sterling pieces constituting the remainder. Pierre Chouteau in 1793 possessed fifteen *couverts* of silver. The inventory of the Cerré estate in 1802 listed more than 700 piastres (dollars) worth of silver.[9]

It is not to be wondered at, then, that Captain Amos Stoddard, the first American commandant, should write home to his mother in Connecticut that the people of St. Louis "live in a style equal to those in the large sea-port towns." Poor Stoddard, having been lavishly entertained by the Spanish lieutenant governor, Charles de Hault de Lassus, as well as by the principal citizens, politely entertained in his turn; his party cost him $622.75 (he borrowed $400 from Pierre Chouteau to pay his bills). It was possibly to this party that William Clark came down from Wood River with Meriwether Lewis on April 7, 1804. On arrival in town he "Dressed & Dined with Capt. Stoddard & about 50 Gentlemen, A Ball succeeded, which lasted untill 9 oClock on Sunday."[10] William Henry Harrison, Governor of Indiana Territory (to which St. Louis belonged at the moment), was likewise impressed by his first view, in the autumn of 1804, of this outpost in the wilderness. Many of the houses, he found, were "large & convenient. . . . Some of the Inhabitants are very rich   Most of them in easy circumstances—The ladies are remarkably handsome genteel & well bred & the Society may be considered altogether as a polished one. A few of the Citizens live in a style of elegance scarcely inferior to those of the first rank in Philadelphia or New York." This was life on the raw "confines of the wilderness."

Schools were simple and few, but Captain Stoddard had been pleasantly surprised to find "no want of education" among St. Louisans. Many, of course, were illiterate, but twenty or thirty of the leading citizens had come from solid middle-class French families. Sons of merchants and professional men, they had had a good share of schooling. In turn they looked to the education of their sons. Silvestre Labbadie, Jr., was at school in France when his father died in 1794. Bernard Pratte

[9] The uniform prescribed by Lieutenant Governor de Leyba in 1779 for a newly organized cavalry company of militia—"coat and breeches, red; cuffs, waistcoat, lapel and collar, blue; buttons, gilt"—is indicative of interest in style at this frontier post. Lawrence Kinnaird, ed., *Spain in the Mississippi Valley* (Washington, D.C., 1949), I, 348.

[10] Ernest S. Osgood, *The Field Notes of Captain William Clark, 1803-1805* (New Haven, 1964), 30.

and some of the sons of Auguste Chouteau were sent to seminaries in Canada. Other boys were sent to New Orleans. Auguste Pierre Chouteau and Charles Gratiot, both born in St. Louis, had been sufficiently schooled to be qualified for appointment in 1804 to the U.S. Military Academy at West Point; Gratiot, remaining in the service, eventually rose to be chief of the Corps of Engineers.

There was no dearth of books in colonial St. Louis. Fifty or sixty households established before 1804 owned among them in those early years 2,000 or 3,000 books. Hector St. John de Crèvecoeur, who was to become famous for his *Letters from an American Farmer,* visiting the three-year-old village in 1767, was interested to find books in this remote settlement on the western edge of the world. Distance and difficulty put no stop to the importing of books: in the cargo that Laclède brought from New Orleans in 1778 was a twelve-volume history of the Roman emperors.

One of the earliest visitors to St. Louis, British Captain Harry Gordon (1766), observed that Laclède had been "very well educated." Evidence enough is found in the collection of more than 200 volumes that he left at his death in 1778. More than half of these were "useful" works on hydraulic engineering, the care of horses, the military code, agriculture, business law, finance, taxes, the kitchen garden, medicine. Among the others were a French-English grammar, the dictionary of the French Academy, and twenty-four volumes in Spanish. Surely it is exciting to know that in this little town of his Laclède had on his shelf Benjamin Franklin on electricity, Bacon's *Essays,* Locke *On the Human Understanding,* and the philosophy of Descartes, that deep into this wilderness he had brought Rousseau's *Nouvelle Héloïse* and *Contrat social,* works published since he had left France.

In one house or another in this frontier town could be found almost any classical author, any standard French author, and more than a few English and Spanish writers. *Tom Jones, Gil Blas, Don Quixote, Robinson Crusoe,* the plays of Racine, Cook's *Voyages,* the *Mémoires* of the Cardinal de Retz, the *Confessions* of St. Augustine, the works of Ovid. Most enlightening, perhaps, was the prevalence of the French freethinkers of the eighteenth century. John Mason Peck was to observe in 1818 that, though the French of St. Louis were nominally Catholics, "every Frenchman, with whom I formed an acquaintance, of any intelligence and influence, was of the school of French liberalists—an infidel to all Bible Christianity . . . the casual correspondence held with France, where infidelity was demolishing the thrones of political and religious despotism, and tearing up the foundations of superstition, led them to regard all religion as priestcraft, necessary perhaps for the ignorant, superstitious, and vicious, but wholly unnecessary for a gentleman —a philosopher." Evidence of these ties with the writers of the Enlightenment are found from the first years of the town. Montesquieu's *Spirit of the Laws* was a common favorite, but his other works were known too. Diderot, Buffon, Mably, Mirabeau were in the colonial libraries. And more widely represented than any others were the works of Rousseau and Voltaire. So independent in their thinking were these frontier French that one finds a quarter of the books in the library of Auguste Chouteau on the Catholic Church's index of prohibited books.

I have attempted to give in brief some idea of the development of business and the state of culture in St. Louis before 1804, when it was still quite a small place a thousand miles from anywhere, truly a frontier spot.[11] Rough, shiftless, indolent, illiterate, uneducated, dull-witted people lived there certainly—misfits and roughnecks—half-civilized woodsmen and boatmen and peasants. But there were also men of education, breeding, and enterprise who dominated the town and the region, who furnished the credit and the business drive which sustained Upper Louisiana. Settlers came into the surrounding countryside and cleared farms here, as elsewhere, because they had a town ready to supply them and to provide a market for their produce. The town existed first, but of St. Louis or of other towns in the Ohio or the Mississippi valleys Turner had hardly a word to say.

It is the close study of local records in recent years that has shown that St. Louis was not the crude backwoods settlement typically associated with the frontier in the minds of many. This experience suggests that intimate study of other frontier towns may produce equally interesting results. The early attempts at settling the Boon's Lick country in central and western Missouri had been thwarted by Indian troubles in the War of 1812, but in 1816-17 the town of Franklin was laid out and by 1819 1,000 persons were living there. It became the emporium for a rapidly filling country as well as the last outfitting place for the Santa Fe trade. In 1819 it had a newspaper, the third established in Missouri. In 1820 a traveler passing through noted that his landlord's daughter amused herself (perhaps self-consciously) by playing on the piano from time to time through the day. Silks and satins and books were in stock in

[11] For further details consult John Francis McDermott, *Private Libraries in Colonial Saint Louis* (Baltimore, 1938), and Charles E. Peterson, *Colonial Saint Louis: Building a Creole Capital* (St. Louis, 1949).

the stores. Franklin flourished for a decade only, for the Missouri River ate the town away, but it should be studied as a representative new town on the very edge of civilization.[12] So, too, should Boonville, which soon overtook Franklin. The early history of Lexington and St. Joseph farther up the Missouri will also show how important were these centers of business in the development of the frontier, how spontaneously a culture grew, and how shaky is any theory of the significance and character of the frontier that ignores them.

The towns on the Mississippi will reward close scrutiny. Keokuk at the rapids above the Des Moines was a tiny, disreputable, and nameless place until after the titles to the lands of the "halfbreed tract" were cleared; the town founded in 1837 swiftly grew into an amazing little city. Except in the most general way we still do not know what Hannibal was like in its earliest years. Alton, Quincy, Burlington, Davenport —studies of river towns such as these will produce a new understanding of the early West, will give us facts to supplant hypotheses. And they will all illustrate the prime importance of commercial enterprise in the development of the frontier.

When we really know the facts of life in these towns in their early years, when we know the economic, cultural, and intellectual conditions existing and the cultural and commercial relations between town and countryside, then we can begin to speak with some assurance of the frontier and its character and influence.

But it is not the towns alone that must be examined. To know the frontier we must re-examine the pioneer—or at least the stock idea of the pioneer, the frontiersman. Support enough can be found for the common concept of the Turnerian frontiersman but it does not tell the whole story about the men of the frontier.

We can go on a walking tour into the Ozarks with Henry Rowe Schoolcraft in 1818 and look in at the last cabin to be found on a west tributary of the White River:

... the first object worthy of remark which presented itself on emerging from the forest, was the innumerable quantity of deer, bear, and other skins, which had been from time to time stretched out, and hung up to dry on poles and on trees around the house. These trophies of skill and prowess in the chace were regarded with great complacency by our conductor as we passed among them, and he told us, that the house we were about to visit, belonged to a person named Wells, who was a forehanded man for these parts, and a great hunter. He had several acres of ground in a state of cultivation, and a substan-

[12] For a sketch of Franklin see John Francis McDermott, *George Caleb Bingham, River Portraitist* (Norman, 1959), 4-15.

tial new built log-house, consisting of one room, which had been lately exchanged for one less calculated to accommodate a growing family. Its interior would disappoint any person who has never had an opportunity of witnessing the abode of man beyond the pale of the civilized world. Nothing could be more remote from the ideas we have attached to domestic comfort, order, neatness, or conveniency, without allusion to cleanliness, order, and the concomitant train of household attributes, which make up the sum of human felicity in refined society.

The dress of the children attracted our attention. The boys were clothed in a particular kind of garment made of deerskin, which served the double purpose of shirt and jacket. The girls had buckskin frocks, which it was evident, by the careless manner in which they were clothed, were intended to combine the utility both of linen and calico, and all were abundantly greasy and dirty. Around the walls of the room hung the horns of deer and buffaloe, rifles, shot pouches, leather coats, dried meat, and other articles, composing the wardrobe, smoke house, and magazine of our host and family, while the floor displayed great evidence of his own skill in the fabrication of household furniture. A dressed deerskin, served up much in the shape the animal originally possessed, and filled with bear's oil, and another filled with wild honey hanging on opposite sides of the fire-place, were too conspicuous to escape observation. . . . After supper we made many inquiries respecting the region we were in . . . topics upon which [our host] readily gave us information. He was even anxious to show that he knew something of civilized society . . . [and] told us that he . . . lived within *a hundred miles of a justice of the peace,* and by way of proving this, showed us a summons he had himself lately received. He desired us to read it (a thing neither himself nor any member of his family could do). . . . I tried to engage our hostess and her daughter in small talk, such as passes current in every social corner; but . . . they could only talk of bears, hunting, and the like. The rude pursuits, and the coarse enjoyments of the hunter state, were all they knew.

Among such people, Schoolcraft noted later in his account, "in manners, morals, customs, dress, contempt of labour and hospitality, the state of society is not essentially different from that which exists among the savages. Schools, religion, and learning are alike unknown . . . a man's reputation is measured by his skill as a marksman, his agility and strength, his boldness and dexterity in killing game, and his patient endurance and contempt of the hardships of the hunter's life."[13]

These are Turner's first-wave frontiersmen, but I suggest that there is no evidence that they have "returned to primitive conditions"; rather, they give strong evidence that they have never been at any higher level than they here exhibit.

If all men of the frontier had been like these, the frontier would

[13] The Schoolcraft quotations are from his *Tour into the Interior of Missouri in the Years 1818 and 1819* (London, 1821), entries for Nov. 30 and Dec. 8, 1818.

never have been conquered, the West would never have been pioneered. The brothers Auguste and Pierre Chouteau were first-wave pioneers and men of the frontier, but their business not only took them far up the Missouri and down into the Southwest, it kept them in close contact with Montreal and Philadelphia and New Orleans. Dr. Antoine Saugrain, Paris-born physician and scientist, who loved to read the French dramatists, had adventures enough in Louisiana, on the Ohio River, and in Missouri between 1783 and 1820 to warrant a place on the role of pioneers. Manuel Lisa, with whom Henry Marie Bracken-ridge read *Don Quixote* on a trading voyage up the Missouri in 1811, William Ashley, who led his own fur-hunting parties into the mountains, Kenneth McKenzie, bourgeois of Fort Union, called "King of the Upper Missouri," Charles Gratiot, who in the 1790's traveled from St. Louis to New York, Montreal, London, and the Continent in an attempt to establish an international fur trade cartel—these were men of the frontier quite as much as any of the mountain men who have of late become so romantically popular. Certainly they contributed far more to the development of the West that the rough illiterates, the "reckless breed," who provide historians today with "color."

General Thomas A. Smith was not born in Missouri but, following his resignation from the U.S. Army, he became one of the first citizens of Franklin; in 1819 he had a two-story brick mansion in that new little city and a short time later opened a showplace farm in Saline County. Nathaniel B. Tucker, lawyer and litterateur, was one of his neighbors. Another was John Hardeman, a lawyer by training but a botanist by preference, "fond of books, of poetry, of polite literature, of philosophy, and the study of nature," a deist who "liked to live among his books and flowers." These are all representative of the men of the new country, their accomplishments somewhat greater than those of Mike Fink or John Colter or Old Bill Williams.

Another subject that calls for study is class distinction. Turner and other historians have spoken with easy assurance of a frontier democracy where all men were equal, but on the frontier as elsewhere we will find that some were more equal than others. Opportunity to advance was greater in the new country. Many a poor man became comfortably well-to-do through his own efforts. Ability, energy, intelligence could make a man one of the leaders of his community, give him social importance. But the point is that there was always an awareness of social distinctions. This was clearly evident in the eagerness of the American democrat for titles which announced one's own attainments and position to the world and when applied to friends called attention to the high tone of the associations of a man who could greet acquaintances as "Judge" or "General" or "Governor."

This class stratification was noticeable from the beginning. No doubt at all that in tiny colonial St. Louis everyone was on easy speaking terms with everyone else, but official documents underscored class distinction when one man was referred to as *le sieur Tel-et-Tel* and another was merely *le nommé Tel*. One cannot imagine a hunter or workman or petty trader traveling to the Indians addressing Laclède except as Monsieur de Laclède or calling the Chouteaus or Labbadie or Gratiot or Papin by their given names. Their lives may all have been intimately intertwined, but there was still a distinction of class to be recognized and not to be intruded upon.

This was as true out in the wild country as well; the mountains were no more egalitarian than the towns. A young scholar some fifteen years ago was scornful of what he thought was snobbishness on the part of Washington Irving when in *Astoria* he would refer to one man on that hazardous enterprise as "Mister" and would mention another by his surname only or by a nickname. Had this young man been better read in contemporary diaries and letters he would have seen that these distinctions of class were commonplace on the frontier.

At the great trading posts all men might eat in the common room, but, as in the great hall of the medieval castle, some were above the salt and some below, some ate at the first table and some at the second. The bourgeois and his clerks and distinguished guests were one class; the *engagés,* the hunters and trappers and boatmen and other hired employees, quite another.

The young Swiss artist, Rudolph Friederich Kurz, who spent the winter of 1851-52 at Fort Union, describes the class distinctions which existed there: "All employees are furnished board and lodging free of charge; that means, engagees are provided with nothing but meat, a place to sleep, and one raw buffalo hide. Hunters and workmen eat at the second table, i.e., meat, biscuit, and black coffee with sugar. Clerks are served with the bourgeois at the first table, which is, on an average, a well-furnished table for this part of the country." While it was quite possible for an able man to rise in the fur trade hierarchy, Kurz observed that "A common engagee is . . . not worthy of notice."[14]

John James Audubon mentions this same attitude toward the

[14] J. N. B. Hewitt, ed., *Journal of Rudolph Friederich Kurz* . . . (Bureau of American Ethnology Bulletin 115, Washington, D.C., 1937), 236, 203.

lower classes. Traveling up the Missouri in a fur company steamboat in 1843, he noted that the *engagés* being taken to Fort Union and other posts were "spoken to as if slaves and treated much as if such, but the more so, the better they seemed to like their employers." These hired men slept on the deck wherever they could find room and were positively forbidden to enter the passenger cabin. It was not expected that they would presume even to address their betters without permission.[15] Class distinction in the wilds was an accepted fact which surprised no one.

I find, then, the frontier hypothesis of Frederick Jackson Turner unsatisfying, for it fails to take into sufficient account such aspects of frontier life as I have put forth briefly here. It was not the runaways from civilization skulking in the forests or the ax bearers striding forward in manly chorus, rifle in hand, bearing the light into the wilderness, but the men of capital and enterprise who opened the western country. It is from a study of their lives and works, of the towns they built and the countryside over which they operated, of the culture they brought with them, that we will come at last to a knowledge of the frontier world as it really was.

[15] John Francis McDermott, ed., *Audubon in the West* (Norman, 1965), 72.

The
American
Entrada

A Spanish Point of View

DONALD JACKSON

UNIVERSITY OF ILLINOIS

In the spring of 1807, a band of Mexican horsemen and foot-soldiers were patrolling the western slopes of the Sangre de Cristo Mountains in northern New Mexico. They were keeping an eye on the passes, and peering up the valley of the Rio Grande, watching for clouds of dust or other signs of movement, because they thought they were about to intercept an American expeditionary force.

No Americans were in the area at all, except a scattering of traders and wanderers in Santa Fe or strung out along the Camino Real leading down to Chihuahua. These men included a small detachment of U.S. soldiers led by Captain Zebulon Pike. Having been picked up by a Spanish patrol at his camp on the west side of the Rio Grande, Pike was in custody. And one of his soldiers had told a story—which he seemed to believe, himself—that the U.S. Army was coming in force to rescue the hapless Pike and his detachment. Intelligence reports about U.S. activities were not so plentiful in those days that Spanish officials could afford to ignore even this thin tale from a ragged private. The governor of the province of New Mexico called out the militia.

For several weeks, Lieutenant Nicholas de Almansa led a little army of a hundred or so men, including soldiers, Mexican civilians, and Indians, up and down the arroyos. He was instructed to expect perhaps 3,000 or 4,000 U.S. soldiers. He was not to attack them, of course, but was to persuade them to halt, if he could, and bring their commanding officer to Sante Fe for a council.

Lieutenant Almansa's patrol looked for this mythical invading force from mid-April until June, and then it disbanded. Later the commanding general of the Interior Provinces of New Spain, Nemesio Salcedo, submitted a substantial bill to the U.S. government, attempting to collect all costs of maintaining the patrol.[1]

The fact that a highly placed Spanish civil servant would react so keenly to an unverifiable report of border violation is evidence that Spanish nerves were on edge. For four years Spain had been adjusting to the fact that she had a different set of neighbors on the east. The enormous Louisiana Territory no longer had an absentee landlord—Napoleon—but had been purchased by the United States, a country whose citizens were living on the premises, building, and talking of expansion.

In the period just before the Louisiana Purchase of 1803, the areas of contact between New Spain and the United States were not as large or as sensitive. The irritations were political, the confrontations mainly between chargés d'affaires and other officials. Now and then the encounters did become more personal and violent. Philip Nolan took a band of men into Texas, ostensibly to trade for wild horses; but his relationship with the double-dealing commander of the U.S. Army, James Wilkinson, made him a potential spy. He lost his life in 1801, and those of his men who survived were still under detention in Mexico when Pike was there six years later. The Venezuelan revolutionary, Francisco de Miranda, was allowed to mount a naval expedition against his own country from the port of New York. He failed, and no Spaniard could forget that without U.S. aid he might never have set sail.

The Spanish reacted with special vigor to a particular kind of penetration from the United States. This was the official government expedition, the sending out of exploring parties for the avowed purpose of mapping, observing, collecting—the kind of trip that Thomas Jefferson liked to call, in the parlance of his time, a "literary expedition." The Spanish knew well that after the explorer came the rancher, the plantation developer, the squatter, and others; that exploring parties tended to make the Indians confused about their loyalties, and often carried medals and trade goods for that exact purpose; and that, worst of all, an exploration into new country gave the sponsoring government a claim of ownership on the region.

Three U.S. expeditions which aroused Spanish resistance, soon after

[1] Joaquín del Real Alencaster to Nemesio Salcedo, April 15, 1807, *legajo* 1787-1807, *cuaderno* 15, Secretaría de Guerra y Marina, Mexico; typed transcript at the Illinois Historical Survey, Urbana, hereafter cited as Cunningham transcripts. For Spanish efforts to receive U.S. payments for this venture, see Valentín de Foronda to James Madison, March 22 and Nov. 28, 1808, in notes from the Spanish legation, Miscellaneous Letters, Department of State, National Archives.

the Louisiana Purchase, are the subject of the present study: those of Lewis and Clark, of Thomas Freeman, and of Zebulon Pike.

The official Spanish policy was to forbid all such expeditions. But the men who had to administer this policy were hundreds, even thousands, of miles apart. In St. Louis there was Carlos Delassus, Lieutenant Governor of Upper Louisiana. In New Orleans there was the Marqués de Casa Calvo, the boundary commissioner. In Philadelphia lived the Marqués de Casa Yrujo, who was chargé d'affaires (or rather, *encargado de negocios*) with the Spanish legation. Finally, very far away indeed, was the most important man of all, Pedro de Cevallos, the foreign minister to the King of Spain. Usually, by the time the foreign minister had learned of an impending U.S. action, it had long since been carried out.

When Jefferson began to plan the Lewis and Clark expedition, late in 1802, the project was protested by the Spanish chargé and a passport was denied the explorers. When the expedition reached St. Louis, passage was again denied Lewis and Clark, and the Spanish lieutenant governor wrote to New Orleans for instructions. Someone there, probably Casa Calvo, wrote back that the expedition should be permitted to ascend the Missouri. The next man to be heard from was General Salcedo in Chihuahua. He wrote to the foreign minister on May 8, 1804, saying he had heard that a certain "Captain Merry," meaning Meriwether Lewis, was about to ascend the Missouri. He objected to this violation of territories under his command, and said he was sending a party of Indians to see if they could cut off the expedition. By September 24, Foreign Minister Cevallos was writing back that the king had approved Salcedo's position and his course of action. But of course Lewis and Clark were well out of reach.[2]

The fact that during this period the Louisiana Territory passed from France to the United States was not a factor, in Spanish eyes, because the Spanish were protesting not only the extent of the territory but the legality of the purchase itself. It seems likely that the change of control did persuade Casa Calvo that the expedition should be permitted to pass; but of all Spanish officials concerned, he alone held this view.

The problem was not all politics; some of it was geography. Even if

[2] Many of the exchanges between Spanish officials in regard to Lewis and Clark are in A. P. Nasatir, ed., *Before Lewis and Clark . . . 1785-1804* (St. Louis, 1952), and Nasatir's translations are also in Donald Jackson, ed., *Letters of the Lewis and Clark Expedition* (Urbana, Ill., 1962). See especially, in Jackson, documents 9, 97, 106, 111, 118, 132.

the Louisiana Territory had been well defined on paper—which it was not—there was not a man alive who knew what it meant in terms of square miles, who knew where the principal mountain ranges lay and where the great rivers ran. One dispatch from the Spanish court in 1804 speaks of the Missouri River as passing through a part of the province of Texas.[3] And let us have a look at the geographical knowledge of General Salcedo, to whose command all the vast upper portions of New Spain were assigned. Having failed to intercept Lewis and Clark on their way up the Missouri, he planned to cut them off on their return trip by organizing a party of friendly Indians for the purpose. He considered the Missouri to be the northern boundary of his territory, even as high as present Montana and North Dakota, and especially he felt that he controlled the river "west of its confluence with the Platte." Of course it does not run west there, but north.[4]

Salcedo's attempt to use the Indians against Lewis and Clark is significant. Now that there was no natural barrier between the two countries, the various bands of Indians along the Missouri, the Platte, the Arkansas, and the Red River were considered by both nations to be a convenient buffering factor. The Pawnee tribes make a good example, for they roamed the plains just about midway between the populated western frontier of the United States and such Spanish towns as Santa Fe and Taos.

In the fall of 1805, acting under instructions from Salcedo, the governor of New Mexico sent two traders up from Santa Fe to visit the Pawnee villages. Pedro Vial and José Chalvet were to spend the winter with those Indians on the Republican and Platte rivers, near the present Kansas-Nebraska boundary. Not only were they to look into the problem of heading off Lewis and Clark, but also were to strengthen the allegiance of the tribes to Spain. "To that end," Salcedo said, "there suggests itself, as the most powerful inducement, that we give them gifts on our behalf, urge their chiefs to come frequently [to Santa Fe], and . . . give them once again proof of the affection which they owe us; and, in case they do indeed go to Santa Fe, you will proceed not only to inspire in them horror toward the English and Americans, but also to persuade them to deny openly their relationship with those nations. . . ."[5]

The mission failed because Vial, Chalvet, and their party were at-

[3] Statement of Pedro Cevallos, March 17, 1804, Archives of New Mexico, Santa Fe.
[4] Salcedo to Alencaster, Sept. 9, 1805, Cunningham transcripts.
[5] *Ibid.*

tacked at the confluence of the Arkansas and the Las Animas by an unidentified party of Indians (which Vial convinced himself had been aroused against him by the Americans).[6] Yet, in the following summer when Zebulon Pike called on the Pawnee, he found that a large band of Spanish horsemen had recently been there—and that the Pawnee chiefs were very much pro-Spanish.

While General Salcedo was scheming to cut off Lewis and Clark, in the fall of 1805, he heard of another Jeffersonian plan—that of sending a small expedition up the Red River. The project was arranged by William Dunbar, who already had explored portions of the Red and the Ouachita, but the civilian leader of the group was to be a surveyor, Thomas Freeman. Military command was to be under Captain Richard Sparks, and there also was to be a botanist, Dr. Peter Custis, and a detachment of about nineteen enlisted men.

Salcedo wrote a letter of protest to Casa Calvo in New Orleans, saying he had heard that the marqués had already issued a passport. "I consider the expedition both unnecessary and very dangerous to the interests of our government," he wrote, "and not only do not give my permission for you to aid the operation, but I must protest against your doing so."

Here was his reasoning. "The results for geography and other sciences are unnecessary because we are in possession of thorough knowledge of the said rivers from their sources to their confluence with the Mississippi." That would have been news to Baron Alexander von Humboldt, whose famous map of New Spain showed the middle course of the Red River as a blank and the headwaters completely misplaced. "It cannot escape Your Excellency's fine wit that Mr. Dunbar's expedition has one difficulty: that the rights and possessions of His Majesty in those regions being indisputable and generally recognized, there exists no authority for any foreign power to examine those lands without His Majesty's permission, whatever may be the objective." Thus General Salcedo, having asserted that the Red River region in the south was Spanish, and the Missouri River region in the north was Spanish, had in his own mind whittled the Louisiana Purchase down to a rather small parcel of real estate.

Then he gave this order: "The governors of the provinces adjacent to the United States are to suspend the operations of any and all expedi-

---

[6] Alencaster's report of the Vial failure, with a copy of his instructions to Vial and a brief diary of the trip, are in the Cunningham transcripts.

tions which may present themselves within the Provinces, and therefore it is to be expected that the expedition of Mr. Dunbar will be so treated. . . ."[7]

But the Freeman expedition, masterminded by Dunbar, did not get the word. It left Fort Adams on the lower Mississippi in April, 1806, and only when it was under way did rumors of possible Spanish intervention reach the travelers. In July they encountered a substantial Spanish force which Salcedo had sent out especially to intercept the expedition. About 600 miles from the mouth of the Red River, Freeman, Sparks, and the others were made to turn back.[8]

Even before Salcedo had learned that his men had successfully terminated the Red River expedition, another venture came to the general's attention. If there was a single act committed by the Americans in this period that caused the Spanish the most pain it was the expedition of Captain Zebulon Pike. It was painful because it involved the commanding general of the U.S. Army, James Wilkinson, and the Spanish from time to time had considered him *their* man. Figuratively, at least, they had check stubs to support their belief, for Wilkinson had been receiving a pension from Spain.

This is not the place to study the motives of that complex man, Wilkinson, or that rather simple soldier, Pike. I have done so elsewhere, and although the evidence is inconclusive I believe that Pike was basically an honest and loyal officer.[9] Here we are not concerned with the motives of the general and his young protégé, but rather with what the Spanish government understood those motives to be.

Salcedo is said to have learned of Pike's impending expedition from a source in Natchez—very likely Stephen Minor, a longtime associate of Wilkinson's. Wilkinson himself may have sent the word, hoping to get Pike captured so that he could spy on the Spanish. Once again Salcedo

[7] Salcedo to the Marqués de Casa Calvo, Oct. 8, 1805, Bancroft Library, Berkeley.

[8] For an account of the Red River expedition, see Isaac Joslin Cox, *The Early Exploration of Louisiana* (Cincinnati, 1906), chap. 6. Many of the letters exchanged during the period between Thomas Jefferson and William Dunbar, in the Jefferson Papers, Library of Congress, provide background. The four-month expedition on the Red and Ouachita rivers, conducted by Dunbar and Dr. George Hunter in 1804-05, is significant in the history of the trans-Mississippi frontier but did not proceed far enough west to antagonize the Spanish. See Cox, *Early Exploration of Louisiana,* chap. 5, and John Francis McDermott, ed., *The Western Journals of Dr. George Hunter, 1796-1805* (Philadelphia, 1963).

[9] See Donald Jackson, "How Lost Was Zebulon Pike?" *American Heritage* (Feb., 1965), 10-15, 75-80. Also Donald Jackson, ed., *The Journals of the Zebulon Montgomery Pike Expedition* (Norman, 1966).

dispatched a force of cavalrymen, under Lieutenant Facundo Melgares. Melgares first took his troops, on 300 white horses, down the Red River to intercept the Red River expedition if the previous attempt had failed. Then he headed north, all the way to the Pawnee village on the Republican River, at the present Nebraska line. But he was too early to intercept Pike, who was not to arrive for several weeks. Melgares worked hard at his other assignment—that of impressing the Pawnee with Spanish strength and influence. And those 300 horses left a very impressive trail which Pike was able to follow at least part of the way westward to the Rockies.[10]

Having delivered some Osage Indians to their village on the headwaters of the Osage River, and gone up to counsel with the Pawnee, Pike set out in the late summer of 1806 to finish his mission. He was to find the Comanche Indians and try to bring them under U.S. influence, and he was to reconnoiter the Red River from its source down to the U.S. post at Nachitoches, in present Louisiana. So again we find the Spanish and the Americans badgering each other in exactly the same way: going into disputed territory to win over the Indians and explore the land.

As an explorer, Pike ran into nearly insurmountable difficulties, and as a Comanche-finder he had no luck at all. By late fall he had seen and approached Pike's Peak, had lost the trail of the Spanish horsemen, and had wandered up north between the Front range and the Sangre de Cristo range of the Rockies; his men were suffering from frostbite and hunger. After an incredible period of probing and backtracking, Pike crossed the Wet Mountain Valley, found a pass in the Sangre de Cristos, trailed out across the San Luis Valley, and encountered a river. He thought it was the Red River, and he believed—along with men such as Jefferson—that the waters of the Red were within the boundaries of the Louisiana Territory. But it was the Rio Grande, much farther west, and the Spanish were not being unreasonable in considering it to be firmly within their boundaries—and besides, Pike was encamped on the west side of the river.

With his capability for being just a little too obvious, he had built a stockade with a moat around it, on the west side of the river, and had run up the U.S. flag. Then he did something which was more than obvious, unless he was definitely seeking to be captured; he allowed a member of his party, Dr. John H. Robinson, to wander off to the west, allegedly to collect a bill from an expatriate American. When Robin-

[10] Pike's account of the Melgares expedition is based upon later talks he had with that officer in Mexico. See Jackson, *Pike Journals,* I, 323-325.

son was found and taken to Santa Fe by friendly Indians, he told a poor lie about the nature of the party he had been traveling with, and aroused the suspicions of the governor, Joaquín del Real Alencaster. It was then that the governor sent a patrol up the Rio Grande valley to find Pike and bring him in.

Confronted by his captors in Santa Fe, and later in Chihuahua where he and his men were taken for further interrogation, Pike was unconvincing. He said he had been lost, and thought he had been encamped on a branch of the Red River. Yet he had with him a letter to Wilkinson, written after his departure, in which he said he *planned* to get "lost."[11] Then his talkative orderly, Private Daugherty, filled the governor's ear with that tale of several thousand U.S. troops coming to the rescue.[12] Finally, Dr. Robinson wrote to Salcedo, telling a tale that the general could not accept. He said he had come to Mexico hoping to stay; that he wanted to become a Roman Catholic and work for the good of Spain. He claimed to have some geographical information of value. And, incidentally, he asked the general, will you please not tell Captain Pike of my plans to defect?[13]

There are some comic aspects in all this, until it is realized that Pike's men were ragged and exhausted, some had lost their toes to frostbite and had been temporarily abandoned in the mountains, and all were apprehensive about the treatment they would receive from the Spanish. The episode took on a truly tragic aspect at the presidio of Carrizal, where some stragglers from Pike's detachment were being held. In a fit of rage, heightened by the effect of brandy, Sergeant William Meek argued with Private Theodore Miller, then killed him with a bayonet.[14]

General Salcedo was in a quandary over what to do with Pike. He could either release him, and risk the ire of his superiors, or he could detain him for the many months it would take to receive further instructions. He surely had no desire to detain a young officer who was a favorite of Wilkinson's, and whom Wilkinson may have promised to

[11] *Ibid.*, document 55.

[12] Alencaster to Salcedo, April 15, 1807, Cunningham transcripts. The troops were to come if Pike had not appeared by Christmas Eve, Daugherty told Alencaster through an interpreter. Alencaster said he checked the story by having Daugherty tell it also to Nicholas Cole, an American tailor living in Santa Fe.

[13] Robinson to Salcedo, April 8, 1807, copy in *Estado, legajo* 5557, *expediente* 10, Archivo Histórico Nacional, Madrid.

[14] See the account of the murder and Meek's subsequent trial in Jackson, *Pike Journals,* document 103.

come and rescue. His decision was probably a good one: he confiscated Pike's papers, sent transcripts in English and Spanish to his superiors, then had Pike and most of his men escorted out of Mexico.

There is no evidence in any contemporary document that Salcedo ever knew of Wilkinson's Spanish pension. The letters which the Spanish general wrote to Philadelphia, New Orleans, and the court of Spain were filled with irritation over Wilkinson's dispatch of the Pike expedition, particularly as news of the abortive Aaron Burr undertaking had reached the general's ears, with its implication of Wilkinson as a probable partner in that intrigue against Mexico.

Spanish officials in the United States and Europe pored over the transcripts of Pike's papers, hoping to find something incriminating. When Wilkinson writes to Pike about observing the satellites of Jupiter, as a source of navigation, they suspect it is a possible code. "I cannot do less than add . . . that in one of the documents which were found on Pike, there is talk of Jupiter, of telescopes, of sextants, etc.; that in another there is again talk of the said Planet and of its satellites, and then it suddenly shifts to Miranda, which makes me believe that it is a cipher; that the fears of Don Nemesio Salcedo ought to have been excited by the Astronomy which Wilkinson explains in his instructions to Pike; for he could not have missed this dilemma, that either Pike knows how to make astronomical observations or he does not. If he knows, Wilkinson's lesson is not useful to him; if he does not, so summary an instruction would not have been of any service to him."[15]

What the Spanish thought was another code symbol proved to be no more than a little device which the translator in Chihuahua was using to denote that he had omitted some minor portions of Pike's papers.

From all he had done to terminate the Pike expedition, General Salcedo might have expected a commendation from the king. Instead, he got a reprimand, forwarded through the office of the foreign minister. The king said he recognized the generous motivation which had prompted Salcedo to give Pike his freedom, but that Pike had also been afforded the very thing he may have wanted—a good look at lots of Mexican territory. What Salcedo should have done, he was told, was to detain Pike until the United States should ask for him, and admit the imprudence of violating the Spanish border.

After this rebuke, Salcedo proposed a partial remedy. He still had several of Pike's men in custody—including a murderer. How about

[15] Foronda to Madison, March 22, 1808 (see note 1).

holding them until the United States should make sufficiently obsequious overtures? It would not be fair, said the foreign minister, to hold some of the men when others, including the commanding officer, had already been released.

At one point in this exchange, there is a marginal note in the hand of Cevallos, asking whether Wilkinson was still being paid a pension in view of his unfriendly action toward Mexico. A further check revealed that nobody in the Spanish court seemed to know how recently the pension had been paid, or even which department had been paying it. Wilkinson's potential value to Spain dated from an earlier time, and he was no longer in favor.[16]

The dialogue between Spain and the United States in the Pike affair was carried on between Secretary of State James Madison and the newly appointed chargé d'affaires for Spain, Valentín de Foronda. The burden of Foronda's complaint: you violated our border and you owe us an apology plus the money it cost our government to conduct Pike back to his own territory. The gist of Madison's attitude—bolstered by occasional conferences with Jefferson and Secretary of War Henry Dearborn—was that the border between the two countries was not clearly established, that Zebulon Pike had lost his way, it had been a friendly expedition, and the United States felt obliged to pay only the $1,000 which had been advanced to Pike in cash.

It was clear from the start that Jefferson, Madison, and Dearborn had no intention of paying the nearly 22,000 pesos asked by Spain, a total which included such items as these:

"Six pesos 4 reales supplied . . . for repairs to Pike's saddles."

"For one dead horse 10 pesos."

"To Francisco Polanco for 10 baggage-carrying animals which he furnished to the Lieutenant and his Troop as far as Chihuahua, at 5 pesos a day each, total 50 pesos."

The exchange of notes ran on for a while, then dwindled. All the men in Pike's command eventually got back home, including Sergeant Meek the murderer, although he was held for fourteen years.

In considering Spanish reaction to all these expeditions, it is well not to lose sight of one factor: these were not just two opposing forces facing each other, but rather they were men, and on either side there were men both venal and good. There were men confused by the necessity of

---

[16] See a series of minutes from the files of Cevallos, various dates, *Estado, legajo* 5548, *expediente* 20, Archivo Histórico Nacional, Madrid.

administering lands which their imaginations could not encompass, of making decisions alone and far from the counsel of their governments, of resisting forces which they only hazily understood. If we recognize the position of General Salcedo in Chihuahua, who sincerely believed it his duty to intercept Lewis and Clark when they were headed for the wild rivers of Oregon, and who believed that Indian tribes in what are now Kansas and Nebraska were legitimately his to use as geopolitical pawns, then we shall have begun to recognize the Spanish point of view when U.S. citizens began to enter what Spain then called her "interior provinces" and what we now call the American West.

The Jumping-Off Places on the Overland Trail

MERRILL J. MATTES

NATIONAL PARK SERVICE, SAN FRANCISCO

Of literature on the Central Overland Trail, the great migration route up the Platte River westward, there is no end, but in all this profusion there is little that illuminates the Missouri River border towns commonly referred to as the "jumping-off places." In the mid-nineteenth century an overland trip from the States to the Pacific Ocean, over vast treeless plains, the awesome Rocky Mountains, and scorching deserts must have seemed roughly equivalent to today's venture into outer space. So what of the Cape Kennedys—the launching platforms—of 1849?

It is not that we are ignorant of the river towns. Every traveler to the far West had to start somewhere, and almost every emigrant journal (several hundred of which are now available to students) describes or mentions one such place. It might be Independence, Missouri, or Council Bluffs, Iowa, or any one of several places between these two extreme points along a stretch of some 200 miles. There is ample material on these catalytic—and sometimes cataclysmic—communities. What is lacking is a panoramic view of these places in the total trans-Missouri frontier picture, their geographic and strategic relationship, and their relative importance at different periods between 1820, when Lieutenant Long made the first westward journey up the Platte, until 1869, when the Union Pacific and Central Pacific railroads were joined, and transcontinental travel by wagon became obsolescent.

The significance of the jumping-off places has been obscured by two factors. First, during the heyday of transcontinental wagon traffic the spotlight was on the overland adventure and the supposedly glamorous destinations—Oregon, California, Utah, Colorado, or Montana. Second, since covered wagon days the Missouri River towns which played such significant roles have, for the most part, grown into sprawling modern communities, overlaid with concrete and stone and steel, with little trace left of their historic beginnings.

Lewis and Clark suggested that a fort be built at the mouth of the Platte River, and in the 1860's a town named Plattsmouth did materialize there; however, the great migration route up the Platte did not begin at its mouth at all, but actually at Fort Kearny, about 200 miles inland. There were five major approaches to Fort Kearny from the east, radiating inward from five principal points where emigrants collected themselves to prepare for their voyage over the dimly charter wilderness. These points are now roughly equivalent to the modern communities of Kansas City, Weston-Leavenworth, St. Joseph, Nebraska City, and Council Bluffs–Omaha.

The complex of sites around Kansas City were on the west side of the river to begin with, so there one had the immense advantage of starting off, at least, on dry land. Weston, St. Joseph, the Nebraska City ferry, and Council Bluffs were rallying and recruiting points on the east side, the departure from which first required the dangerous crossing of the Missouri by flimsy rafts or ferries at the mercy of its brown turbulence.

At one stage or another all of the five main river ports were reached by precarious St. Louis steamboats. Indeed, the Kansas City and Weston jump-offs were normally approached by steamer, and overland travel to them from the east was the exception. Quite the reverse was true of St. Joseph, Nebraska City, and Council Bluffs, which were mainly the objectives of wagon trains fanning out from points throughout the upper Mississippi valley. But it would be best to examine each of these five points of prairie embarkation separately before considering them collectively.

Kansas City

Kansas City was the best known, partly because this area was the principal jump-off for the highly sentimentalized Oregon migration, partly because it had been in the business of outfitting explorers, fur traders, and emigrants longer than any of its rivals. Kansas City was important because of a simple accident of geography. It was located at the point where the Missouri River, after its westward course through the state of Missouri, makes a sharp bend northward to Nebraska, hence was a seemingly logical place to get out of a boat and pursue one's westward objectives overland.

Greater Kansas City today, approaching a population of 1,000,000, has all but obliterated the evidence of its origins. Within this metropolitan area, complete with skyscrapers, elaborate trafficways, and jet planes overhead, there were once four focal points of covered wagon concentration. The earliest of these was Fort Osage, a government factory established in 1808 at a point recommended by William Clark, several miles downstream from downtown Kansas City, and now restored as a Jackson County park. Next came François Chouteau's trading post of 1821, below the mouth of the Kansas or Kaw River, on the rock ledge now occupied by an interstate viaduct and cloverleaf intersections, at the foot of a steep hill once timbered and harboring Indian spies, but now occupied by the city's towering business district. In time Chouteau's Landing, moved frequently by floods, evolved into the historically obscure settlements variously tagged Kansas, Kansasmouth, Kanzasville, and Westport Landing.

Independence became the third and far more important point of overland departure. Independence today is a separate city, the metropolis of western Jackson County; however, for all visible purposes it is a suburb of Kansas City, the principal connecting artery, Truman Road, going by the name of its most distinguished citizen. A modern shopping center surrounding a splendid brick courthouse (built on the site of the 1849 courthouse) now dominates the square which once echoed to the braying of mules, the bellowing of oxen, and the epithets of their drivers. The only tangible links with the past are a protected "emigrant spring," a log cabin dubiously represented as the original 1827 courthouse, and the restored Jackson County Jail and Marshall's House, of 1859 vintage.[1]

In 1827 Independence succeeded Franklin as the eastern terminus of the Santa Fe Trail, and for several decades freighters assembled here for the harrowing journey to Council Grove and up the Arkansas River, either to Bent's Old Fort near La Junta or to the Cimarron Cutoff west of Dodge City. Independence itself was several miles from the river, on the fertile upland between the Big and Little Blue rivers (Missouri version). Steamboat cargoes and passengers unloaded at nearby wharves, known as Independence Landing or Wayne City, and had to climb or be hauled up the river bluffs. From Independence the Santa Fe Trail headed southwest over the prairie to intersect the boundary between the United States proper and Indian territory (now the Missouri-Kansas line), at a point called Little Santa Fe, near present 120th Street and State Line. When travel to Oregon became the vogue in the 1840's, the

[1] Records of the Jackson County Historical Society, Independence.

new breed of emigrants followed the convenient Santa Fe Trail as far west as present Gardner, Kansas, then left it and turned northwestward to cross the Kaw near present Topeka, and reached the Platte via the Big and Little Blue rivers (Kansas version). Thus when the California Gold Rush erupted, Independence was ready, as a springboard for the Argonauts.

Westport town was on the uplands between Turkey Creek and Brush Creek, four miles south of Westport Landing and just inside the state line. Old Westport, now virtually annihilated by Kansas City, once occupied ground which is now roughly bounded by 39th and 43rd streets, between Central Street and the Southwest Trafficway, and its hub was the intersection of present Westport Road and Pennsylvania Avenue.

In 1831 Isaac McCoy and Johnston Lykins founded this community, across the state line from their Baptist mission to the Shawnee Indians. John McCoy set up a trading post for the Indians, and in 1836 a trail was completed to rival Independence, about ten miles to the northeast. This trail tapped the lucrative Santa Fe trade, diverting much of it from the original route along Blue Ridge. In the 1840's the Westport Trail became the main line to Oregon, and present Westport Road is that section of the old trail which took freighters and emigrants through the town.

Aside from the ancient homes of Colonel Jack Harris and the Rev. Nathaniel Scarritt, almost the only bona fide structural survivor is the decrepit Westport Inn at 500 Westport Road, built in 1837 by the Shawnee Chief Captain Joseph Parks, and unquestionably the oldest structure in Kansas City.[2]

Weston–Leavenworth

Fort Leavenworth was founded in 1827, fronting the Kansas wilderness some thirty miles north of Chouteau's Landing. At first this was strictly a military affair, to impress the Sac, Fox, Missouri, and Potawatomi Indians. Fur traders, often with cargoes of illicit whiskey, gave the place a wide berth, and citizen emigrants were at first not imagined. When the Oregon migration focused attention on Platte River Road, Army engineers pioneered a patrol line northwestward from the fort, which reached the Independence-Westport Road, via Grasshopper

---

[2] Records of the Westport Historical Society. Other contemporary sites of the old Westport countryside, now difficult to find in sedate residential areas, include the Shawnee mission in Johnson County, Kansas, the 1856 Alexander Majors home at 81st Street and State Line, and the West 55th Street home of William Bent and Seth E. Ward, both fur trade notables.

Creek, at the Big Blue. In 1849 a substantial number of gold seekers started off on the Leavenworth Road, looking upon this as a shrewd way to avoid congestion at Independence and St. Joseph.

Weston, Missouri, had been founded in 1837 by Joseph Moore, an ex-Dragoon from Fort Leavenworth, and was prospering three years later as a tobacco market, the river port on the east shore serving Fort Leavenworth. An influx of emigrants from central Europe, building picturesquely on the steep hillsides, gave this town the nickname of "Little Switzerland." During the Gold Rush as many as eight steamboats would be docked here at one time. Outfitting and supplying both soldiers and emigrants brought Weston's population in 1858 to more than 5,000. For a few years it was second only to St. Louis among Missouri towns in population, but it rapidly shrank when it was stranded by the railroad boom of the 1860's, together with the shift of the Missouri River channel to the west bank.

Today Weston is a relaxed community, largely ignored by tourists and historians alike, but distinguished for its tobacco auctions, its 1856 whiskey distillery founded by David Holladay (brother of famed Ben), and a number of well-preserved homes that go all the way back to the Gold Rush. Typical of these is the Sebus home, a brick dwelling complete with slave quarters, that was built by Weston's own Captain Charles Murphy, a Pied Piper who led a contingent of Forty-Niners to California and then disappeared.[3]

St. Joseph

Joseph Robidoux, who established a trading post at the Blacksnake Hills about 1825, was a man of vision. He anticipated not only an influx of settlers, but also the need for a trail to the west which would join the Blue River and the Platte. Blacksnake Hills had it all over Independence, being substantially closer to the Platte River; two extra days by steamer would save two weeks by ox team. So when in 1843 the canny French-Canadian laid out the city named for his patron saint, little time elapsed before Yankee traders arrived, bought lots, and started the metropolis of northwestern Missouri.[4] Legally it was St. Joseph, but in everyday parlance it was always St. Joe.

There was some Oregon business in the 1840's but it was in 1849 that St. Joe was rocked by explosions of human vitality, and the trail to the

[3] Records of the Weston Historical Museum.
[4] Roy E. Coy, "The Early Years," *Museum Graphic,* XVII, No. 2 (1965), 6-12.

Big Blue Crossing—the St. Joe Road—became the royal road to California riches. In 1859 the Hannibal and St. Joseph railroad arrived, and in 1860 the fleet Pony Express began its meteoric career here.

While prosperous enough, St. Joe is no longer a boom town; its population of around 75,000 has remained fairly constant for many decades. The community makes a big thing of the transitory Pony Express, commemorating it by statues and monuments, and the preservation of three ancient buildings—a stable, a hotel, and an office—which were used by the entrepreneurs Russell, Majors, and Waddell. Unfortunately the civic memory of the much more significant Gold Rush is short. Its only discernible trace is the unmemorialized river bank at the foot of Jules and Frances streets, named for old Joe's offspring. Once jammed with emigrants waiting their turn for the makeshift ferry boats, the locale is now the setting of the Goetz brewery, an iron foundry, and other impedimenta of the twentieth century.

A few miles north of St. Joe, in 1849 and later, there were several other ferry-boat operations, which developed as the result of the insufferable overcrowding and jostling in the town. The modern rural communities of Amazonia, Savannah, and Oregon have evolved from gold rush days, when the human torrent overflowed in the improvisation of frontier river crossings. The westward trails from these towns all converged, sooner or later, at the Big Blue Crossing, near Marysville.

Nebraska City

The U.S. Army created not only the Fort Leavenworth crossing, but also the Nebraska City crossing. In 1846 Colonel S. W. Kearny and his Dragoons were transported to the mouth of Table Creek and there erected a crude fort, named Fort Kearny (the first Fort Kearny, not to be confused with the second, more permanent Fort Kearny at Grand Island on the Platte, some 180 miles west). Table Creek was the point on the Missouri which was directionally closest to the point where the Independence–St. Joe Road reached the Platte; the Army supposed that this was the logical place to station troops to protect the Oregon migration, and at the same time be supplied by steamboat.

The first Fort Kearny did not get beyond the blockhouse and log cabin stage before it was replaced, in 1848, by the second Fort Kearny. Two things contributed to this. First there was the war with Mexico, which skeletonized the Table Creek garrison. Second, there was the superior logic of the fact that the heavy traffic was from the Independence and St. Joe areas, up the Blue and the Little Blue, and the place for a fort was where the covered wagons were, at the point of their convergence with the Platte, not some hypothetical point on the Missouri River.

Even so, the existence of abandoned old Fort Kearny was magnet enough, somehow, to bring a respectable number of emigrants up the Missouri River to Table Creek, by steamer in some cases, but mainly by wagon overland northward from St. Joe, across the Tarkio and Nishnabotna rivers. In 1849 there was a ferry of sorts at old Fort Kearny, and another one called Duncan's Ferry a few miles south thereof. The way west from Table Creek was over rolling grassy uplands via Salt River to the Platte, joining the Independence–St. Joe Road some ten miles east of the new Fort Kearny.[5]

In 1853 John Boulware had a ferry here and a small settlement began around his post office on the Iowa side. The Kansas-Nebraska Act of 1854, however, creating a territory out of the Indian lands, put the old Fort Kearny port of entry back in business, so to speak, and Nebraska City arose Phoenix-like from the figurative ashes of the abortive Army post. Founded by land speculators, Nebraska City benefitted from the sharp increase in Missouri River steamboat traffic, and burgeoning demands of the U.S. Army for provisioning by freighting contract. With the Utah War of 1857 and the Colorado Gold Rush of 1859, Nebraska City took on boom proportions. In the late fifties and early sixties, come springtime, its streets were alive with sweating humanity and the crack of bullwhips and revolver fire, all prelude to the outflow of ox-drawn freighters and gold seekers.

Nebraska City today is a solidly respectable county seat, with a conventional town square and courthouse, stately frame houses, and gigantic elm trees. Its hesitant beginnings as an Army post are suggested only by a 1938 blockhouse replica, some distance from the original site at 5th and Central. Its rambunctious career as the premier outfitter for the Pike's Peak and Virginia City gold rushes is suggested only faintly by a few venerable brick buildings, onetime warehouses and saloons, which survive from the sixties.[6]

Council Bluffs–Omaha

At the northern end of the Missouri River jumping-off axis is the Greater Omaha area, which embraces portions of Douglas, Washington,

[5] Best known of the old Fort Kearney entrants is J. G. Bruff, *Gold Rush,* G. W. Reid and R. Gaines, eds. (New York, 1944).

[6] Records of the Otoe County Historical Society, Nebraska City.

and Sarpy counties in Nebraska and Pottawattomie County in Iowa.[7] Omaha proper, with a population of one-third of a million, was not in existence until 1854, but Bellevue at its southern edge, old Florence at its northern city limits, Fort Atkinson a few miles farther north, and Council Bluffs on the Iowa side go back to the beginnings of historic time.

Bellevue, at the mouth of Papio or Pappilion Creek, now global headquarters for the Strategic Air Command, was the site of an American Fur Company post beginning in the 1820's, and a Presbyterian mission to the Omaha Indians in the 1830's, actually the first permanent settlement in Nebraska.[8]

Council Bluffs is a name given by Lewis and Clark to the site of their Indian parley of 1804 some twenty miles north of Omaha, on the Nebraska side. In 1819 Fort Atkinson was established at these same original Council Bluffs, but among fur traders this gradually became a generalized name for the entire district.[9] In the fullness of time it became relocalized on the Iowa side, opposite present Omaha. Although Council Bluffs, Iowa, has come to be associated with the Mormon exodus from Illinois-Iowa to Utah, its career as a frontier community started well before and continued well after the passage of Brigham Young. In 1837 Captain D. B. Moore and Company C of the First Regiment of Dragoons came up from Fort Leavenworth and erected a blockhouse on a bluff to protect the Potawatomi from alleged enemies. In 1838 Father Pierre J. De Smet arrived here to assist in setting up a mission among these Indians. With the permission of Colonel Kearny, the Jesuits converted the blockhouse into a chapel, and the three log cabins of the halfbreed trader, Mr. Caldwell, became their dwellings. The blockhouse-mission was within the area now bounded by Broadway, Voorhis, Union, and State streets, in the Council Bluffs downtown area.

In 1841 the Council Bluffs mission was closed, given up as hopeless because of Sioux hostilities and the scourge of alcohol among the Potawatomi.[10] Less than five years later, early in 1846, the advance guard of Mormon refugees from their Illinois Babylon straggled down Indian Creek and Mosquito Creek into the Missouri River bottom

[7] Reference to Brownville, Plattsmouth, and other possible late-period jump-offs is omitted, since their role in Platte River migration was negligible.

[8] William John Shallcross, *Romance of a Village; Story of Bellevue, the First Permanent Continuous Settlement in Nebraska* (Omaha, 1954).

[9] Sally A. Johnson, "Fort Atkinson on the Council Bluffs," reprinted from *Nebraska History*, XL, No. 1 (1959).

[10] Gilbert J. Garraghan, *Jesuits of the United States* (New York, 1938), I, 422-446.

below the old Jesuit mission, and knocked together the first log cabins, which they dubbed Millersville or Miller's Hollow. By June several thousand Saints were encamped here. Anxious to get beyond the reach of unsympathetic Gentiles, and violating the law against settling on Indian lands, Brigham Young made a deal with the Omaha to protect them against the Pawnee, and promptly ferried his sizable flock across the Missouri. He erected a log and dug-out village where his people died like flies during the following winter, but which in 1847 became the base of his triumphant journey to the Salt Lake Zion.[11] This so-called Winter Quarters, sacred in Mormon history, later became the townsite of Florence, now annexed to Omaha.

In 1848 the Mormons who did not migrate to Zion were compelled by the government to return to the Iowa side, and Millersville was renamed Kanesville for a Mormon benefactor, Thomas L. Kane. When the Gentiles came in 1849, bound for California, the Mormons were outnumbered and outvoted, and Kanesville rapidly evolved into Council Bluffs. So populous was the California migration from this point that the trail north of the Platte was always, in its day, known as the Council Bluffs Road.

There were three principal river crossings in the Council Bluffs area. The first and earliest was the one at Trader's Point, eight miles downstream from Council Bluffs, which enabled travelers to touch the mission at Bellevue. The second was a similar distance to the north, the Mormon crossing opposite Winter Quarters. The third, which became the primary crossing after 1854, was the direct route over the river bottom to the new settlement of Omaha. Today these three crossings coincide approximately with the three bridges called Bellevue, Mormon, and Ak-Sar-Ben. The trails from these crossings converged west of the Elkhorn River, in the vicinity of present Waterloo.

Except for the beautiful Mormon cemetery, on the bluff above old Winter Quarters, and a few ancient structures in Bellevue going back to the 1850's, almost nothing survives in urbanized Omaha–Council Bluffs to remind us of the great northern jumping-off place.[12]

If we were to construct a graph showing the use pattern of the jumping-off places, the Council Bluffs area would begin the scale, for it was at Fort Atkinson, at the original Council Bluffs, that the first west-

---

[11] Wallace Stegner, *Gathering of Zion* (New York, 1964).

[12] The site of Fort Atkinson, by the present town of Fort Calhoun, has been identified archeologically. It is to be developed as a state park.

bound trip up the Platte began, the Long expedition of 1820; and from this same point William Ashley in late 1824 launched the Rocky Mountain fur trade overland. Sarpy's Post at Bellevue became the staging area for mountain expeditions of the American Fur Company, beginning with the one Warren Ferris records in 1830.[13] The trips of 1835 and 1836 captained by Thomas Fitzpatrick from Bellevue are chronicled by the Oregon missionaries. John Sutter traveled with Andrew Drips up the north route in 1838.[14]

Despite the earlier action at Council Bluffs, the complex of sites at Kansas City combined to hold undisputed leadership from 1830 to the Mormon hegira of 1846. The celebrated Smith-Jackson-Sublette collection of carts and dearborns in 1830 was launched overland from St. Louis via Independence.[15] Captain Bonneville made up his three-year expedition in 1832 at old Fort Osage.[16] Nathaniel Wyeth in 1832 and 1834, Sublette and Campbell in 1834, and the later American Fur Company caravans which were decorated by the company of Sir William Stewart all made Independence their base. The fur company caravans of 1839 and 1840, publicized by Wislizenus and Father De Smet respectively, were organized at Westport, while this was likewise the point of departure for Bidwell's pioneer emigrant train of 1841, and the White-Lovejoy enterprise of 1842 (both piloted by Fitzpatrick).[17] Captain Frémont's first two expeditions, in 1842 and 1843, were launched at Chouteau's or Westport Landing.[18]

Independence was apparently the exclusive starting point of all involved in the first sizable Oregon migration in 1843; at least no journalist of record disputes this, although Peter Burnett started from Weston before joining the train, thus providing the earliest reference to this town as an emigration point.[19] In 1844 James Clyman's party for Oregon followed the Independence Road, but John Minto, Washington

[13] Warren A. Ferris, *Life in the Rocky Mountains*, P. C. Phillips, ed. (Denver, 1940).

[14] Rev. Samuel Parker, *Journal of an Exploring Tour* (Ithaca, 1844); W. H. Gray, *A History of Oregon* (Portland, 1870).

[15] John E. Sunder, *Bill Sublette* (Norman, 1959), 84-85.

[16] Washington Irving, *Adventures of Captain Bonneville*, E. W. Todd, ed. (Norman, 1961), 13-14.

[17] Bernard DeVoto, *Across the Wide Missouri* (Boston, 1947); John Bidwell, *A Journey to California* (San Francisco, 1937); A. J. Allen, *Thrilling Adventures* (New York, 1859).

[18] John C. Frémont, *Report of the Exploring Expedition, to the Rocky Mountains, 1842, and to Oregon and California, 1843-1844* (Washington, D.C., 1845); Theodore Talbot, *Journals*, C. H. Carey, ed. (Portland, 1931).

[19] Peter H. Burnett, *Recollections* (New York, 1880), 97-99.

Gilliam, and several others made the crossing at St. Joe, the first emigrants of record from this point.[20] In this year also at least three emigrants, including Moses Schallenberger, California Trail pioneer, record departures from Bellevue, proving that the Council Bluffs crossing
was in no sense a Mormon discovery.[21] In 1845 this same mixed pattern
obtains, with most travelers of record, including Joel Palmer, leaving
from Independence, but others as well from St. Joe and Bellevue.[22] In
this year also the Leavenworth Road to the Platte came into its own
when Colonel Kearny led his Dragoons to South Pass.

Travel from Independence in 1846 is vividly recorded by Parkman,
Thornton, Lienhard, and others.[23] At the same time the St. Joe crossing
is reported by at least three minor journalists,[24] while the U.S. Army
created a new jump-off at Table Creek, and the Mormons laid claim to
the Council Bluffs territory. The year 1846 was the last year in which
the Kansas City jump-offs—Independence included—served as the number one funnel for Platte River travelers. The year 1847 was clearly a
Council Bluffs year, with Brigham Young's pioneer trek to Salt Lake.
Of the six non-Mormon journals of record, four are from St. Joe and
two from Independence.[25] In the off-year 1848 we find no one leaving
Independence, but two—Riley Root and James D. Miller—going from
St. Joe to Oregon, and probably 4,000 Mormons and 500 Oregonians on
the Council Bluffs Road.[26] In 1848 Bruce Cornwall is the first emigrant

[20] James Clyman, *Frontiersman*, C. L. Camp, ed. (Portland, 1960), 67; John Minto,
"Reminiscences," *Oregon Historical Quarterly*, I (1900), 73-104; Washington Gilliam,
"Reminiscences," *Transactions of the Oregon Pioneer Association, 1905* (Portland,
1906), 411-423.

[21] Moses Schallenberger, *Opening of the California Trial*, G. R. Steward, ed. (Berkeley, 1953); William Case, "Reminiscences," *Oregon Historical Quarterly*, I (1900),
269-277; Edmund Bray, MS, Bancroft Library, Berkeley.

[22] Joel Palmer, *Journal of Travels* (Cincinnati, 1847); Jesse Harritt, "Diary,"
Transactions of the Oregon Pioneer Association, 1911 (Portland, 1914), 506-526; Sarah
Helmick, "Recollections," *Oregon Historical Quarterly*, XXVI (1925), 444-447.

[23] Francis Parkman, *Journals*, M. Wade, ed. (New York, 1947); J. Quinn Thornton,
Oregon and California in 1848 (New York, 1849); Heinrich Lienhard, *St. Louis to
Sutter's Fort*, E. G. Gudde, ed. (Norman, 1961).

[24] Joseph Aram, "Reminiscences," *Journal of American History*, I (1907), 617-632;
Anson Cone, "Reminiscences," *Oregon Historical Quarterly*, IV (1903), 251-259;
Polly Jane Purcell, "Autobiography" (n.p., n.d.), Huntington Library, San Marino,
Calif.

[25] Isaac Pettijohn, MS, Bancroft Library, Berkeley, and Chester Ingersoll, *Overland
to California*, D. McMurtrie, ed. (Chicago, 1937), represent St. Joe and Independence
departees respectively.

[26] Riley Root, *Journal of Travels* (Oakland, Calif., 1955); James D. Miller, "Early
Oregon Scenes," *Oregon Historical Quarterly*, XXXI (1930), 56-68.

of record to trace a new pattern of overland travel by going first overland, northward from St. Joe to Council Bluffs, thus testifying to the
popular appeal of the northern route.[27]

During the California Gold Rush the diary keepers and letter writers, who provide the only statistical yardstick on the jumping-off places,
swell predictably. Reference to the official register at Fort Kearny suggests over 25,000 Argonauts in 1849. We know that all approaches to
Fort Kearny were crowded, but the only clue to the comparative traffic
count lies in analysis of 145 Forty-Niner journals accounted for: 58
from St. Joe, 38 from Independence-Westport, 15 from Council Bluffs,
and the balance from old Fort Kearny, Weston, or unknown.[28]

In 1850 the migration exceeded 55,000, double that of famous '49.
The number of discovered diaries is proportionately far less, but on the
assumption that these are still a reasonably accurate gauge to distribu-
tion, Council Bluffs and St. Joe, with about thirty-five recorders each,
take a commanding lead. Fewer than ten writers left Independence-
Westport, and only token numbers from Weston and Table Creek.

In 1852, the second biggest year of California traffic on the Platte,
with a probable count in excess of 50,000, a distinctly new pattern
emerges. To recapitulate. Independence-Westport was dominant to
1846. In 1847-48 Council Bluffs became the principal jump-off, while
in the premier gold rush years 1849-51 St. Joe made off with statistical
honors. Now, in 1852, there is every evidence that Council Bluffs re-
gained the championship. We may discount as literary extravagance the
many descriptions of the immense throngs waiting for the ferries. (Ezra
Meeker describes the waiting covered wagons in the distance as "a big
white flat iron"; Mary Ackley's party had to wait in line for three weeks
to make this ferry crossing).[29] But we cannot discount the fact that of
some eighty emigrant journals of 1852, over half relate to Council
Bluffs alone.

When Omaha and Nebraska City materialized in 1854, with the creation of Nebraska Territory, Nebraska's lopsided dominance of Platte
River traffic was reinforced. During the late 1850's lower fares and
technical improvements in steamboat transportation to Nebraska

[27] Bruce Cornwall, *Life Sketch* (San Francisco, 1906).

[28] Beginning with the emigrant flood of 1849, it is impossible, of course, to document these figures by footnotes. A complete overland bibliography will be included
in a planned book-length publication.

[29] Ezra Meeker and Howard R. Driggs, *Covered Wagon Centennial* (New York,
1932), 33-34; Mary E. Ackley, *Crossing the Plains* (San Francisco, 1928), 11-25.

points, combined with a saving of 200 miles of land transportation, led to a sharp decline of covered wagon traffic out of St. Joe and Kansas City. Military, freighting, and stage line travel from Fort Leavenworth and Atchison increased, of course, during this period, but the bona fide covered wagon pre-railroad emigration shifted to and stayed in Nebraska Territory.

The Pike's Peak gold rush was largely a Nebraska City–Denver affair. The bulk of Montana gold seekers overland were of Omaha origin, as were those who traveled in the sixties on their own to Utah, California, or Oregon before the completion of the Union Pacific.[30]

Thus the wheel came full circle. Council Bluffs was the jump-off for Stephen H. Long and William H. Ashley, who in the 1820's initiated western travel up the Great Platte River Road. Council Bluffs–Omaha and Nebraska City were the primary points of embarkation on the prairie sea for seventeen years prior to the advent of transcontinental train travel. If the Missouri cities are remembered most vividly as the jump-off points during the climax years to Oregon and California, the Nebraska towns should be remembered as the first and last of the jumping-off places, and over the decades they launched the greatest number of those who followed the western star.

[30] Over seventy-five journals have been identified for the late migration period, 1858-66.

Trails, Rails, Paddlewheels, and Frederick Jackson Turner

OSCAR O. WINTHER

INDIANA UNIVERSITY

Permission by our editor John Francis McDermott to use Frederick Jackson Turner as a launching pad rather than as a co-pilot in this present flight into the outer spaces of western history is an act of great magnanimity. I am sure, however, that McDermott was fully aware that he really had no other choice. Certainly no other American historian has been more explored, deplored, revered, and reviled than Turner, and in the course of this adulation and denunciation the printed books and articles dealing with Turner's frontier hypothesis have reached adequately monumental proportions. The late E. E. Edwards' *References on the Significance of the Frontier in American History*[1] listed 124 items pertaining to this one essay alone. An updated bibliography of this would show no leveling off with the passing years. During the relatively brief period that I have served as editor of the *Mississippi Valley Historical Review* and its successor, the *Journal of American History,* fresh articles on Turner (some too fresh) have continued to come to my desk. And not only did the modest Turner inspire this outpouring about his thesis, but Turner's stimulating thoughts and ideas about the West as a whole have generated an even loftier mountain of special studies. In 1942 I published a guide to the trans-Mississippi West periodical literature containing a list of 3,501 articles. In 1961 an updated edition lists 9,244 articles dealing with the trans-Mississippi West alone.[2] It is left to others to compile a comparable bibliography relating to the Atlantic and the

[1] Everett E. Edwards, *References on the Significance of the Frontier in American History,* 2nd ed. (United States Department of Agriculture, Bibliographical Contributions No. 25, Washington, D.C., 1939).

[2] Oscar O. Winther, *The Trans-Mississippi West: A Guide to Its Periodical Literature* (Bloomington, Ind., 1942); *A Classified Bibliography of the Periodical Literature of the Trans-Mississippi West, 1811-1957* (Bloomington, Ind., 1961, 1964).

trans-Allegheny frontiers, but the evidence would remain the same, a gigantic and unceasing outpouring of literature on the American West. And in spite of all this, or perhaps because of it, there is currently being produced by Holt, Rinehart and Winston an eighteen-volume frontier history series under the general editorship of Ray A. Billington. It is little wonder that in his Mississippi Valley Historical Association presidential address Billington should have been moved to explain—with Turner in mind—why some historians rarely write history.[3]

The problem, then, is where and how to open new vistas, how to heed our editor's instructions "not to attack Turner but to discuss aspects of the frontier not accounted for by him." It is in keeping with this admonition that the present remarks are addressed to Turner's observations on the role of transportation as a factor in frontier development and to what, in light of present hindsight, appear to have been his oversights and his shortcomings.

One does not normally associate Turner's writings specifically with the subject of transportation. He wrote no separate essay on this subject. Only one chapter, chapter 27 of *Rise of the New West,* entitled "Internal Improvements and Foreign Trade," comes close to being a published discussion of this subject. Moreover, nowhere in unpublished papers does there appear to exist a separate file on the subject of transportation.[4]

This is not to imply that Turner was either indifferent or unmindful of the role of transportation in our national life. The reader of his books and essays quickly discerns that he rarely developed any topics at length. Few, if any, of the things he wrote are labeled. He much preferred to carry forward a variety of subjects simultaneously, piece by piece, and upon close examination one finds a goodly number of brief but widely scattered allusions to transportation that reveal a keen awareness and understanding of this subject. And in view of the fact that Turner directed the doctoral programs of students who did work on transportation, one might contend that the great master at least begat studies in this field of frontier history. Turner was conscious of the latter. He maintained a special file of his graduate students with classifications that included "land transportation," "commerce," and

[3] Ray A. Billington, "Why Some Historians Rarely Write History: A Case Study of Frederick Jackson Turner," *Mississippi Valley Historical Review,* L (1963), 3-27.
[4] I am deeply indebted to Wilbur R. Jacobs for information contained herein on the Turner Papers in the Huntington Library, San Marino, Calif.

"internal trade." In the transportation folder he listed U. B. Phillips, Archer B. Hulbert, James B. Hedges, and Solon J. Buck. He listed Grace Nute under "commerce." Significantly enough the names of Phillips and Buck reappear under "politics."[5]

Only one of these—Hulbert—became a major historian of transportation in the West, and Hulbert alone produced works which, combined, comprise a monumental contribution in the field of transportation, or perhaps more accurately stated, roads.[6] However, C. H. Ambler, whom Turner classified as a political historian, wrote on the subject of transportation in the Ohio valley.[7]

Turner was, of course, as loyal to his students as they were to him, but following the publication of Hulbert's prize-winning *Forty-Niners* (Boston, 1931)—a synthetic diary of the Gold Rush migration to California—Turner expressed his doubts about the propriety of producing what he referred to as fictional or composite history, saying to Hulbert:

> Whether one who has read many of the original journals would feel the sense of reality, is doubtful, in my mind; but I can see that your unique experience in having gone through a vast collection of these journals, having traversed the ground yourself, and having worked out the trails so carefully, gives you an exceptional position for attempting such a composite picture. Perhaps because I am now one of the older generation, I must confess that the review by Nevins, the historian, seems to me to be more nearly in accord with my own impressions than are the reviews of your literary critics. The combination of fiction and history, even in skillful hands like yours, finds me somewhat unconvinced.[8]

In the area of transportation, as in most areas involving the West, Turner's approach is more subtle than overt, more implicit than explicit, more in the nature of miscellaneous profound explanations and observations, than it is a cohesive exposition of the role of transportation in the development of the West.

In a sense Turner's entire frontier concept was one based on movement, an ever-moving line of settlement, rather than one that envisioned a static situation. Turner leaves little doubt that his ever-shifting succession of "Wests" was augmented by the means of transportation available at given periods in our history. Moreover, he believed

---

[5] Wilbur R. Jacobs to the author, September 23, 1965. This classification appears in the Turner Papers, TU Box 56.

[6] Archer B. Hulbert, *Historic Highways* (Cleveland, 1902-05); also numerous other special studies.

[7] Charles H. Ambler, *History of Transportation in the Ohio Valley* (Glendale, Calif., 1932).

[8] Turner to Archer B. Hulbert, February 2, 1932, Turner Papers.

that transportation was closely intermeshed with sectionalism and sectional rivalries. Very early in his classic essay, "The Significance of the Frontier in American History," there appears, in beautifully poetic words, Turner's portrayal of this constantly moving, shifting transportation picture: "The buffalo trail became the Indian trail, and this became the trader's 'trace'; the trails widened into roads, and the roads into turnpikes, and these in turn were transformed into railroads. The same origin can be shown for the railroads of the South, the Far West, and the Dominion of Canada."[9] In this essay he refers as well to the role of "rising steam navigation on western waters, the opening of the Erie Canal" in adding new states to the Union. He alludes also to the need for improved means of transportation as the frontier "leaped over the Alleghanies" and then "skipped the Great Plains and Rocky Mountains" to re-emerge on the West Coast. Wrote Turner: "Railroads, fostered by land grants, sent an increasing tide of immigrants into the Far West."[10] Moreover, transportation was basic to Turner's ideas on sectionalism. Even though railroads are mentioned but once in his book, *The Significance of Sections in American History* (New York, 1950), this one statement is highly significant in that he contends that railroad construction provided the foundation for economic empires, or sections, and as such provided the grist for "political power."

This contention had also been expressed earlier but with less finality in his essay, "The Middle West," in which he pointed out how the railroad system of the 1850's bound the Mississippi to the North Atlantic seaboard, leaving New Orleans to give up (in spite of continued river traffic) her commercial hegemony to New York City. It remained for the late Albert L. Kohlmeier to detail this subject in his book, *The Old Northwest: Keystone to the Arch of Federal Union* (Bloomington, Ind., 1938). Also, in his essay entitled "The Problem of the West," first published in the *Atlantic Monthly* in 1896, Turner injected another of his penetrating observations by stating: "Railroads, fostered by government loans and land grants, opened the way for settlement and poured a flood of European immigrants and restless pioneers from all sections of the Union into the government lands."[11]

Interspersed in Turner's collected essays and books are a considerable number of brief, and as such tantalizing, pronouncements—a pattern that pertains as well to the newly published *Frederick Jackson*

[9] Frederick Jackson Turner, *The Frontier in American History* (New York, 1920), 14.
[10] *Ibid.*, 7, 8, 9.
[11] *Ibid.*, 218.

Turner's Legacy, edited by Wilbur R. Jacobs. In this welcome book appear but six rather minor references to transportation; each in turn is broad in its implications. In one of these heretofore unpublished essays or lectures Turner makes the significant statement that the improvement of transportation will assist in breaking down the "importance of the state" just as the radio "will diminish localism." He implies that such improvements will foster nationalism, as indeed they have done in Europe. Reversely (and here he assumes the role of a prophet), improvements in transportation, as for example the development of the St. Lawrence waterway, "will be resisted by New England in behalf of the port of Boston and by the harbor of New York on the plea that the Erie Canal should be improved instead. . . ."[12] In another portion of this collection of odds and ends of Turnerana appears the statement: "As means of transportation by steamboat, canal and railway penetrated the west, the farmer could raise a surplus of the market, and was no longer obliged to depend upon a product which could walk to market."[13]

All that has been said of Turner's published writings seemingly applies as well to the great mass of unpublished letters, class notes, and ephemera that make up the Turner Papers at the Huntington Library. I make no pretense of having worked in the Turner Papers even though I have perused some of them under the loving and generous guidance of Ray A. Billington and Wilbur R. Jacobs. When in a moment of weakness I accepted McDermott's invitation to prepare this paper, I fully intended to dash out to the Huntington in search of materials. But in advance of actually making such a trip there ensued a somewhat extended correspondence with Jacobs, then ensconced in the Turner room at the Huntington.

At first Jacobs held out at least slight hopes that a fresh search among the Turner Papers would be rewarding. "It is hard to say how much you might benefit from a personal trip," wrote Jacobs. "Sometimes you might read dozens of letters with no reference to transportation and then come across a gem." Jacobs did, however, discover a brief series of 3 × 5 cards classified "transportation," mostly bibliographical references to the subject. But this, he wrote, is "all that I have found labeled 'transportation' among FJT's notes, letters, 3 × 5 file and larger file drawers. . . . But why not come out for a trip?"[14] I did.

[12] Wilbur R. Jacobs, ed., *Frederick Jackson Turner's Legacy: Unpublished Writings in American History* (San Marino, Calif., 1965), 62, 69.
[13] *Ibid.,* 174.
[14] Jacobs to the author, September 10, 1965.

So this brings the discussion to the McDermott injunction: to discuss aspects of the frontier—in this case transportation—not accounted for by Turner, and to this one might add, by Turner's students.

The subject, as viewed within Turner's broad spectrum ranging from the buffalo trail to the railroad and within the context of middle and far West history, offers many opportunities for research that were either ignored or unwittingly bypassed by the Turner school. To say this carries with it neither blame nor indictment, because the post-Turner era has opened up new and previously undreamed-of opportunities for research, has been the legatee of new bodies of source materials, and has been the benefactor of many new inventions—all of which have given special advantages to the present-day historians of transportation. Moreover, historians who today criticize Turner possess the advantages that come not only from hindsight but that accrue from the rich harvest of source materials.

In any event the subject of frontier transportation today encompasses something more than it did in Turner's day. Research and publication in railroad history, for example, range widely over the whole field— from the solid core of finance and business management to sordid episodes associated with Indians and bad men. Research and writing in steamboat history have reached out from the main rivers to long-neglected western waters. The study of roads embraces not only turnpikes but military roads; federal, state, and local public roads; the relationship of military and public roads. Recent studies concern the good roads movement, such as RFD and the good roads movement, the farmer and the good roads movement; also the cyclists and the motorists and the good roads movement. Travel and travelers are also topics in which there is currently much interest, and in this connection tourism, hotels and inns, not to mention the folklore of travel, are subjects of books and special studies either out or in the making.

Historians—amateur and professional—busy themselves with a host of specialized topics that include cycling, canals, Indian travois, windwagons, buggies, balloons, and hiking. A reworking of old subjects has embraced a dissection of the Conestoga wagon and the Concord coach. One might add rebuilding, for recently I received a phone call from a business executive at South Bend, Indiana, who asked where he might locate a broken-down Concord—"anywhere in the U.S.A." He wanted to buy it and use it as a model for rebuilding a new one—before he died. The most recent books on the Conestoga and on wagons generally are basic anatomic descriptions, down to the last bolt, felloe, and skein.

Turner and his students had much transportation material available to them, but the truly great repositories—now open and within reach of the scholar—have come into full and effective use within relatively recent years: the Huntington (I say this in spite of Turner's residence there after retirement from Harvard), the Hopkins Transportation Library at Stanford, the opened archives of the Burlington and the Illinois Central at the Newberry, the Baker Library at Harvard, and the Bureau of Railroad Economics Library of the Association of Railroad Economics, Washington, D.C. All these holdings, physically, are of breathtaking proportions.[15] Not only have these magnificent collections altered the complexion of transportation history since Turner's death; they stand as an open invitation for younger generations of scholars who will find in these libraries relatively untouched materials associated with such things as the automobile, the airplane, the truck, and, to a lesser degree, vehicles now used for travel in outer space.

In addition to writing new history of transportation, there remains the challenge of discovering trends or patterns of development, and the always stimulating mental exercise of attempting to reinterpret the past. One recurrent pattern in frontier transportation is monopoly. This pattern in railroad development is so familiar it needs no telling here. It was, however, a pandemic situation among most transportation businesses in the free-enterprise West. In the realm of river steamboat operation the struggle among operators was for control. No sooner had steamboats invaded the California rivers during the 1850's than the California Steamship Company battled its way to mastery over its competitors. The scores of independent steamship operators on the Columbia River and its tributaries fought a life-and-death battle for a control that was eventually garnered by the Oregon Steam Navigation Company. The counterpart of these two companies on the "Old Muddy" was the Missouri River Transportation Company; on the upper Mississippi it was the Keokuk Northern Packet Company; on the lower Mississippi there was an ever-changing scramble for control.

Among the hundreds of small individual expresses on the West Coast there emerged two giants, Adams and Company and Wells, Fargo and Company, with a winner-take-all battle that in 1855 ended with Wells,

[15] The Hopkins transportation collection, for example, takes up one floor of the main stacks in the Stanford Library. The Burlington archives comprise 1,000,000 letters, 1,500 bundles of miscellaneous materials, and 2,000 bound ledgers. See Elizabeth C. Jackson, comp., *Guide to the Burlington Archives in the Newberry Library, 1851-1901* (Chicago, 1949), 374 pp. The Bureau of Railroad Economics Library consists of approximately 300,000 items. Others are of comparable size.

Fargo the victor. In freighting Russell, Majors and Waddell were triumphant, whereas in the overland staging business there emerged a succession of monopolists such as Ben Holladay's Overland Mail and Express Company on the central plains, John Butterfield in the Southwest, the California Stagecoach Company on the West Coast, and on the eve of the Pacific railroad completion Wells, Fargo and Company (in the staging as well as the express field). About the only frontier transportation enterprise that escaped monopolistic control were the lowly mule trains.[16] But these were usually run by the Mexican *cargador,* who was more content to put his trust in God and his energies into pacifying recalcitrant mules than be concerned about acquiring a monopoly of the packing business.

Another aspect of frontier transportation about which one might speculate concerns Turner's previously mentioned, beautifully poetic account of the orderly development of transportation history from the buffalo trail to the railroad. Was not the pattern of development much less orderly and less precise? The transportation picture on a given new frontier strikes one as having been that of chaos, or at least spontaneous evolvement. Pioneers often drove their wagons over unblazed trails and, as a rule, everything happened at once: wagon freighting emerged; stagecoach lines blossomed; express businesses sprang up with the same facility and frequency as saloons; steamboats all but moved overland in valiant efforts to serve newly formed communities; and if railroads were not made in a day, plans for them were.

It is, moreover, important to note this—and to the best of the reader's knowledge Turner does not do so: railroads were the destroyers of the frontier. For a brief time the horse-drawn operations lived side by side, served as a feeder, but sooner or later they withered on the vine. Steamboats could really not travel on land nor could they travel fast enough to satisfy the West, and they too gave way to the iron horse.

Then, finally, it may be contended that, so far as the transportation frontier is concerned, the year 1890 is a meaningless date. In no sense did the transportation frontier end with the passing of an unbroken line of settlement in 1890. Frontiers in transportation represent a continuous process and no termination of this process is in sight.

[16] See Oscar O. Winther, *The Transportation Frontier* (New York, 1964).

The Image
of the American West
at Mid-Century (1840-60)

A Product
of Scientific Geographical Exploration
by the United States Government

HERMAN R. FRIIS

THE NATIONAL ARCHIVES

By mid-nineteenth century the image or public impression of the area of the United States west of the Mississippi valley was undergoing decisive and far-reaching modification. The unprecedented migration of large numbers of people into this area to settle in the newly found oases and fertile valleys and to search for and mine the auriferous gravels and fabulous lodes demanded an acceleration in the extent, accuracy, and completeness of geographical and cartographical information.

The U.S. government, especially through the Topographical Bureau of the War Department, responded quickly and efficiently to this clamor for geographical information by directing a large number and a wide variety of expeditions whose primary objective was topographical surveying and landscape description. Leading civilian scientists and topographical engineers and their assistants combined their talents for observation, analysis, and interpretation to produce a surprisingly large treasure trove of objective, on-the-spot information about the New West that significantly modified the then current concept of an inhospitable, resourceless, sterile environment. The products of these expeditions, the survey field notes, maps, landscape sketches, reports, and correspondence, cover a wide variety of subjects of fundamental interest to historians and historical geographers. It is surprising that so little of this resource potential has been published and that so few of our specialists in western history have used it. Most of the extant contemporary manuscript records are in the National Archives in Washington, D.C.

This discussion is restricted to but a few, a very few, of the representative highlights. Emphasis is on the graphic record, of which the map is the best composite evidence.

Most of the maps of the western United States in the 1820's and 1830's that were available to and were viewed by the public included much misinformation that was based on fancy rather than on fact. Indeed, before the 1840's the federal government had surprisingly little accurate terrain information about this region in its Topographical Bureau files because most of the bureau's activities were directed to surveys for internal improvements in the populous eastern United States. This lack of fundamental accuracy is perhaps best illustrated by House Geographer David H. Burr's official "Map of the United States of North America with Parts of the Adjacent Countries," compiled and printed for the House of Representatives of the United States in July, 1839 (Figure 1).

The key to initial scientific geographical exploration of the West was the availability of accurate knowledge of the composition and arrangement of the primary physiographic features, especially the passes and interfluves. By 1840 the principal breaks in the Rocky Mountain Front leading into the interior were well, though not accurately, known. An excellent example of the detailed cartographic information on one of these passes, South Pass, is the relief map by Captain Washington Hood (Figure 2). He was a topographical engineer officer and compiled it from survey notes and sketch maps in the military headquarters office in Independence, Missouri, in 1839.

One of the most notable of Lieutenant Charles Wilkes's many contributions that resulted from the extensive surveys by his U.S. exploring expedition in the Pacific basin in 1838-42 was a detailed relief map of Oregon Territory (Figure 3). It was compiled from surveys by his field parties in 1841. One of these parties under Joseph Drayton explored inland along the Columbia River some 300 miles to its confluence with the Snake River near Fort Walla Walla. This party returned with "the materials for the construction of a map of the Columbia river, above the Cascade. . . . "

John C. Frémont contributed more than any other explorer of the American West in the 1840's to the accurate description and cartographic delineation of the primary physiographic features. He was the leader of five far-ranging expeditions. His reasonably accurate observations and broad interpretations of the geographic landscape and his cartographic contributions were both timely and facilitative, coming as they did on the eve of the great migrations of the 1840's and 1850's. In 1842 Frémont was ordered by the War Department to complete the survey of the Oregon or Emigrant Road westward from Independence, Missouri, to Fort Walla Walla in Oregon Territory in order to effect a tie-in at that point with the surveys by Wilkes previously noted. This remarkable accomplishment in October, 1843, completed the first full transect of the United States for mapping purposes. It made available a large fund of general geographical information about a vast hinterland lying as an imagined inhospitable threshold between the Pacific coast and the Great Plains. On the western portion of Frémont's map we note the details of terrain that were observed and about which he left to posterity a remarkably accurate geographical description and on-the-spot interpretations (Figure 4). A route to the western ocean had been blazed and its geographical landscape had been mapped and described for the use of a steadily increasing volume of emigrants that trod its many miles of wearying terrain.

The historic Oregon Road, that nature endowed and Frémont mapped westward from Independence, Missouri, through some 2,300 miles of terrain comprising a wide variety of landforms and environment to the Pacific coast, became a highway of unparalleled importance to the development of the new image and to the settlement of the West. Frémont's detailed large-scale map of the road was of inestimable value to settlers and to travelers. In addition to being a reasonably accurate topographic expression, this map, published in seven sheets, includes statements about natural resources, favorable camping sites, and weather. Sheet 4 of this series covers the historic milepost of the Continental Divide (Figure 5).

A second transcontinental route to the Pacific coast led from Fort Leavenworth in eastern Kansas to San Diego, California, by way of El Paso, Texas. In 1846-47 Lieutenant William H. Emory conducted a reconnaissance along this route, which included collecting and identifying materials in the natural sciences, observing weather and climate and astronomical and geographical phenomena, and mapping the terrain. The principal results of this survey were expressed as detailed reports by the scientists and as a series of overlapping sheets of the route, together comprising a large-scale topographic map. An example of the cartographic products adjacent to El Paso is shown on sheet 9 of Emory's final manuscript compilations of the entire route of survey (Figure 6).

On February 2, 1847, the Senate of the United States directed Lieutenant John C. Frémont to prepare a map of Oregon and California from his field notes and topographical surveys, and from such other reputable information as was available (Figure 7). Although the map was drawn by Frémont's assistant, Charles Preuss, Frémont notes in his "Geographical Memoir" that accompanies the map: "It [the map] is believed to be the most correct that has appeared of either of them [Oregon and California]; and it is certainly the only one that shows the structure and configuration of the interior of Upper California."[1]

Later in the same report Frémont discusses in meaningful physiographic terms the "Great Basin" that spreads across so much of the thermal barrier comprising the southwestern United States:

East of the Sierra Nevada, and between it and the Rocky mountains, is that anomalous feature in our continent, the GREAT BASIN, the existence of which was advanced as a theory after the second expedition, and is now established as a geographical fact. It is a singular feature. . . . Partly arid and sparsely inhabited, the general character of the GREAT BASIN is that of desert, but with great exceptions, there being many parts of it very fit for the residence of a civilized people; and of these parts, the Mormons have lately established themselves in one of the largest and best. . . .[2]

In 1848 gold was discovered near the base of the western slope of the Sierra Nevada in northern California. A young officer, Lieutenant William T. Sherman, who was stationed at Monterey in California, accompanied Colonel R. B. Mason on an official tour of the gold fields in the summer of 1848. Lieutenant Sherman prepared three maps of the gold fields on the American River, which were sent to Washington, D.C., with Colonel Mason's report. Mason's report, perhaps the first official account and description of the region and of its mining activities, is an excellent source of on-the-spot information about the landscape at that time. On one of his three sketch maps Sherman shows the site on which gold was discovered and the location of Sutter's mill (Figure 8).

One of the most remarkable sustained migrations of peoples into the West was made by the Mormons, who in the 1840's successfully settled in and intelligently adapted to the arid environment of the western foothills of the Wasatch range that fronts onto the Great Salt Lake. These Mormon settlements were located at or near the intersection of

[1] John C. Frémont, "Geographical Memoir upon Upper California in Illustration of His Map of Oregon and California . . . Addressed to the Senate of the United States," *Senate Miscellaneous Document No. 148*, 30th Cong., 1st Sess., Serial 511, 1848, 67 pp. Map at end of document. For manuscript version see in Records of the U.S. Senate in the National Archives, Washington, D.C.

[2] *Ibid.*, 7.

primary travel routes that carried the emigrants through the many wearying miles to the far West. Mindful of its responsibilities to survey accurately the metes and bounds of lands that had been settled, and just as mindful of its maximum need to obtain comprehensive geographical information about that region, the federal government in 1849 ordered Captain Howard Stansbury to make a detailed topographic survey and to prepare a report. Stansbury's report of the "Exploration and Survey of the Valley of the Great Salt Lake of Utah, Including a Reconnoissance of a New Route Through the Rocky Mountains" gives one of the first accurate descriptions and objective appraisals of terrain in the northeastern portion of the Great Basin and includes a large-scale detailed topographic map of the region (Figure 9). His description of the terrain relates particularly to the construction of roads through the Rocky Mountains and the Uinta and Wasatch ranges and to the mode and extent of Mormon settlement. Stansbury's "Map of the Great Salt Lake and Adjacent Country in the Territory of Utah" gives the first reasonably accurate view of this vital oasis threshold area as surveyed in 1849 and 1850.

On Monday, August 27, 1849, Stansbury recorded his first impression of the Great Salt Lake as follows: "Descending the pass through dense thickets of small oak-trees, we caught the first glimpse of the GREAT SALT LAKE, the long-desired object of our search. . . . A gleam of sunlight, reflected by the water, and a few floating, misty clouds, were all, however, that we could see of this famous spot. . . . "[3] With most of the government exploring expeditions were artists who were responsible for making sketches of the terrain along the route. A sketch in Stansbury's report shows the view he describes in the preceding quotation (Figure 10).

During the decade of the 1840's the U.S. Army, particularly the Topographical Bureau, expanded its field operations west of the Mississippi River. Some of the expeditions were of a punitive nature, though the large majority were primarily responsible for a progressive, systematic survey of the Great Plains, the Rocky Mountains, and the vast interior that spread west toward the sea. In 1850 the Topographical Bureau compiled and published a relief map of "the United States and Their

[3] Howard Stansbury, "Exploration and Survey of the Valley of the Great Salt Lake of Utah, including a Reconnoissance of a New Route Through the Rocky Mountains," *Senate Executive Document No. 3*, 32nd Cong., Special Sess., Serial 608, 1852. 487 pp. Map at end of document. For manuscript version see in Records of the U.S. Senate in the National Archives.

Territories Between the Mississippi and the Pacific Ocean," based on the most authentic information available in the files of the federal government (Figure 11). Most of the available usable information consisted of maps and field survey reports of topographical engineer officers and others that were on file in the archives of that agency, a few representative examples of which we have just discussed. It was, of course, immediately obvious that most of the West in 1850, especially that beyond the Rocky Mountains, was inadequately explored and erroneously known. There is little question but that this map pointed up the needs for and ushered in a new era of intensive exploration and mapping, especially by the Topographical Bureau. This was the official image of the West in 1850, perhaps the first reasonably accurate map of the broad general physiographic features. The sudden universal interest in this West, clearly sharpened by the discovery of extensive mineral deposits and by the proof, as in the Mormon oases and the Willamette valley settlements, that rich agricultural potentialities existed, presaged a new and a highly productive era of geographical exploration.

During the decade of the 1850's the federal government initiated a major program of systematic exploration and mapping of the West. This program included especially (1) exploration to determine accurately the precise location, extent, and composition of the primary landform features, (2) exploration and surveys of the principal river systems, and (3) exploration and surveys for civilian and military transportation. We have space only to show a representative example of each one of these.

One of the large little-known areas was the Colorado Plateau. Within this extensive area and measuring its length and breadth was the deep, sinuous gorge of the Colorado River and its wide-ranging tributaries, which served as a major obstacle to the direct east-west route of migration and trade, especially along the southern perimeter. The Topographical Bureau, intent on solving this problem, in the 1850's launched a succession of land and water expeditions to trace these riverways and to survey the circumjacent arid, deeply dissected Colorado Plateau. An example of one of these surveys is that by Lieutenant Lorenzo Sitgreaves, who in 1851 made a topographic reconnaissance of the Colorado Plateau between the Gila and Colorado rivers (Figure 12). With his informative report are large-scale topographic maps, the manuscript compilations of which are in the National Archives.

In 1858 Lieutenant Joseph C. Ives was ordered "to ascertain the navigability of the Colorado with especial reference to the availability for

Figure 1

MAP
exhibiting the practicable passes of the
ROCKY MOUNTAINS;
together with the Topographical features of
the country adjacent to the head waters of the
MISSOURI, YELLOWSTONE, SALMON,
LEWIS' & COLORADO
RIVERS;
BY
WASH: HOOD
CAPT. ENG.rs

Figure 2

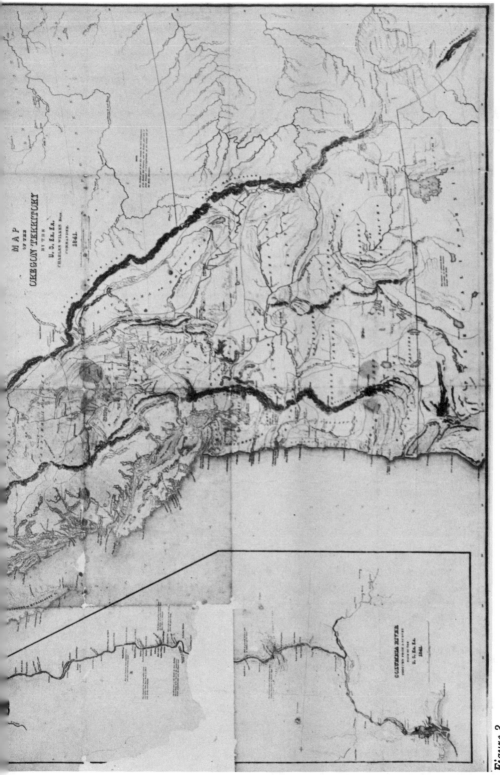

MAP
OF THE
OREGON TERRITORY
BY THE
U. S. Ex. Ex.
CHARLES WILKES Esqr.
COMMANDER.
1841.

COLUMBIA RIVER
REDUCED FROM A SURVEY
BY THE
U. S. Ex. Ex.
1841.

Figure 3

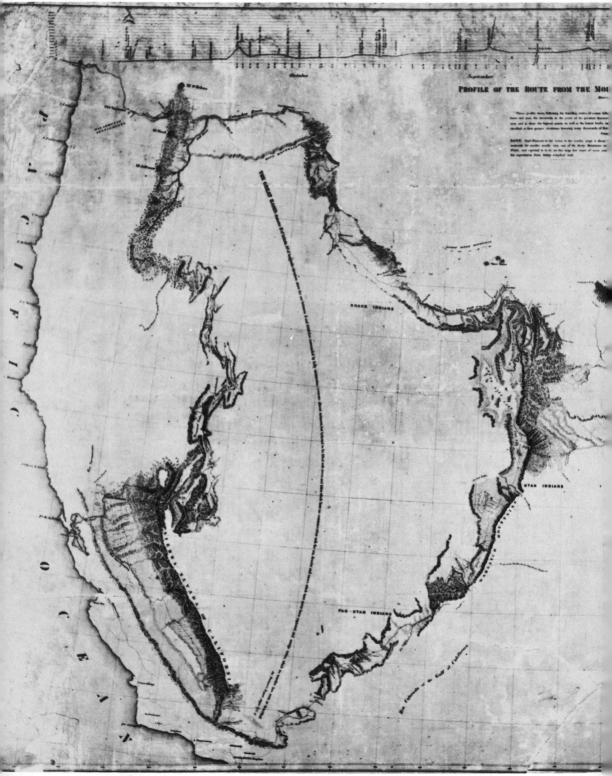

Figure 4

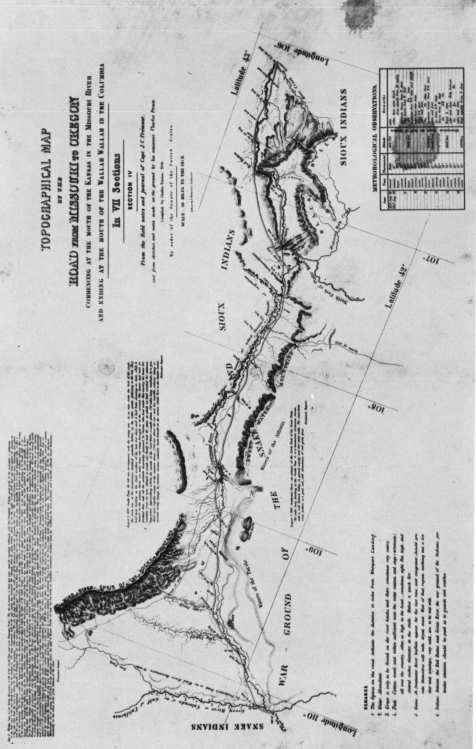

Figure 5

Figure 6

Figure 7

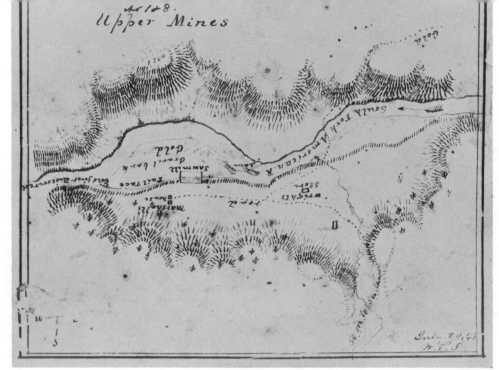

Figure 8

Figure 9

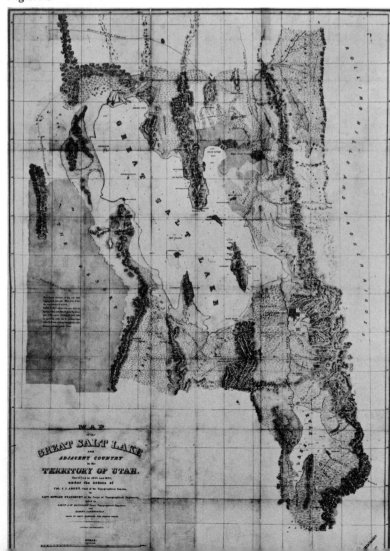

Figure 10

Figure 11

Figure 12

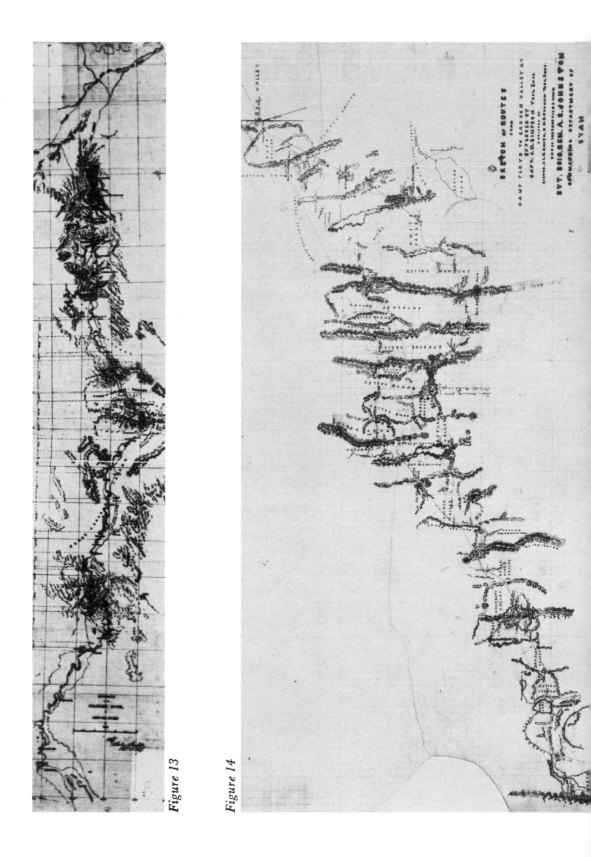

Figure 13

Figure 14

Figure 15

Figure 16

Figure 17

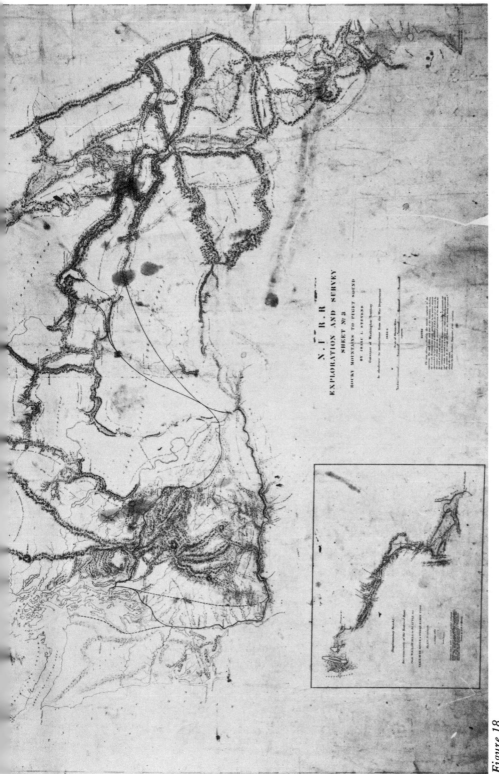

Figure 18

Figure 19

Figure 20

Figure 21

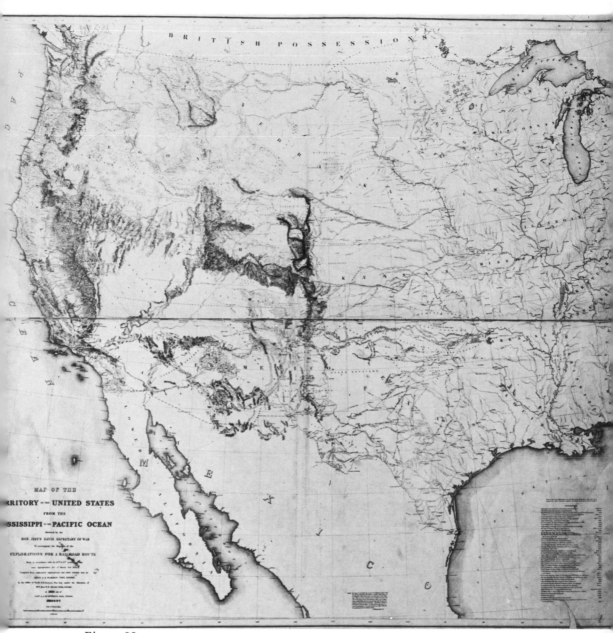

Figure 22

Figure 23

the transportation of supplies to the various military posts in New Mexico and Utah." In addition to preparing a well-illustrated, scientific report of the expedition, Ives compiled a map of the area covered by the reconnaissance (Figure 13). His map shows the track of the reconnaissance and, as accurately as the surveys and generalization permit on a small scale, the course of the lower Colorado.

Most of the emigrants following the California Trail through the Humboldt River maze of alkaline-silted valleys of the Basin Range Province between Utah and California succored the finding of a more hospitable environment and a more direct route. In 1858 and 1859 Captain James Hervey Simpson, a topographical engineer officer with considerable experience and competence in road building, directed a detailed reconnaissance for and discovered a more favorable route south of the much-traveled California Trail. On his generalized manuscript map of the region he shows the line "for a direct wagon route from Camp Floyd, Utah, to Genoa, in Carson Valley, California" (Figure 14).

With his official manuscript report, one of the first accurate on-the-spot scientific appraisals of the geographical features and natural resources of the region, Simpson includes eight beautiful landscape views in water color, prepared by artists from detailed field sketches of topographer-artists who accompanied the expedition. An excellent example of these sketches is that of "Carson Lake from the East, Sierra Nevada in Distance," prepared by J. J. Young from a field sketch by H. V. A. von Beckh (Figure 15). Interestingly, these remarkably lucid and graphic portrayals of the geographical landscape of selective and representative areas were not reproduced with the official report.

The call for a transcontinental railroad between the Mississippi River and the Pacific, a whisper in the 1830's, a promise and a hope in the 1840's, became a national issue of formidable proportions by the early 1850's. By now the question was not so much shall a railroad be constructed; rather, it was how and where? To complicate the issue further, sectional feelings were aroused and sentiments ran high as to the preferred route. In 1853 Congress authorized the Secretary of War to undertake a systematic survey along each of four east-west routes from the Mississippi River to the Pacific Ocean to determine the best, most practicable route for a railroad (Figure 16). A fifth route was to be run in California. These reconnaissance surveys constituted the government's first concerted attempt at a comprehensive and systematic geographical examination of the American West along predetermined belts of latitude. The resulting terrain information made possible the first reasonably accurate topographic map of the West, while the reports, sketches, survey field notebooks, and other records comprise a remarkable reservoir of geographical information about the area at that time. The Secretary of War noted in his remarks that the instructions given to the survey parties directed them "to observe and note all the objects and phenomena which have an immediate or remote bearing upon the railway, or which might seem to develop the resources, peculiarities, and climate of the country; to determine geographical positions, obtain the topography, observe the meteorology . . . make a geological survey of the lines; to collect information upon, and specimens of, the botany and zoology of the country; and to obtain statistics of the Indian tribes which are found in the regions traversed. . . ."[4]

In addition to the military and their civilian assistants, each survey party included botanists, topographers, geologists, civil engineers, surveyors, astronomers, naturalists, meterologists, and artists. At convenient intervals each survey party transmitted to Washington the products of their reconnaissances, graphic, cartographic, textual, and related records.

The Secretary of War was given responsibility for the surveys and the preparation of the reports. In order to achieve the prescribed goals he wisely established an Office of Explorations and Surveys, which became in effect a kind of detached office of the Bureau of Topographical Engineers. Operating out of this office were the several field parties. Although the primary objective of each party was to prepare accurate large-scale detailed topographic maps and profiles of the belt of terrain astride the prescribed route of survey, each party also was to observe, record, and report on the total geographic landscape through which the surveys were run.

The principal published product of these explorations was a thirteen-volume document comprising a large number of descriptive reports, maps, colored and black-and-white lithographs of landscape views and archeological, ethnological, and zoological subjects, profiles and cross sections, tables of statistics, and other graphic materials. This document, entitled *Reports of Explorations and Surveys to Ascertain the*

[4] Jefferson Davis, "Report of the Secretary of War, Dated Washington, February 27, 1855," in "Reports of Explorations and Surveys to Ascertain the Most Practicable and Economical Route for a Railroad from the Mississippi River to the Pacific Ocean . . . ," *Senate Executive Document No. 78,* 33rd Cong., 2nd Sess., Vol. I, 1855, 30 pp. For quotation see pp. 7-8. For manuscript version see in Records of the U.S. Senate in the National Archives.

Most Practicable and Economical Route for a Railroad from the Mis-sissippi River to the Pacific Ocean, was published by the federal government. These volumes and the cartographic, graphic, and textual records constitute a primary source of information about the physical and cultural landscapes of the West extant in the decade of the 1850's. There is little question but that these thirteen volumes, published between 1855 and 1861, together with the large number of books, articles, and other scientific publications on the results of these explorations authored by responsible and professionally competent persons, played a substantial role in giving the world a more accurate and objective view of the West. Indeed, the scientific results, the large number of mineral, rock, zoological, and other specimens, the landscape sketches and maps, and the variety of the reports encouraged scientists subsequently to so augment their field work and research in the West that their publications found international recognition. We should point out that publication of the thirteen volumes of reports alone cost between $1,000,000 and $1,200,000, as compared with some $400,000 that were expended on the field surveys. A representative example of an illustration is found within Governor Isaac I. Stevens' published report for 1853 of the detailed surveys of Oregon and Washington (Figure 17). The illustration is of Palouse Falls of the Palouse River in eastern Washington.

An excellent example of one of the final manuscript compilations of sectional topographic maps covering these routes is sheet 3 of the rugged terrain between the Rocky Mountains and Puget Sound on the Pacific coast, derived from surveys under the direction of Isaac I. Stevens in 1853-54 (Figure 18). This sheet was one of several overlapping sheets on the same scale covering the entire route of survey from St. Paul, Minnesota, to the Pacific coast. Similar series of overlapping sheets of compilation covered each of the other four routes.

But there is a real question as to whether the final printed and published lithographic reproductions of these remarkable landscape views are completely accurate and do faithfully reflect the "manuscript original" prepared in the field by the artist. We are fortunate that among the relatively small number of manuscript and press proof copies of these illustrations that are in the National Archives there are at least two items that justify this concern. One of these is the pencil field sketch by Charles Koppel which bears the notation "Ravines in the bed of the ancient lake" (Figure 19).

The aforementioned pencil sketch apparently was sent to the reliable engraving firm of August Hoen in Baltimore with appropriate instructions by Lieutenant Gouverneur K. Warren, who was directly in charge of the work of the Office of Explorations and Surveys. A comparison of available field and office landscape sketches and maps with their counterparts in final published form reveals the extent to which engravers took liberties with the manuscript, presumably in the interests of better composition and perhaps even to satisfy their own urge to be final editor. This is especially well illustrated by a comparison of the foregoing manuscript sketch and the corresponding lithographic or printer's proof (Figure 20).

During the 1850's several of the exploring expeditions in the West included photographers who obtained landscape views especially for use by cartographers in more accurately rendering their maps. But photography was costly, the equipment needs were considerable and bulky, and most expedition leaders felt the product was far inferior to the artist's "as-seen" sketch. Within the published Pacific Railroad Survey reports are numerous landscape sketches that are of particular value to a historian and to a historical geographer. An excellent example is the lithographic copy of a landscape view of Fort Vancouver, Washington Territory, about 1853, prepared by the artist-cartographer Gustav Sohon to accompany the "General Report" of the surveys under Isaac I. Stevens (Figure 21).

Perhaps the single most important product of these extensive field surveys and office activities directed to the publication of the scientific results of the geographical explorations was the compilation of an accurate landform "Map of the Territory of the United States from the Mississippi to the Pacific Ocean" on a scale of 1:3,000,000 or about fifty miles to an inch (Figure 22). This was Lieutenant Warren's immediate and primary responsibility. On March 1, 1858, Warren transmitted to his superior, Captain A. A. Humphreys, a letter and a report or memoir to accompany the foregoing map. In his letter he notes: "In compiling the 'map . . . ' my instructions were to carefully read every report and examine every map of survey, reconnoissance, and travel which could be obtained, to ascertain their several values, and to embody the authentic information in the map. This duty is now to the best of my ability completed."[5]

In his brief, simple, straightforward manner Warren transmitted to his superiors a memoir and a map that must rank as one of the most

[5] Gouverneur K. Warren, "Memoir to Accompany the Map of the Territory of the United States from the Mississippi River to the Pacific Ocean . . . ," *ibid.,* Vol. XI, 1861. 115 pp. For quotation see unnumbered p. 9.

significant contributions in the history of American cartography. In modest, self-effacing sentences he assumes responsibility for errors in research, compilation, and engraving, and justifiably gives full credit to his draftmen, E. Freyhold and F. W. Egloffstein, for their very large share in the final compilation.

Here indeed was a new and accurate map that became a datum upon which to revise periodically as more correct and detailed information was received. This map was based on a wide variety of carefully selected and evaluated cartographic and related records in the federal government, particularly those of the Topographical Bureau. Frequent new editions on a scale of about one inch to fifty miles were issued by the War Department, even into the present century. This terrain map represents the new look of the macromorphology of the primary elements of the geographical landscape of our West—a new image if you will—at mid-century. This was the base upon which to portray in relatively accurate relationship the patterns of settlement specifically and the ingredients of cultural geography generally. Indeed, here was a different West from that shown in "A mapp of Virginia discovered to ye Hills . . . " by Virginia Farrer, published in London at mid-century 200 years earlier. You will note that on this map the West extends from the Appalachian Mountains to the Pacific Ocean as a gently sloping plain "ten dayes march . . . from the head of Ieames River . . ." (Figure 23). This map represents fancy; our 1857 map represents fact. Yet each is a record of a geographic concept at a specified moment in time. Each has its rightful place in recorded history and certainly in the writings of historians and geographers. Each *must* be viewed and used with the knowledge of what it is and why it was made.

I believe that we will agree that by 1857 the cartographic image of our West was both reliable and objective, for it was derived from field surveys and observations, or fact rather than fancy.

Most of us, if not all, will agree that any concept of the American West must include as its very base a geographical consideration. As interpreters and as objective writers of history we cannot escape the fact that fundamentally we are dealing with time and space, or we might better say, respectively, with history and geography. One of the most useful records which combines these two elements of time and space is the cartographic representation—the map. We have seen representative examples of a few of these that are in the National Archives in the foregoing presentation. As geographers and as historians we make appallingly little use of this vast invaluable resource in our research and in our writing. A review of Frederick Jackson Turner's writings, for example, reveals that he was at heart a theoretician who emphasized the importance of the map. Yet he rarely allowed himself the opportunity to use the cartographic record as an expression of his geographical *Lebensraum,* the frontier and the American West, in which to apply his theories. Surely the map of the West in 1857 which we have seen would have been a favorable graphic background upon which both to describe and to appraise the West during that eventful decade straddling the mid-century.

But Turner's failing is not alone. Far too many historians and even geographers over the past century or more have neglected their research in and their objective use of cartographic and graphic records for what they are—a composite of a wide variety of information about the physical and cultural landscape at a moment in time. Too often, far too often, these materials have been selected simply as random illustrative materials, as in the case of the historian who came to my office in the National Archives some years ago and pleaded: "Please, I have but two hours between trains. My publisher has told me to stop off here and get a dozen or so maps and views to dress up my book." But really objective writers should know that good scholarship is not a product of mail-order selection. Good scholarship requires the application of the same rigorous and objective research, appraisal, and selection of materials to cartographic and graphic materials as it does to the textual. Surely we cannot excuse this lack of appreciation and use by leaning on the crutch of ignorance. There *is* a considerable and variant treasure trove that goes begging for the using.

Descriptive List of Illustrations

Each of the illustrations (except 23) is a reproduction of the official record item on file in the National Archives (NA). The agency of origin and the file notation of each item is indicated. Measurements in inches are to the edge of the sheet; the vertical dimension is given first. The scale given is of the "original" and not of the reproduction.

1. "Map of the United States of North America With parts of the Adjacent Countries. By David H. Burr. (Late Topographer to the Post Office.) Geographer to the House of Representatives of the U.S." 1839. Scale 1 inch to 60 miles. 38 × 51 inches. Colored manuscript Plate 1 with David H. Burr's *Atlas . . . 1839* in the Records of the Post Office Department, in NA.

2. "Map exhibiting the practicable passes of the Rocky Mountains; together with the Topographical features of the country adjacent to the head-waters of the Missouri, Yellowstone, Salmon, Lewis' and Colorado Rivers; by Wash:

Hood Capt. T. Engrs. 1839." Scale 1 inch to 43 miles. 16½ × 22 inches. Reduced print of colored manuscript US 110 in the Headquarters Map File of the Office of the Chief of Engineers, in NA.

3. "Map of the Oregon Territory by the U.S. Ex[ploring] Ex[pedition] Charles Wilkes Esqr. Commander. 1841." Scale 1 inch to 50 miles. 26 × 38 inches. Printed map CA 347 in the Records of the Bureau of Indian Affairs, in NA.

4. "[Western Half of a] Map of an Exploring Expedition to the Rocky Mountains in the Year 1842 and to Oregon and North California in the years 1843-44 by Bvt. Capt. J. C. Frémont of the Corps of Topographical Engineers Under the orders of Col. J. J. Abert, Chief of the Topographical Bureau." Scale not given but computed to be 1 inch to 32 miles. 30¼ × 50¼ inches. Printed map US 130 in the Headquarters Map File of the Office of the Chief of Engineers, in NA.

5. "[Sheet 4 of a] Topographical Map of the Road from Missouri to Oregon Commencing at the Mouth of the Kansas in the Missouri River and Ending at the Mouth of the Wallah-Wallah in the Columbia. . . . From the field notes and journal of Capt. J. C. Frémont, and from sketches and notes made on the ground by his assistant Charles Preuss . . . 1846 By order of the Senate of the United States." Scale 1 inch to 10 miles. 16 × 26 inches. Printed map US 155(4) in the Headquarters Map File of the Office of the Chief of Engineers, in NA.

6. "[Sheet 29 of a Map of the] Boundary between the United States & Mexico. . . . Astronomically determined and surveyed in 1855, under the direction of William H. Emory, U.S. Commissioner. . . . Projected and drawn by F. Herbst. . . ." Scale 1 inch to 1 mile. 26 × 39 inches. Printed map to accompany U.S.-Mexico Boundary, Treaties of 1848-53, Department of State, in NA.

7. "[Topographic] Map of Oregon and Upper California From the Surveys of John Charles Frémont And Other Authorities Drawn by Charles Preuss Under the Order of the Senate of the United States Washington City 1848." Scale 1 inch to 48 miles. 32¾ × 26½ inches. Annotated printed map W 37 in the Headquarters Map File of the Office of the Chief of Engineers, in NA.

8. "[Map of] Positions of the Upper and Lower Gold Mines, on the South Fork of the American River, California. July 20, 1848, W. T. S[herman]." Scale 1 inch to 3 miles. 10½ × 18½ inches. Manuscript map W 8(2) in the Headquarters Map File of the Office of the Chief of Engineers, in NA.

9. "Map of the Great Salt Lake and Adjacent Country in the Territory of Utah. Surveyed in 1849 and 1850, under the orders of Col. J. J. Abert, Chief of the Topographical Bureau, by Capt. Howard Stansbury of the Corps of Topographical Engineers. . . . Drawn by Lieut. Gunnison and Charles Preuss." Scale 1 inch to 4 miles. 43¾ × 30¼ inches. Colored printed map in the published record set in the Headquarters Map File of the Office of the Chief of Engineers, in NA.

10. "First view of Great Salt Lake Valley, From a Mountain Pass. . . ." 5½ × 8¾ inches. Tinted printed lithograph in Howard Stansbury, "Exploration

and Survey of the Valley of the Great Salt Lake of Utah . . . ," *Senate Executive Document No. 3,* 32nd Cong., Special Sess., Vol. II, opposite p. 268, in NA.

11. "Map of the United States and Their Territories Between the Mississippi and the Pacific Ocean; and of Part of Mexico. Compiled in the Bureau of the Corps of Topgl. Engs. under a Resolution of the U.S. Senate. . . . 1850." Scale 1 inch to 50 miles. 43 × 38½ inches. Printed map in the published record set in the Headquarters Map File of the Office of the Chief of Engineers, in NA.

12. "[Part of a Map of a] Reconnaissance of the Zuñi, Little Colorado and Colorado Rivers. Made in 1851 under the direction of Col. J. J. Abert Chief of Corps of Top. Engrs. by Bvt. Capt. L. Sitgreaves. T.E. Assisted by Lieut. J. G. Parke, T.E. and Mr. R. H. Kern. Drawn by R. H. Kern. 1852." Scale 1 inch to 10 miles. 26½ ×48½ inches. Manuscript map W 20 in the Headquarters Map File of the Office of the Chief of Engineers, in NA.

13. "[Part of a Map of] Exploration of the Colorado River, by Lieut. Ives, Topl. Engs. in 1858. . . . Copy [by] Charles Churchill 1st Lt. 3d Arty." Scale 1 inch to 6 miles. 12 × 66½ inches. Manuscript map US 324(80) in the Headquarters Map File of the Office of the Chief of Engineers, in NA.

14. "Sketch [Map] of Routes from Camp Floyd to Carson Valley U.T. Explored by Capt. J. H. Simpson Topl. Engs. Assisted by Lieuts. J. S. K. Smith, & H. S. Putnam Topl. Engs. Under Instructions from Bvt. Brig. Gen. A. S. Johnston Commanding Department of Utah Survey and Sketch by Lt. Putnam 1859." Scale 1 inch to 16 miles. 14½ × 28 inches. Colored manuscript W 67(1) in the Headquarters Map File of the Office of the Chief of Engineers, in NA.

15. "Carson Lake from the East, Sierra Nevada in Distance. . . . [By] J. J. Young from a Sketch by H. V. A. v. Beckh. Journal Plate VI." *Ca.* 1859. 9¾ × 21½ inches. Colored manuscript landscape sketch Misc. 120(5) in the Headquarters Map File of the Office of the Chief of Engineers, in NA.

16. "Principal routes of surveys and explorations for a railroad from the Mississippi River to the Pacific Ocean: 1853-1857," compiled in January, 1958, by Herman R. Friis. Scale 1 inch to 112 miles. 20 × 32 inches. Annotations on a printed relief map of the United States in color published by the U.S. Geological Survey in 1916, reprinted in 1934, in NA.

17. "Peluse Falls. . . . [By] Stanley Del[ineator]." 8 × 11 inches. Lithographic reproduction in color. From *Reports of Explorations and Surveys to Ascertain the Most Practicable and Economical Route for a Railroad from the Mississippi River to the Pacific Ocean, Made Under the Direction of the Secretary of War, in 1853-57* (Washington, 1860), Vol. XII(1) , opposite p. 151, in NA.

18. "N.P.R.R Exploration and Survey. Sheet No. 3 [Topographic Map of the Area from the] Rocky Mountains to Puget Sound by Isaac I. Stevens, Governor of Washington Territory . . . 1853-4." Scale 1 inch to 18 miles. 25 × 37 inches. Drawn by John Lambert, topographer of the expedition. Manuscript map in the Records of the Office of the Secretary of the Interior, in NA.

19. "Ravines in the bed of the ancient lake . . . from a sketch by Charles Koppel." *Ca.* 1855. 8× 11 inches. Manuscript pencil and ink wash sketch in the Records of the Office of the Secretary of the Interior, in NA.

20. "Ravines in the bed of the ancient lake. . . . From a sketch by Chs. Koppel." *Ca.* 1855. 8 × 11 inches. Proof of a lithographic copy in the Records of the Office of the Secretary of the Interior, in NA.

21. "[Landscape View of] Fort Vancouver, W[ashington] T[erritory, *ca.* 1853], G[ustav] Sohon Del[ineator]." 8 × 11 inches. Lithographic reproduction in color. From *Reports of Explorations and Surveys to Ascertain the Most Practicable and Economical Route for a Railroad from the Mississippi River to the Pacific Ocean, Made Under the Direction of the Secretary of War, in 1853-57* (Washington, 1860), Vol. XII(1), opposite p. 154, in NA.

22. "Map of the Territory of the United States from the Mississippi to the Pacific Ocean Ordered by the Hon. Jeff'n Davis. Secretary of War To accompany the Reports of the Explorations for a Railroad Route. . . . Compiled from authorized explorations and other reliable data by Lieut. G. K. Warren. Topl. Engrs. In thc Office of Pacific R.R. Surveys. War Dep. under the direction of Bvt. Maj. W. H. Emory, Topl. Engrs. in 1854 and of Capt. A. A. Humphreys, Topl. Engrs. 1854-5-6-7." Scale 1 inch to 50 miles. 42¼ × 46 inches. Printed map in the Records of the Office of the Secretary of the Department of the Interior, in NA.

23. "A mapp of Virginia discovered to ye Hills, and in it's Latt: From 35. deg: & ½ neer Forida, to 41. deg: bounds of new England. Donuna Virginia Farrer Collegit. . . . [London,] 1651." Precise scale not possible. 10¾ × 14 inches. Printed map on paper in the Map Division, Library of Congress, Washington, D.C.

The Great Revival, the West, and the Crisis of the Church

RALPH E. MORROW

WASHINGTON UNIVERSITY

The Great Revival always has held an important place in historical writing on frontier religion. The publication of Catherine Cleveland's *The Great Revival in the West, 1797-1806* during World War I marked the advent of academic interest in the topic, but her book was preceded by a hundred-year procession of narratives which described the revival with greater or lesser fullness.[1] Academic studies of the revival improved on the earlier accounts by carefully charting its erratic course, analyzing its social milieu, and borrowing insights from social and medical science to interpret the extravagant behavior with which it was punctuated. In one respect, however, much of the academic writing fell short of that of the nineteenth century. Earlier chroniclers often had a lively sense of movements of religion in history and, moreover, entertained convictions that such movements tended toward the fulfillment of a cosmic purpose. Consequently, they tried to fit the Great Revival into a comprehensive scheme of religious development. Among their academic successors, however, the imagination has been kept firmly reined. The bulk of twentieth-century writing on the revival has been done by historians who worked within tight regional frames of reference. One result is that the full dimensions of the revival have been obscured by the magnification of its western phases.

---

[1] Basic bibliographies of nineteenth-century literature on the Great Revival are in Catherine C. Cleveland, *The Great Revival in the West, 1797-1806* (Chicago, 1916), and Walter B. Posey, *The Presbyterian Church in the Old Southwest, 1788-1838* (Richmond, 1952). Among other academic studies which give attention to the Great Revival are R. Carlyle Buley, *The Old Northwest: The Pioneer Period, 1815-1840* (Indianapolis, 1950); Charles A. Johnson, *The Frontier Camp Meeting: Religion's Harvest Time* (Dallas, 1955); Walter Posey, *The Development of Methodism in the Old Southwest* (Tuscaloosa, 1933); and William W. Sweet, *The Presbyterians, 1783-1840 (Religion on the American Frontier,* II, New York, 1936).

Yet the turn-of-the-century revival deserves to be restored to a more elaborate setting. It quickly came to be called "great" not only for the intense feelings which were aroused but because it was nationwide. Besides the heavings in Kentucky and Tennessee, Connecticut had "a shower of refreshing" so heavy that it was promptly dubbed the Second Awakening, and from these centers in the East and West the swells of piety reached far outposts in northern Ohio, Nova Scotia, and Georgia. In naming the visitation the Second Awakening New Englanders were historically correct as well as descriptively accurate, for the first had prepared the way for it. The Great Awakening and the Great Revival are joined, however, not only by the nexus of revivalism but by that of the institutional church. In respect to the latter, the two revivals stand as the fore and after brackets of a period of mounting confusion over the nature, purpose, and functions of the church. It is within this larger context of time, space, and meaning that the revival in the West finds its special place. In the western states the ambiguities and cross purposes which had been accumulating for half a century came into sharpest focus, and there also the most earnest attempts to eliminate them were made.

Theologians often lament and church historians confirm that ecclesiology has been the branch of theology most neglected by Americans until recent years. Nevertheless, it is possible to outline a minimal body of agreement among Protestants in the early eighteenth century on the character and functions of the church. John Calvin's dictum that it was "necessary . . . to know . . . the visible church" for "there is no other way of entrance into life"[2] was an article of faith in the churches established in the English colonies and in the unestablished offshoots of European state churches. Moreover, it was not under serious challenge outside these churches. Theology and universal history furnished one support to the church, the necessities of man and society another. The ministrations of the church enabled man to understand himself and to fulfill his destiny, at the same time furthering peace and stability in society. These practical considerations of service to the Commonwealth and the citizens thereof entitled the church to nurture and protection by the civil government. The discharge of these private and public responsibilities by the church, however, depended upon the right ordering of its internal affairs. A church could serve man and society as they should be served only if it remained pure in doctrine, kept its ministra-

[2] Hugh T. Kerr, Jr., ed., *A Compend of the Institutes of the Christian Religion* (Philadelphia, 1939), 154.

tions orderly and regular, and paid heed to those intellectually qualified and properly commissioned to lead.

This common ground of opinion, however, failed to survive the colonial period. Virginia, in the decade before the Revolution, afforded a vivid but by no means exceptional example of how far the divergence of views had progressed. There, Thomas Jefferson, who respected the church as a socially useful human contrivance, Jonathan Boucher, who viewed it as part of a divinely ordained plan for the government of mankind, and Francis Asbury, who saw it chiefly as a community of redeemed men, all belonged to the Anglican communion. In two important respects, the fragmentation of attitudes which occurred between the Great Awakening and the revolutionary period anticipated dominant patterns of the Great Revival. First, the agreement which prevailed in the early eighteenth century was not broken by assault from outside. Neither in the colonial period nor later was the church in America pressed to defend itself against sustained attacks from "enemies of religion." Instead, the traditional conceptions were undermined inside the church by the influences of rationalism and pietism. Second, the differences which arose over the church seldom were tried in the fire of open and searching debate. Individuals and groups protested particular exercises of authority in the name of the church, and skirmishes over the doctrine of the church erupted along with conflicts which centered on other theological issues. The total effect of this, however, pales beside the great discussions of the church known to other times and peoples. Comparing the latter to the course of debate in America, one is tempted to conclude that ancestral views of the church were not destroyed, they were merely forgotten.[3]

Uncertainty and disagreement within the church do much to explain the hesitant and wavering attitudes which its spokesmen exhibited during the movements for separation of church and state and the establishment of religious freedom. One historian has written that separation and freedom produced "the most profound revolution . . . in the entire history of the church . . . on the administrative side"[4] since Constantine, but disarray prevailed in ecclesiastical ranks as the new era approached.

[3] This discussion of the church is built upon two brilliant essays by Sidney E. Mead, "From Coercion to Persuasion; Another Look at the Rise of Religious Liberty and the Emergence of Denominationalism," *Church History*, XXV (1956), 317-337, and "American Protestantism During the Revolutionary Epoch," *Church History*, XXII (1953), 279-297.

[4] Winfred E. Garrison, "Characteristics of American Organized Religion," *Annals of the American Academy of Political and Social Science*, CCLVI (1948), 17.

The churches with traditions of state support were unable to present an unbroken front either for or against change and even groups without such traditions were not entirely united. In New England the compromise of multiple establishment, which persisted into the nineteenth century, not only was unsatisfactory to most Baptists but to some Congregationalists as well. In Virginia, the alignments of groups and individuals on the questions of church and state shifted bewilderingly during the ten-year struggle which preceded the adoption of the statute of religious freedom in 1786. The inability of churches to agree within and among themselves left political leaders in charge of organizing and directing the movements both for and against reform. Despite the burning relevance of the issues, hardly any churchmen won prominence for political generalship and none left a memorable exposition on church-state relations to stand as an intellectual monument to the struggle.[5]

In view of these disruptive changes "the first task of the American churches after the Revolution" could not have been "to follow [the] westward moving population over the Alleghenies. . . ."[6] Their "first task" was to make the ancient idea of "the body of Christ" relevant to the times. Specifically, the church, or the various visible fragments thereof, had to keep contact with a population free to choose religion or not, establish an identity by which it could know itself and be known, retain its cohesiveness in a society remarkably open and free, resettle relations to civil government, and secure a place in the social order. These and kindred problems raised temptations for churchmen to withdraw into a fastidious concern for doctrinal and ecclesiastical orthodoxy or else lunge into theocratic adventures in politics. Both tendencies were clearest in New England, the first in the "Unitarian controversy" and the second in the anti-Jeffersonian alliance between the Congregational clergy and the Federalist party.

The thesis that religious organizations were too deeply involved in problems of internal repair and external adjustment after the Revolution to take up the challenge of the frontier does not, however, rest solely upon inference. It is supported by their record of activity in the region. The vacillating, uncoordinated, and spasmodic character of missionary work in the trans-Appalachian West contrasts sharply with

[5] M. Louise Greene, *The Development of Religious Liberty in Connecticut* (Boston, 1905), 212; H. J. Eckenrode, *The Separation of Church and State in Virginia* (Richmond, 1910), *passim*.

[6] William W. Sweet, *The Story of Religions in America* (New York, 1930), 5.

the rational and expeditious methods applied in extending civil government to the region. The Methodists and Baptists appear to have given neither special consideration to the area nor awakened to the opportunities it opened to them until they were into the Great Revival. The Protestant Episcopal Church for many years after its organization in 1789 more closely resembled an executor settling the bankrupt estate of the old Anglican establishment than the heir of a rich and vital religious tradition. The Plan of Union of 1801 between the Presbyterians and Congregationalists, which looms large in most studies of religion in the Mississippi valley, was less a plan for a joint missionary campaign than a solution for dealing with the results of campaigns to come. Past 1820 the missionary efforts of the Congregationalist party to the compact were limited largely to New York. Elsewhere in the West they had advanced little beyond the dispatch of scouts to reconnoiter the state of religion.[7]

The only exception to this general pattern of ecclesiastical response was Presbyterianism, and the alertly organized action of this church was as continuous with its late eighteenth-century history as the indifference, hesitation, or aimlessness of other groups. "Never . . . has American Presbyterianism been so much a church in history," one of its recent historians has written, as during the late colonial, revolutionary, and confederation periods.[8] Its unity, growth, and expansion stand out in an epoch ridden by factionalism and retrenchment. From its main base of strength in the middle Atlantic states Presbyterian ecclesiastical forms by 1786 reached to the perimeters of American settlement; and whether in western Pennsylvania, on the Georgia frontier, or in Kentucky, the extension of the Presbyterian system meant the founding of schools as well as the organization of congregations. In Kentucky, at-

[7] The statement on the Congregationalists is based upon Colin B. Goodykoontz, *Home Missions and the American Frontier* (Caldwell, Idaho, 1939), 19-48, and that on the Episcopalians on W. W. Manross, *History of the American Episcopal Church*, 2nd ed. (New York, 1950), 98-136. As for the Methodists, Francis Asbury's *Journal* does not indicate that the West caught his imagination or especially engaged his attention before 1800. He visited the region irregularly and the lack of effective supervision helps to explain why the Methodists claimed fewer members in the West in 1798 than five years earlier. The Baptists are a more difficult case because of their rigid practice of congregational autonomy. The Baptist growth in the West before the Great Revival was slight, however, compared to that afterwards. The early nineteenth-century Baptist historian, David Benedict, credited the increased growth to zeal generated by the revival. David Benedict, *A General History of the Baptist Denomination in America* (Boston, 1813), II, 20-21, 232.

[8] Leonard J. Trinterud, *The Forming of an American Tradition* (Philadelphia, 1949), 308.

tempts to act on the presumption that nothing in society was exempt from the concern of the church and, particularly, that the church could legitimately use the resources of the state to fulfill its responsibility to educate the citizenry brought outcries against "theocrats dabbling in politics" almost as soon as Kentucky became a state.[9]

These actions reflected the persistence of ideas of the church which had been commonplaces of Protestant thought early in the eighteenth century. Since the Great Awakening, however, it had not been possible to view the church only in traditional institutional terms. If the founding of Princeton and many less lustrous colleges, a sense of civic obligation, and an insistence upon regular ecclesiastical forms constituted one strain of Presbyterian history, another was the continuing effort shaped in the Great Awakening to "spread among the people the gospel of conviction, conversion and pardon." The initial phase of Presbyterian development in Kentucky and Tennessee was institutional, but the second and more fateful grew from "going down among the people." Of the many vectors of influence which triggered the western revival the Presbyterian unquestionably was the most conspicuous, and, as in the Great Awakening, the heightening intensity of the revival precipitated conflict and division. Unlike the Great Awakening, however, the nature of the church itself emerged as the crucial issue and on this question the lines of past and future drew together.

In the revival, tradition suffered the perverse fortune of having only the case against it presented fully and explicitly. The discussion of the church was introduced and prolonged by the revivalists. The anti-revivalist faction, while standing as defender of the church, based its case on charges that the revival was being promoted by mistaken views of human ability. The revivalists were accused of holding that "man could believe in Christ at any time," that "man's assurance of salvation was perfect and complete," and that "examining into evidences of salvation" was inconsistent with Scripture.[10] While these doctrines, by affirming the sufficiency of human effort, raised fundamental questions of the role of the church in the plan of salvation, the connection was not explored. That the opponents of the revival defined the issue as divine

[9] The activities of Presbyterianism in early Kentucky are described in Robert H. Bishop, *An Outline of the History of the Church in the State of Kentucky, During a Period of Forty Years: Containing the Memoirs of Rev. David Rice* (Lexington, Ky., 1824), and more fully in Robert Davidson, *History of the Presbyterianism in the State of Kentucky* (New York, 1847).

[10] John P. MacLean, *A Sketch of the Life and Labors of Richard McNemar* (Franklin, Ohio, 1905), 8-9,

sovereignty rather than the church was due not only to theological traditions in the Calvinist family but also to the climate of opinion outside
the church. The key doctrines of Calvinism were targets of mockery in
the "open, catholic and liberal" society of Kentucky as they were in
similar circles over the nation. Against these "insidious influences of
infidelity" many of the Calvinist clergy of the West, as of the Northeast,
had risen in the last decade of the eighteenth century. As a consequence, the burgeoning revivalism encountered opinions already highly sensitized on the issues of human agency and divine will.[11]

The "liberal and catholic" spirit, however, was not more welcome
in the revivalist household than in the other. In fact, one of the chief arguments offered in defense of the revival was its effectiveness in stop-
ping the seepage of "false beliefs in religion" from the "idle and indul-
gent" classes into the "population at large." This front of interest was
broken, however, by the relentless probe after evidences of theological
deviation. The anti-revivalist group carefully avoided a blanket con-
demnation of the revival, but as one witness described it: "Persistent
questionings and quibblings raised doubts in new converts, impugned
the integrity of faithful ministers, threatened the progress of the work,"
and at last excused "Outrageous abuses of the religious rights of free
men."[12] The conflict swirled for two years until in 1803 six clergymen
who were in the van of the revival movement in Kentucky withdrew
and founded a new organization.

To this point the controversy had progressed along eighteenth-century lines. The kindling of religious enthusiasm, the attempt to impose
order on it, the protest against the attempt, separation and the formation
of a new sect formed a sequence of events known to Americans if not
yet monotonously familiar. But those made secessionists by the Great
Revival quickly struck out in a new direction. In 1804 they dissolved
the organization founded the previous year, renounced "the carnal
bonds of ecclesiasticism," and in a thunderous shower of sermons and
pamphlets scourged virtually every attribute which custom ascribed to
the visible church. "Creeds," "written confessions of faith," "articles of
discipline," "ceremonies," "hired ministers," "theological subtleties,"
and "distinctions of rank among Christians" alike were consigned to
"the rubbish heap of human invention on which Christ was cruci-

[11] Niels H. Sonne, *Liberal Kentucky, 1780-1828* (New York, 1939), 46-77.
[12] Barton W. Stone, *An Apology for Renouncing the Jurisdiction of the Synod of Kentucky to Which is Added a Compendius View of the Gospel, and a Few Remarks on the Confession of Faith, by the Presbytery of Springfield* (Lexington, Ky., 1804), 4.

fied."[13] These repudiations in detail almost hid a more fundamental repudiation which, though not coherently argued until later, nevertheless razed the orthodox foundations of organized religion. No institution mediated "saving truths"; hence, no institution had a right to bind man or to review his judgments of things religious.

Of the several possibilities which this repudiation opened, Barton W. Stone developed the one most portentous for organized religion in America. Stone is an apt case study in the sociology of religious radicalism, for his early life was a microcosm of the fluid social conditions of the southern back country in the late eighteenth century. Born in Maryland of a family of erratic fortunes, he migrated with his parents to southeastern Virginia in order to escape the turmoil of the Revolution. His piecemeal education was capped by study at a Presbyterian "log college" in North Carolina, after which he taught in an academy in Georgia and served as an itinerant evangelist in the Carolina Piedmont. He came to Kentucky in 1798 to fill the pastorate of the church at Cane Ridge, where in 1801 the Great Revival reached an emotional crescendo that fifty years later Peter Cartwright still called the greatest since Pentecost. Never contented with ordinary pastoral duties, Stone was utterly dedicated to the pursuit of "causes" in religion.[14] Until he came under ecclesiastical censure during the Great Revival the question of the church does not seem to have had high priority in Stone's thought. After he was stung by ecclesiastical criticism, however, he turned to concentrate on it with an intensity seldom seen in America since Roger Williams.

Current historical interest in Stone centers on his pioneering efforts in the field of ecumenicity. A recent biography of him carries the subtitle "Early American Advocate of Christian Unity"[15]—an interpretation which both relates Stone to strong movements in the modern church and faithfully represents his central concern after the Great Revival even though the result of his work was not greater unity but another addition to the Protestant denominational fold. Stone is a figure on

[13] These enumerations are culled from the writings of the two principal foemen of orthodoxy, Richard McNemar and Barton W. Stone. In addition to Stone's *Apology*, see John Rogers, *The Biography of Elder Barton W. Stone, Written by Himself: With Additions and Reflections by Elder John Rogers* (Cincinnati, 1847), and Richard McNemar, *The Kentucky Revival, or A Short History of the Late Extraordinary Outpouring of the Spirit of God in the Western States of America* (reprinted New York, 1847).

[14] Rodgers, *Stone,* 9-27.

[15] William G. West, *Barton Warren Stone: Early American Advocate of Christian Unity* (Nashville, 1954).

which to pivot American church history, however, not so much for his ecumenicalism as for the radical conception of religious liberty which lay at the heart of his proposals for a reordered church as well as his objections to the old.

The iconoclastic potential of Stone's idea of religious liberty stands out most clearly if it is distinguished from another woven into eighteenth-century history. In one of its acceptations religious liberty meant the civil right to choose or not to choose affiliation with a church. In this sense, it was not necessarily incompatible with institutional ideas of the church. As a matter of fact, many men of the eighteenth-century Enlightenment in America found in the civil guarantee of choice the solution to a practical dilemma. The enmity of state-supported churches to the supreme value of the Enlightenment, the autonomy of the human mind, they believed to be fully established. In his famous *Remonstrance,* James Madison blamed the established church "for fifteen centuries" of "superstition, bigotry and persecution."[16] Therefore, the protection of human dignity and freedom required the separation of church and state. Yet they also recognized the importance of the church, albeit suitably divorced from the state, in fostering virtues necessary to the stability and prosperity of a republican society. This consideration kept Benjamin Franklin paying a subscription to a church throughout his adult life even though the doctrinal tenets it advanced were thoroughly repugnant to him. The civil guarantees of religious liberty bridged the gap between personal freedom and the social need. The church could continue to fill its necessary role in civil society, the autonomy of the human mind was protected, and the individual and institution were left free to negotiate a basis on which to meet.

Stone, however, had little interest in religious liberty defined as the right to choose among churches or systems of belief. So defined it implied a detachment toward religion entirely alien to him. The issue to Stone was freedom of choice within the church; the right of "regenerate men to enjoy the liberty wherein . . . they have been set free." The converted man, he argued, needed no guidance from theologically trained clergymen, no supervision by ecclesiastical authorities, no creedal sureties of belief, for he was guided, supervised, and enlightened "by the Spirit." "To deny this," wrote Stone, "is to degrade God." "By conversion man is restored to the image of God and made capable of hearing . . . understanding and obeying His commands." Devastating as this view

[16] Gaillard Hunt, ed., *The Writings of James Madison* (New York, 1900-1910), II, 187.

was to organization in religion, Stone, nevertheless, earnestly tried to apply it to the movement which grew up around him. He refused to designate his followers by any other name than "Christian," allowed free reign to belief, asking only that it justify itself by the New Testament, and while admitting distinctions of office among believers, forbade gradations of authority.[17] Stone, in effect, aimed at a second revolution in the church. By the first the church had been separated from the state and, in law, transformed into a voluntary association. Stone demanded that the church carry through a second by recognizing itself as an association of equal and autonomous individuals and reorganizing its internal life accordingly.

Undoubtedly, the climate of revolutionary political speculation helped to shape Stone's views on the church. Analogies between the freedom men enjoy in civil society and the freedom they ought to enjoy in the church are sprinkled through his writing. He owed a larger debt, however, to the pietistic influences which the Great Awakening had set in flow through and around historic American churches. Pietists insisted upon individual autonomy as emphatically as rationalists, with the difference that theirs was the autonomy of feeling. Until the revolutionary era Pietism was under the practical necessity of defending the right to enjoy "heart religion" against the state as well as the traditional churches to which they by and large belonged. Upon the separation of church and state, however, the field of conflict between Pietism and institutional authority narrowed to the church. Stone stood as a culmination of this conflict. His sharp juxtaposition of the church and the individual crystallized positions in the controversy, his assertion of their utter irreconcilability shut the door to compromise, and his bold proposal for reorganizing the church extended Pietism's emphasis upon "the man set free by the Gospel."

Stone's attempts to remake the church carried him on a course that ran convergent with those of other religious movements destined to cut a large swath in American Protestantism. Throughout the Great Revival Stone reveled in the cooperation he received from Methodists and Baptists. He interpreted this working alliance as evidence of revivalism's effectiveness in overcoming "sectarian distinctions," but to a historian it represents a juncture of movements with striking similarities. Like Stone's "Christians," the origins of the Methodists and Baptists were entwined with traditional ecclesiasticism, and their views of the

---

[17] West, *Stone,* 53-109.

church were in part reactions against these traditions. To dead formalism they opposed spontaneous experience; to ceremony and ritual, New Testament simplicity; to the impersonality of an establishment, the fraternity of believers; and to ecclesiastical authority, the assurance of private belief. In view of these similarities and the rapid growth of the Methodists and Baptists, it seems that Stone's program of reform was largely realized, however limited his direct contribution was.

The crisis which the Great Revival brought to a head was not confined, however, to the internal forms of the church. The thrust of "primitive" and "apostolic" religion cut between the church and society and hardened distinctions between them that impoverished both. In the revivalistic patchwork of ecclesiastical history the descent of the church was divided into successive stages of secular contamination. The "primitive gospel" fell prey to Greek thought, primitive democracy to Roman authoritarianism, and the original equality of believers to feudal conceptions of hierarchy. Nor was the Reformation a reversal of this course, for "princes and synods" merely replaced "pope and bishop" as captors of the church. The weight of evangelical rhetoric described the revival neither as a recovery nor a fulfillment of the Reformation.[18] Rather, it was a new beginning, or, more accurately, a return to the beginning, when the springs of religion flowed pure and untrammeled. "The circuit rider," wrote a mid-nineteenth century Methodist chronicler, deserved "a veneration second only to that [felt] for the Saviour." The encomium annihilated most of post-Biblical Christianity because it was conferred for freeing religion "of mystery, subtlety, ornament and complication."[19]

The vision of a New Testament church materialized with astonishing literalness in the early history of the Mississippi valley. The Great Revival was a gigantic exhibition of privatism in religion; a preoccupation which Methodists, Baptists, and smaller evangelistic groups extended into the succeeding decades. Against the view that the church spoke to man in all his relationships they put the practice of promoting personal piety, and, moreover, made success in this effort the touchstone for distinguishing a "true" church from the "false." A "true" church converted and regenerated men, and no historic titles of legitimacy or claims to usefulness substituted for failure on this score. The purpose of the church, a circuit rider mused, was not properly "to serve society" or

[18] See, for example, McNemar, *The Kentucky Revival, passim.*
[19] F. C. Holliday, *Life and Times of the Reverend Allen Wiley* (Cincinnati, 1853), 118-119.

"excite the fancies of the mind" but to "get men justified and pardoned for their sins."[20] The pervasiveness of John Wesley's dictum that the church had "nothing to do but save souls" is an admonition against hastily equating the growth in the membership of evangelical churches in the first half of the nineteenth century with the growth in "church influence." Likely as not there was a proportionality between the increase in numbers and the opinion that the church's influence was limited to cultivating personal feeling and private morality.

While the religious movements which gushed from the Great Revival were optimistic about man's chances for redemption, they entertained a deep pessimism about the possibilities of redeeming society. It is unnecessary to look beyond the volumes of clerical reporting on social conditions in the early West for evidence of this pessimism. This literature has been combed for tidbits of detail but it is also an index to the social perspectives of early evangelicalism. William Beauchamp, whom a circuit-riding brother described as "judicious and temperate," conveyed the dominant mood in this statement: "The world is cursed with a corrupted state of society. . . . The world we inhabit presents such a scene as chills the blood. . . . Corruption reigns in all human associations and inundates human life with a flood of miseries."[21] Eventually, evangelicalism saw the regenerate man as the agent for overcoming the "degenerate and cursed world," but in the early West its primary mission was to rescue him. One of Francis Asbury's favorite sermon topics was "you must come out to be saved"; and from those who obeyed emerged the "gathered church." As institutionally conceived, the church was kneaded into the textures of society and hence responsible for the pious and indifferent alike. The flood tide of early nineteenth-century revivalism, however, tore it loose from these moorings and carried it into the backwaters of estrangement, withdrawal, and separation. There it floated as a kind of alternative to involvement in society.

The company which constituted the church was distinguished by feelings of piety, professions of dogma, and practices of ascetic morality, however, not by intellect and sensitivity. Toward the latter early western evangelicalism was sometimes passively indifferent and sometimes actively hostile, but almost never concerned about nourishing them in the church or in society. Not until after 1830 was there a concerted movement to make even literacy a requirement for entry into the ministry among the Methodists and Baptists in the West. Before then the

---

[20] "Diary of Isaac Conger," MS, Tennessee State Library, Nashville.
[21] "The Misery of Man," *Western Christian Monitor* (April, 1816), 154.

persuasion of being "called" and "gifts promising usefulness" usually sufficed for a commission to evangelize. The average of cultural attainment among the evangelical clergy, except possibly the Baptist, unquestionably far exceeded these minima as well as the level of popular culture, but frontier preachers neither earned recognition for this achievement nor made special display of it. On the contrary, they were famous "for being like the people." On the face of its record in formal education, evangelicalism's disengagement from the traditional concern of the church for intellect and the quality of culture appears almost complete. In 1825 the Methodists, Baptists, and Presbyterian splinter groups which collectively accounted for probably three-fourths of the church members in the West could not claim one college or thriving academy among them.[22]

I admit to selecting only a few designs from the tapestry of early evangelicalism, but for the purpose of underscoring a point. To organizations which addressed themselves to private feeling, defended their purity against a degenerate society, and were unabashed by their cultural nakedness, there could be no problem of colonizing the West. To them the West posed problems of enrolling members, conducting missionary campaigns, developing ecclesiastical machinery, and recruiting clergymen, but not the problems of preserving cultural values or transplanting social institutions such as had challenged Anglicans and Puritans earlier along the Atlantic fringe. In absenting themselves from these concerns the Methodists and Baptists were not acting peculiarly "western," however, for their early histories in the eastern states were much the same. Their indifference sprang from Pietism and dissent, not from the West. They were sects en route to becoming churches but still encumbered by habits acquired under social and religious conditions which had changed greatly by the early nineteenth century. Not until the 1830's did they begin to awaken to the imbalance between their sense of social responsibility and the realities of their position in society.

Presbyterianism alone among the major religious groups active in the West showed a grasp of the problem of acculturation. The history of Presbyterian initiative in supporting public education, establishing parochial schools, and participating in other projects of community betterment is too familiar to require recapitulation. The shadow of the Great Revival, nevertheless, also fell heavily across this church. Be-

[22] Donald G. Tewksbury, *The Founding of American Colleges and Universities Before the Civil War* (Teachers College, Columbia University, Contributions to Education No. 543, New York, 1932), 32-54.

tween 1803 and 1809 the turbulence of revivalism swept away more than half of the Presbyterian clergy and lay members in Kentucky and another severe loss occurred in 1813. This statistical damage, however, was sooner repaired than that done to the Presbyterian capacity for adaptation. The buffetings which the church took in the Great Revival left it resentful of criticism, hostile to innovations in theology and polity, zealous to maintain internal uniformity, and punctiliously observant of the letter of its law.[23] This irresilience carried into Presbyterianism's approach to society. As often as the church wrestled with the problems of society it wrestled with society as the problem. The attack upon Horace Holley's liberal administration at Transylvania University which culminated in his ouster in 1827 and the campaign to prohibit Sunday mails a few years later are well-known examples of a church seeking to impose itself on the social order rather than participating in it.

The ambivalence of Presbyterianism's achievements, the obtuseness of the Baptists and Methodists, and the failure of New England Congregationalists to sustain a western missionary campaign until nearly 1830 combine to leave the strong impression that religious organizations did not enter creatively into the process of western colonization in the first third of the nineteenth century. The most apparent cause of this failure lay in the circumstances of time rather than the West. The "pioneer period" in the Ohio-Mississippi valley overlapped perhaps the most critical era in the history of the Protestant church before World War I. The surge of post-revolutionary migration began as established churches were trying to cope with a mounting tempo of change and other religious movements struggled to gain identity. This pattern of disintegration, division, and incipience was extended willy-nilly to the West, and the Great Revival stirred it into greater confusion. From the mélange stable organizations emerged before 1840 which church historians agree in calling denominations. In the interval between the age of the church and that of the denomination, however, religious groups tended to their own houses first, not to the evolution of western society. Thus, during a half-century of rapid growth, the West was largely without an agency of influence that had proved effective in colonizing other frontiers. The consequences of the breakdown in organized religion for the history of manners, morals, tastes, Indian relations, and population movements in the West deserve to be studied more closely than they have been.

[23] These attitudes permeate the outline history of Kentucky Presbyterianism by Bishop and the more comprehensive one by Davidson.

Fact and Fiction
in the Documentary Art
of the American West

JOHN C. EWERS

THE SMITHSONIAN INSTITUTION

The recent surge of interest in artists' records of the trans-Mississippi West as it appeared before the disappearance of the frontier is a noteworthy development in the study of American history. Scholars may point to the fact that the series of maps accompanying the Census Report of 1890, tracing the extension of the frontier of settlement, decade by decade, from 1790 to 1890, influenced Frederick Jackson Turner in the formulation of his stimulating thesis on the significance of the frontier in the history of our country, as well as in his choice of an 1890 date for the end of the frontier. And surely Turner was not blind to the fact that artists have been contributors to history. Indeed, he once wrote that the data of history must be drawn from "studies of literature and art" as well as of "politics, economics, sociology, psychology, biology, and physiography."[1] Nevertheless, it would be a grave error to suggest that recent studies of the documentary art of the West owe their inspiration to Turner.

As a matter of fact, historians have been slow to recognize that drawings and paintings which portray the American West as it was before the frontier disappeared are documents as worthy of serious, critical study as are the writings and maps produced by explorers, traders, travelers, missionaries, soldiers, and settlers. In fact the geographical frontier had passed several decades before historians began to show a scholarly interest in the pictorial documentation of its history.

The real pioneer in this field of scholarship was not a historian but an anthropologist—David I. Bushnell, Jr., of the Smithsonian Institution's Bureau of American Ethnology. As a student of the cultures of

[1] Merle E. Curti, "The Section and the Frontier in American History: The Methodological Concepts of Frederick Jackson Turner," in Stuart A. Rice, ed., *Methods in Social Science* (Chicago, 1931), 355-356.

the Indians of Virginia, during the first decade of the present century Bushnell found the drawings of John White, executed in 1585 among the Indians of coastal North Carolina, to be exceedingly helpful aids to an understanding of how these Indians lived at the time of early white contact. The White water colors were in the British Museum, but gaining in awareness of the importance of on-the-spot pictorial sources for documenting both the cultures and the history of the Indian tribes of North America, Bushnell began assembling his own private collection of drawings and paintings, and between 1925 and 1940 published in a Smithsonian series no fewer than eight articles, each dealing with the contributions of a single artist. Most of these articles were illustrated, at least in part, with reproductions of original pictures in his own collection, and six of them were concerned with artists who knew Indians of the trans-Mississippi West prior to 1860—Seth Eastman, George Gibbs, Paul Kane, Rudolph Friederich Kurz, John Mix Stanley, and John Webber.[2]

Bushnell "also projected a larger work on artistic representations of Indians and Indian life in the period before 1875 but this undertaking, for which he was supremely well prepared, was unfortunately cut off by his death" in 1941.[3] He bequeathed his fine collection of pictorial originals to the Peabody Museum of Harvard University.

Turner's last frontier of 1890 had disappeared fully a half-century before the late Robert Taft of the University of Kansas began to publish a pioneer series of critical studies on the pictorial history of the Old West in the *Kansas Historical Quarterly* in 1946.[4] Taft was a professor of chemistry whose hobby was pictorial history—he was *not* a professional historian. But he was a thorough scholar with a highly developed critical judgment, who extended the study of the contributions of west-

[2] Bushnell's articles included "John Mix Stanley, Artist-Explorer," *Smithsonian Report for 1924*, 507-512, 7 plates, 1925; "Drawings by John Webber of Natives of the Northwest Coast of America, 1778," *Smithsonian Miscellaneous Collections*, LXXX, No. 10, 12 pp., 12 plates, 1928; "Friederich Kurz, Artist-Explorer," *Smithsonian Report for 1927*, 507-512, 8 plates, 6 text figures, 1928; "Seth Eastman: The Master Painter of the North American Indian," *Smithsonian Miscellaneous Collections*, LXXXVII, No. 3, 18 pp., 15 plates, 1 text figure, 1932; "Drawings by George Gibbs in the Far Northwest, 1849-1851," *Smithsonian Miscellaneous Collections*, XCVII, No. 8, 28 pp., 18 plates, 15 text figures, 1938; and "Sketches by Paul Kane in the Indian Country, 1845-1848," *Smithsonian Miscellaneous Collections*, XCIX, No. 1, 25 pp., 1 plate, 11 text figures, 1940.

[3] John R. Swanton, "David I. Bushnell, Jr." (obituary), *American Anthropologist*, N.S., XLIV (1942), 105-106.

[4] Revised and extended, these articles were reprinted in Taft's book, *Artists and Illustrators of the Old West: 1850-1900* (New York, 1953).

ern artists from the field of Indian culture to that of white men's activities in the frontier West. And he was addressing historians when he wrote that "most of us, whether authors or publishers, fail to treat pictures as an integral part of the record of the past and to subject these sources to the same scholarly identification, explanation, and determination of authenticity as we do more familiar materials."[5]

Only within the last twenty years—since the end of World War II— has there developed a lively and widespread interest in preserving, exhibiting, and interpreting the documentary art of the Old West. But it has progressed with remarkable rapidity. During these two decades a number of new repositories for original pictorial documents have been established. The Gilcrease Institute of American History and Art was opened in Tulsa (1949), the Glenbow Foundation Art Gallery at Calgary, Alberta, was founded in 1955, while the Whitney Gallery of Western Art at Cody, Wyoming, and the Amon Carter Museum of Western Art at Fort Worth, Texas, were established as recently as 1959 and 1961 respectively. The postwar years also have witnessed the acquisition of large and significant collections of western art by the older Joslyn Art Museum of Omaha and the Montana Historical Society at Helena. In addition to these thriving centers for the study of western art history in the West itself, this same brief span of years has brought the establishment of the important M. and M. Karolik Collections in the Boston Museum of Fine Arts and the Western Americana Collection at Yale University, while the American Philosophical Society in Philadelphia has acquired the uniquely significant collection of drawings executed by Titian Ramsay Peale while serving as assistant naturalist on Major Stephen Long's historic exploring expedition of 1819-20.

At the same time private collectors, unable to derive satisfaction from meaningless modern abstract paintings, have turned to the collection of drawings and paintings which readily communicate the color, the romance, and the vitality of the Old West. Competition for the acquisition of the works of some of the most highly publicized artists of the Old West which appear on the market has become so keen as to price them as high as the works of some of the Old Masters of Europe. Even works by western artists which are of little or dubious historical value are in demand.

As yet no comprehensive index of the pictorial holdings of the multitude of museums, libraries, and archives in the United States and Cana-

[5] Robert Taft, "Review of Irving's Indian Sketches, Ed. by John Francis McDermott," *Mississippi Valley Historical Review*, XLII (1955), 322.

da which house one or more of these graphic documents of the West
has been attempted. This is not even to mention the collections in private hands, or the ones in private or public ownership in Europe. The
task of compiling a catalog of these pictorial holdings in the United
States alone would be immense, for they are widely scattered from Boston and Washington, D.C., to the state of Washington and southern
California. The historically significant pictures must total thousands,
and the number of artists represented must exceed 200. I have been collecting information on artists who interpreted the Indians of the West
prior to 1900 for some thirty years, and I still encounter a new name
every few weeks.

The new enthusiasm for the works of artists who pictured the Old
West also has found expression in a flood of books, articles, and exhibition catalogs within the past two decades. Many of these have been
handsomely illustrated in color as well as in black and white. A high
proportion of them have dealt with the creations of a single artist (in
the Bushnell tradition); the texts have been relatively short and in very
large part biographical. No fewer than five books and monographs (including a much better-than-average children's book) have appeared on
George Catlin since the war, while the extensive bibliography on
Charles M. Russell is further extended with virtually every issue of the
quarterly *Montana, the Magazine of Western History.*

I must say that I am much less concerned by the quantity than by the
quality of some of this output. Far too much of it consists of biography
interlarded with laudatory comments on the artist's work which are
more akin to the unrestrained prose of the press agent than to the carefully weighed words of the serious scholar and critic. Too often writers
have applied generalized slogans to the western artists—slogans such as
"he knew the horse," or "he knew the Indian," or "the Mountain
Man," or "cowboy," and such gross judgments have been offered in
place of the much more difficult, scholarly criticisms of the individual
works of the artists under consideration. Too many writings on western
artists have been tapped out on the typewriters of professional writers
or art critics who are ethnologically and historically naive.

In the midst of all this excitement, I should like to introduce a few
words of caution. I feel strongly that many of the works by artists of the
Old West have real value as pictorial documents, and that a goodly
number of them, because of the clear and lasting impressions they leave
upon the mind, are more significant historical documents than written
descriptions can be. But the time has come when hardheaded historical

criticism should be applied more widely and more consistently in appraising the thousands of drawings and paintings created by the hundreds of artists who have attempted to picture the looks and the actions of the Old West. We must try to separate the wheat from the chaff—the fact from the fiction in western art.

Let me illustrate what I am advocating by considering, briefly but *critically,* not the total contributions of any one artist but how *different* artists represented a *few* themes which appear repeatedly in the art of the Old West.

I must apologize in advance because the four themes I have selected for consideration here—the buffalo chase, the Indian attack on the wagon train or stagecoach, the Indian council, and the Indian portrait— all concern Indians. But Indians were an exceedingly colorful and vital as well as an integral part of the western scene prior to 1890, and relatively few artists of the Old West did not picture them. Besides, I am an ethnologist by profession, and I feel on much surer ground appraising artists' handling of Indian subjects than I would their representations of such other recurrent themes in frontier art as cattle drives, railroad building, or the interiors of boom-town saloons. I readily acknowledge, however, that pictures of these latter themes should be appraised just as rigorously as I would the Indian subjects—but by those who possess the detailed knowledge of the actions, peoples, and materials which the artists sought to record on paper or canvas, with brush or pencil.

Few themes in western life have been pictured as frequently or by as many different artists as has the buffalo chase on horseback. This exciting method of big-game hunting was practiced by the Indian tribes of the Great Plains from at least as early as 1700—soon after these red men began to acquire European horses—to the extermination of the bison as a wild species on the western grasslands in the 1880's. Titian Peale's pencil sketch of a buffalo hunt, probably executed in the field while he was with Major Long's expedition to the Missouri, Platte, and Arkansas valleys in 1819-20, may have been the earliest artist's attempt of this subject.[6] But literally scores of artists tackled this theme hundreds of times after 1820. Charlie Russell pictured the buffalo chase—in pen and ink, water colors, or oils—nearly fifty times.

[6] Titian Peale's pencil sketch, "Indians slaying a bison," is reproduced in Robert Cushman Murphy, "The Sketches of Titian Ramsay Peale (1799-1885)," *The American Philosophical Society Library Bulletin,* CI (1957), 524. At least two lithographs and an oil painting were developed from this sketch. See Jessie Poesch, *Titian Ramsay Peale and His Journals of the Wilkes Expedition* (Philadelphia, 1961), Figs. 29, 30, 47.

I have examined in recent weeks the originals or clear photographic reproductions of more than fifty different artists' efforts to picture the buffalo chase. Obviously no artist—no matter how quick his pencil or brush—could have executed the details of this lively action while it was taking place before his eyes. But there were a goodly number of artists who witnessed and some who actually participated in the buffalo chase on the western plains. Beside Titian Peale, they included some well-known and some obscure artists, among them Karl Bodmer, George Catlin, Seth Eastman, Robert Hood, John Dare Howland, Paul Kane, Alfred Jacob Miller, Heinrich Mollhausen, Father Nicholas Point, Peter Rindisbacher, John Mix Stanley, and Charles Wimar.

Of the many renderings of the buffalo chase I have examined, Charles Wimar's oil painting of 1860, which now hangs in Alumni House at Washington University in St. Louis, is most satisfying to me as an authentic document. Wimar had ample opportunity to witness the buffalo chase during his two trips up the Missouri in 1858 and 1859, and although this painting was doubtless executed in his St. Louis studio, it must have been based upon field sketches such as the rough pencil one reproduced here as Figure 1. The portrayal of hunting methods shown in Figure 2 most nearly conforms to the best eyewitness descriptions of this action I have read in the literature and to the detailed accounts of the buffalo chase recalled for me by aged Blackfoot Indians who had chased buffalo in their young manhood. The action appears to be correct—the mounted bowman approaching his kill from the buffalo's right, the lancer from its left. Their mounts are small Indian ponies, not big American horses. Their equipment is accurate—including the hair-stuffed pad saddle. My elderly Blackfoot informants told me they preferred to chase buffalo on pad saddles rather than to ride bareback, for the practical reason that they could move more freely from side to side and better maintain their balance if their feet were in stirrups.

On the other hand we find many pictures of the buffalo chase executed by artists who never saw a buffalo hunt, either because they were born too late or because they never visited the Great Plains when buffalo still ran. One of these is the work of Felix O. C. Darley, probably first drawn in 1842, and certainly reproduced as an engraving in *Graham's Magazine* as early as 1844 (Figure 3). Darley was only twenty-two years old in '44, but he was well on his way to becoming America's outstanding book and magazine illustrator of the mid-nineteenth century. He never went West, although he illustrated Parkman's *The Oregon Trail,*

Cooper's *The Prairie,* and other western books and articles. His knowledge of western life must have been based upon his reading, his study of the works of other artists who did produce works based upon their firsthand experiences, and upon his fertile imagination. As John Baur has pointed out, the action in this particular scene (one of several buffalo chases executed by Darley) was derived from one of George Catlin's paintings, which was reproduced as a line drawing in Catlin's 1841 book, *Letters and Notes on the Manners, Customs, and Condition of the North American Indians.*[7] Darley was too clever an artist to copy Catlin's work precisely, so he turned the buffalo from left to right, and in so doing produced a decorative but inaccurate picture. Catlin's buffalo was goring the hunter's pony from the rear—hence the agonized action of the horse. In Darley's print the horse's action is meaningless.[8]

A noteworthy feature of Darley's illustration is the artist's rendering of plains grasses in terms of a thick stand of tall, wheatlike stems, waist high or higher, which bear not the faintest resemblance to the low, much more sparse ground cover of the short-grass plains, which even in Darley's day was the true home of the buffalo and of his Indian hunters. Darley made this same error in many other pictures of actions on the Great Plains. And a similar rendering of grass appears in the works of other popular mid-nineteenth century artists—such as Arthur Fitzwilliam Tait and Louis Maurer of Currier and Ives fame—who tried to visualize the plains grasslands from the security of their New York studios.

One of the most interesting renderings of a buffalo chase was created in Paris by Rosa Bonheur, the world-famous animal painter. Miss Bonheur's Indians and buffalo were members of Buffalo Bill's Wild West Show which appeared in Paris in 1889. The French artist was fascinated by the show Indians' re-enactment of the buffalo chase. She repeatedly visited the show and made numerous sketches of the buffalo, horses, and Indians, at rest and in action. She was also wise enough to understand that the grass she saw growing in France was not the grass of the Great Plains of the American West. From the Botanical Society of Colorado she obtained dried plant specimens and color notes to assist her in picturing the buffalo and gramma grass of the plains in her "La Chasse aux Bisons" (Figure 4). Consequently, her picture, created more than 4,000 miles east of the buffalo country, and several years after

[7] See Plate 112 in Vol. I of Catlin's book.

[8] John I. H. Baur, "After Catlin," *Brooklyn Museum Bulletin,* X, No. 1 (1948), 17-20.

buffalo were exterminated on the Great Plains, is more accurate than many pictures on this theme which were painted in America in earlier years. Nevertheless, her horse and rider appear to be unusually large in comparison with her buffalo—unless the buffalo of Buffalo Bill's show were young ones.[9]

For dramatic action few western themes could compare with the Indian attack on the overland emigrant train or the lone stagecoach. In reality this enduring symbol of the Old West occurred much less commonly than the host of pictures of it would suggest—including its survival in motion picture and TV form. Surely this violent action took place much less frequently in the wilds of the nineteenth-century American West than do assault and rape in the civilized settings of our big cities today.

During a rapid survey of pictures of the Old West, I found no fewer than fourteen attacks on emigrant trains and seven Indian parties attacking stagecoaches. My survey did not include the numerous portrayals of these themes in murals executed by artists under the WPA Program during the depression years for the Post Office Department in Washington and for large and small post offices in towns and cities elsewhere in this country.

One of the earliest pictures of "The Attack on an Emigrant Train" was painted by Charles Wimar, whose "Buffalo Hunt" I have praised. However, Wimar's "Attack" was executed four years earlier, before he traveled over the plains, and while he was still a student in far-off Düsseldorf. It was inspired by a description in Louis Ferry Gabriel de Bellemarr's book, *Impressions de voyages et aventures dans le Mexique, le haute Californie et les regions de l'or,* published in Brussels in 1851. Although this is a technically competent painting, I agree with Perry Rathbone's opinion that it is "redolent with the atmosphere of the studio, and betrays an absence of direct contact between the artist and his subject matter."[10] In this melodramatic scene, the half-naked Indians in the foreground appear to be partially costumed in garments fashioned from the whole cloth of the artist's imagination, while their comrades on the right are riding fearlessly and furiously forward through a sea of Darley-like tall grass (Figure 5).

This picture should warn us of the folly of generalizing about the historical value of the works of artists who depicted the Old West. Skill

[9] Anna Klumpke, *Rosa Bonheur* (Paris, 1908), 18-24.
[10] Perry T. Rathbone, *Charles Wimar, 1828-1862, Painter of the Indian Frontier* (St. Louis, 1946), 15-16.

Figure 1. A plains Indian buffalo hunt. Pencil sketch by Charles Wimar, 1859.

(Courtesy Missouri Historical Society, St. Louis)

Figure 2. "The Buffalo Hunt." Oil painting by Charles Wimar, 1860.

(Courtesy Washington University, St. Louis)

Figure 3. "Hunting Buffaloe." Engraving for *Graham's Magazine* from a drawing by Felix O. C. Darley, 1844.

(Courtesy Library of Congress)

Figure 4. "Buffalo Hunt." Engraving from a painting by Rosa Bonheur. Published in London in 1898.

(Courtesy Glenbow Foundation, Calgary)

Figure 5. "The Attack on an Emigrant Train." Painting by Charles Wimar, Düsseldorf, 1856.

(Courtesy University of Michigan Museum of Art)

Figure 6. "Indians Attacking Butterfield's Overland Dispatch Coach." Engraving in *Harper's Weekly*, April 21, 1866, from a field sketch by Theodore R. Davis.

Figure 7. "Captain Lewis & Clark holding a Council with the Indians." Engraving by an unknown artist for Patrick Gass's *Journal*, 1807.

(Courtesy Library of Congress)

Figure 8. "Pawnee Council" (October, 1819). Engraving from a field water color by Samuel Seymour, 1823.

(Courtesy Library of Congress)

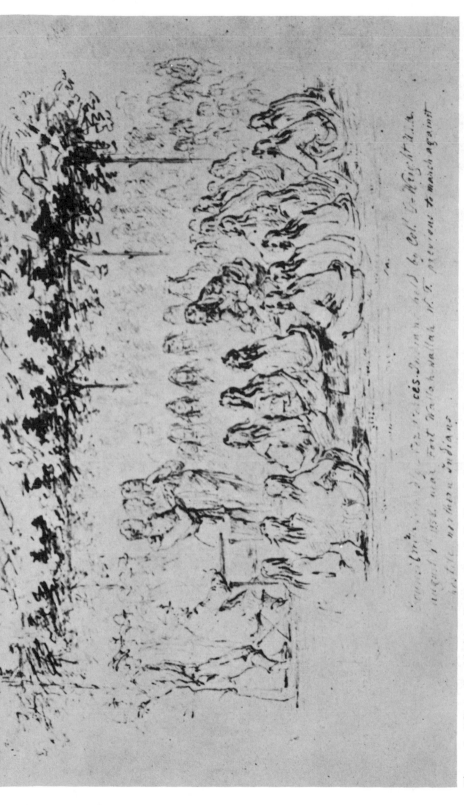

Figure 9. "Council with friendly Nez Percés Indians held by Col. Geo. Wright U.S.A. August 4th 1858, near Fort Wallah-Wallah W.T. previous to march against hostile northern Indians." Pencil sketch by Gustavus Sohon.

(Courtesy Library of Congress)

Figure 10. " . . . Governor Lyon's Treaty with the Sho-Sho-Nee Indians . . . March . . . 1866." Oil painting by Charles. Nahl.

(Courtesy Thomas Gilcrease Institute of American History and Art)

Figure 11. "Custer's Demand." Oil painting by Charles Schreyvogel, 1902.

(*Courtesy Library of Congress*)

Figure 12. The Light, an Assiniboin leader. Oil painting by George Catlin, 1831.

(Courtesy Smithsonian Institution)

Figure 13. Four Bears, Second Chief of the Mandan. Oil painting by George Catlin, 1832.

Figure 14. Big Soldier, Sioux chief. Engraving in Maximilian's *Atlas* from a field water color by Karl Bodmer, 1833.

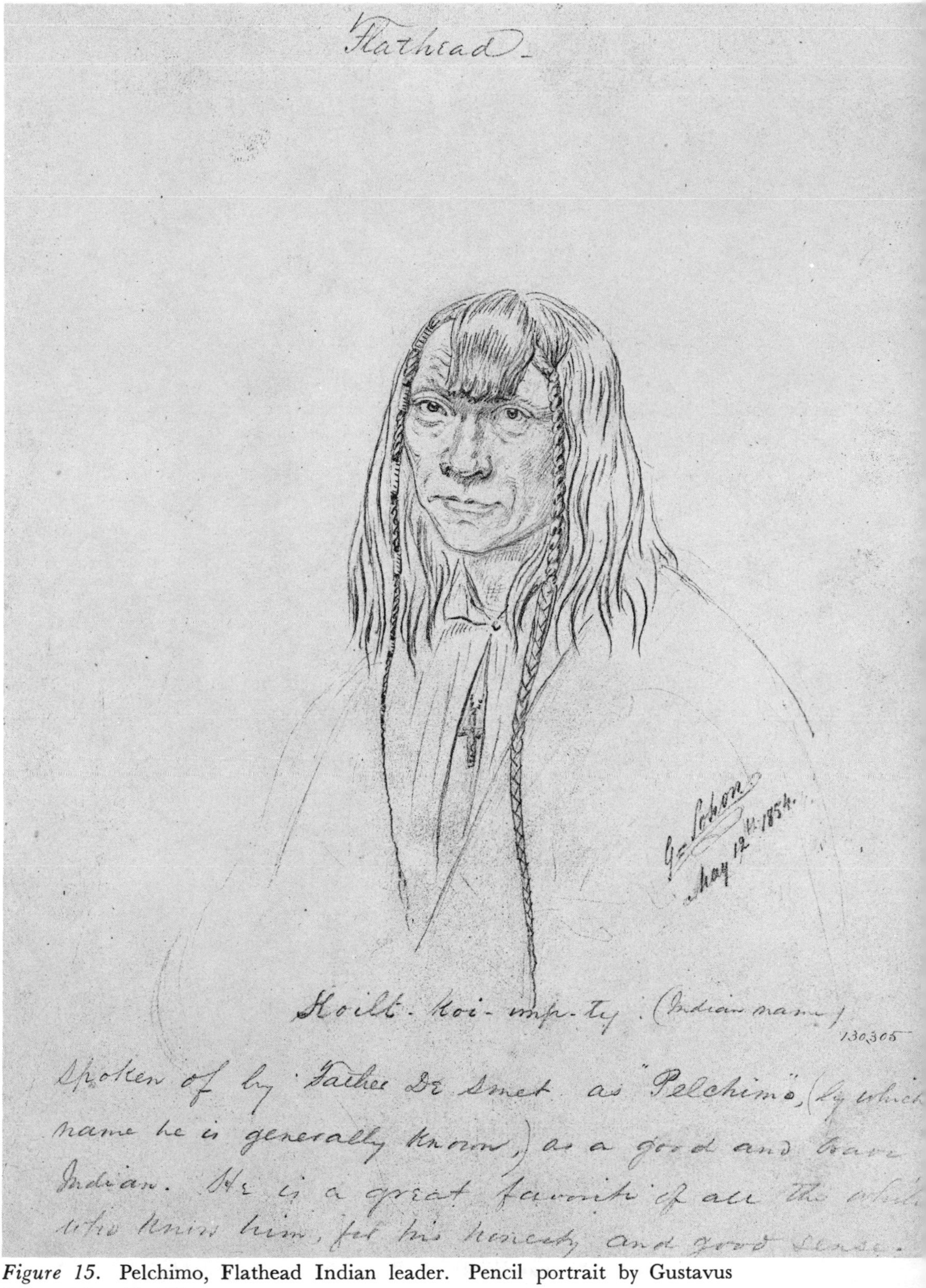

Figure 15. Pelchimo, Flathead Indian leader. Pencil portrait by Gustavus Sohon, May 12, 1854.

(Courtesy Smithsonian Institution)

Figure 16. "Indian Warrior." Pencil drawing by Jules Saintin, *ca.* 1858.

(Courtesy Detroit Institute of Arts)

in drawing, composition, and in applying paint to canvas is not enough. To be a pictorial document of historical value a painting must present its subject accurately. Many of Wimar's later works, based upon firsthand observation, stand in the front rank of the pictorial records of the Old West. They must not be confused with the few spuriously realistic paintings of western subjects he executed prior to 1857, during his student days in Düsseldorf. Indeed, it was quite possible for the same artist, working at different times and under different conditions, to be both a very bad and a very good pictorial historian.

Yet Harry Peters in *America on Stone* referred to a very popular lithograph of Wimar's "Attack on an Emigrant Train" drawn by Leopold Grozelier of Boston in 1860 as a "remarkably fine Western lithograph from every angle."[11] I cannot resist the comment—from every angle except that of authenticity. Unfortunately, neither the popularity of a picture nor the opinions of art critics are much help in evaluating the qualities of a picture as a historical document.

Unquestionably, the outstanding portrayal of an Indian attack on a stagecoach was based solidly upon firsthand experience. In mid-November, 1865, Theodore R. Davis, veteran artist-correspondent for *Harper's Weekly*, was a passenger on the Butterfield Overland Dispatch coach en route from Atchison, Kansas, to Denver, when the coach was attacked by a mounted Cheyenne war party. It was Davis who first sighted the approaching raiders, shouted the alarm, and fired the first shot in defense of his party. His part in this action is attested to in the writings of a fellow passenger as well as in his own.[12] Davis' view of this attack as published in *Harper's* for April 21, 1866 (Figure 6), must be considered a much better-documented portrayal of a stagecoach attack than pictures of this theme by such better-known interpreters of the "wild" West as Frederic Remington and Charlie Russell.

Less exciting and dramatic than either the buffalo chase or the Indian attack was the Indian council. But it was just as typical of life in the Old West during the nineteenth century. Councils between Indians and explorers, traders, Army officers, or treaty commissioners were as common during those years as were battles between Indians and white men—probably more so. They ranged from small-scale parleys of a few individuals to grand gatherings of thousands of Indians from a number of tribes, such as the Fort Laramie Treaty Council on Horse Creek in

[11] Harry T. Peters, *America on Stone* (Garden City, N.Y., 1931), Plate 24 and p. 200.
[12] The background for the precise documentation of this picture is well presented in Taft's *Artists and Illustrators of the Old West*, 62-64, 298-299.

present-day Wyoming in 1851. Unfortunately, no skilled artist was on hand to picture that large, colorful, and historically important council.

Nevertheless, I have found Indian council pictures by at least twenty different artists. The first treatment of this theme must have been attempted by the unnamed illustrator of Sergeant Patrick Gass's *Journal* of the Lewis and Clark expedition of 1804-06 (Figure 7). Simply titled "Captain Lewis & Clark holding a Council with the Indians," this crude work appears to have been based largely upon the artist's imagination. There is no indication which of Lewis and Clark's many councils with Indians is intended to be represented here. But surely the Indians, the Indian costumes, and the peace pipe depicted in this scene do not resemble very closely those of any of the tribes with whom the great explorers conferred during their two years in the western Indian country.

Compare this picture with the engraving of the council with the Pawnee held by Major O'Fallon on the Missouri River above present Omaha in mid-October, 1819, after Samuel Seymour's original water color (Figure 8). Seymour was the first official artist for a U.S. exploring expedition beyond the Mississippi, and his duties, as spelled out by Major Long before the expedition left Pittsburgh for the West, included the execution of pictures of Indians "sitting in council." Seymour's rendering of this scene coincides with written descriptions of it which mention the Indians sitting on "puncheon benches" in "a semicircle, on the chord of which sat the whites, with Major O'Fallon and his interpreters in the centre," while "sentinels walked to and fro behind the benches, and a handsome standard waved before the assembly."[13]

Probably no other on-the-spot artist portrayed as many important Indian-white councils as did Gustavus Sohon, an Army private who accompanied Governor Isaac I. Stevens of Washington Territory on his treaty-making travels in the Northwest during the spring, summer, and fall of 1855. Not only did Sohon picture the arrival of the Nez Percé on the grounds of the Walla Walla Council in early June, but he sketched the first Flathead Treaty Council in session on the Missoula River in July, and the council at which the chiefs of the powerful Blackfoot tribes negotiated their first treaty with the United States at the mouth of the Judith River on the Missouri in October, 1855.[14]

[13] John Francis McDermott, "Samuel Seymour: Pioneer Artist of the Plains and the Rockies," *Smithsonian Report for 1950* (Washington, D.C., 1951), 498-501.

[14] John C. Ewers, "Gustavus Sohon's Portraits of Flathead and Pend d'Oreille Indians, 1854," *Smithsonian Miscellaneous Collections*, C, No. 7 (Washington, D.C., 1948), 5-6.

Nearly three years later this same artist witnessed and sketched Colonel Wright's council with the Nez Percé near Fort Walla Walla, August 4, 1858, at which that officer persuaded thirty-three men of that tribe to march with him and to serve as guides and scouts in a campaign against the hostile Cayuse and their allies (Figure 9). This was one of the earliest successful employments of Indian allies by the Army in an Indian war in the West. And Sohon marched with them to become the first artist to picture a war between the forces of the U.S. Army and Indians of the American West from on-the-spot observations.[15]

There can be no question of the historical value of Sohon's field sketches in the Northwest during the 1850's. But the critical historian must react quite differently to Charles Nahl's starkly "realistic" and finely composed oil painting which purports to depict Idaho Territorial Governor Caleb Lyon's treaty council with a small group of Shoshoni Indians in the Bruneau Valley, April 12, 1866 (Figure 10). This painting has been honored with a two-page, full-color reproduction in *The American Heritage Book of Indians*. And it has been reproduced more recently in black and white in a history of the Shoshoni.[16] The painter, Charles Nahl, was both exceptionally talented and thoroughly trained. He was the outstanding pictorial interpreter of the California Gold Rush, in which he participated. He also knew at first hand the Indians of the California mining country. But there is no reason to believe that Charles Nahl ever saw the Bruneau Valley of Idaho or the Indians who lived there in 1866. The Indians in this painting appear to be exquisitely rendered California types, probably sketched from life with infinite pains. The girl standing at the far left wears a typical California Indian woman's skirt. The baskets, cradles, and other clearly defined Indian artifacts are mostly California types—although the large basket in the right foreground surely is of Pima make, from the Arizona desert.

I do not know how this well-painted but sadly misleading picture came to be executed. Perhaps Caleb Lyon commissioned it some years after the event, to commemorate a memorable day in his undistinguished career. Certainly it was a minor event in the history of the American West—the negotiation of a treaty which was never ratified with a small and obscure group of Shoshoni Indians. Artist Nahl must

[15] *Ibid.,* 8. Reproductions of Sohon's field sketches during the Indian War of 1858 may be found in the Prints and Photographs Division of the Library of Congress.

[16] Alvin M. Josephy, Jr., ed., *The American Heritage Book of Indians* (New York, 1961), 330-331; Virginia Cole Trenholm and Maurine Carley, *The Shoshonis, Sentinels of the Rockies* (Norman, 1964), opposite p. 178.

have pictured what he knew—the Indians of California and artifacts in California Indian collections—rather than the Shoshoni Indians of Idaho whom he had never seen.

In this painting we find another example of the work of a very able artist—one who in other works contributed substantially to the pictorial history of the West—which is spuriously realistic and a historical monstrosity.

Another realistically rendered painting of an Indian-white council was the cause of a bitter controversy between two of the best-known artists who attempted to picture the Old West—Charles Schreyvogel and Frederic Remington. In 1902 Schreyvogel created a historical reconstruction of George Armstrong Custer's parley with the Kiowa chiefs Lone Wolf, Satanta, and Kicking Bird, of the Kansas plains, in 1869 (Figure 11). The enthusiastic praise this painting received aroused the jealousy of Remington, who seemed to regard Schreyvogel's success as a threat to his own pre-eminence as a painter of the Indian-fighting Army in the West. Remington expressed his opinion in the *New York Herald* that Schreyvogel's "Custer's Demand" was "half-baked stuff," and specifically criticized some of the clothing, military equipment, and horse gear which Schreyvogel so precisely rendered in this painting. According to Remington, not only did the Kiowa not wear flowing feather war bonnets at that time, but Custer's hat was the wrong color and his boots incorrect, as were some of the leggings, trousers, pistol holsters, cartridge belts, saddle cloths, stirrup leathers, and saddlebags Schreyvogel so clearly detailed in his painting.

Since the parley portrayed took place when both Remington and Schreyvogel were only eight years old, and more than a decade before either of them ever saw the West, Colonel Schuyler Crosby, who had been present at the council and was pictured in the painting, was called into the hot newspaper controversy—to the embarrassment of both artists. The colonel expressed the opinion that Remington was wrong on several counts (at least four) and Schreyvogel on others (certainly two). It appears that Remington had followed the book—Army regulations— in his criticisms of the soldiers' uniforms and equipment for '69, while it is clear from Colonel Crosby's testimony that Army officers on frontier service in 1869 did not do so.[17]

Certainly the hazards in presenting pictorial reconstructions of historic scenes and events are great. They must be solidly based upon pro-

[17] Taft summarizes this pictorial controversy in *Artists and Illustrators of the Old West,* 228-230, 372-373.

longed and patient research in obscure sources to determine both the exact forms and the colors of all the minute details in a picture—a kind of research few historians care to undertake and few artists are capable of pursuing. I am not opposed to historical reconstructions in the pictorial field. In fact, I believe they can be more accurate today than they were a half-century ago, when Remington attempted to picture the "Great American Explorers," and Russell sought to recreate scenes from the Lewis and Clark expedition. Historical research has progressed in the last half-century, and we can recognize some of the anachronisms that crept into Remington's and Russell's historical reconstructions. I am much impressed by the pictorial reconstructions of fur trade scenes and events by Paul Rockwood in the 1930's which are exhibited in the National Park Service's museum at Scott's Bluff National Monument. And I respect the work Nick Eggenhoffer has been doing in pictorially reconstructing the history of transportation in the American West. I think we need more pictorial reconstructions to help us visualize more clearly some of the stirring actions in the early history of the American West which no artist witnessed and recorded. Ideally an artist and a historian should work closely together in performing the exacting research required as bases for such pictorial reconstructions. And surely each finished work should be both signed and dated, not only to give proper credit to its creator, but to prevent any future viewer from mistaking the picture for a primary pictorial record executed by an eyewitness. It would be a contribution if articles were written to accompany reproductions of completed pictures, listing the basic references used for developing the pictures and bringing out the relationship between written history, collections of historic specimens, and the painting of historical reconstructions.

The mature critic of the pictorial record of the Old West should be keenly aware of the strengths and weaknesses of those artists who were in the field and who worked directly from live models. Even George Catlin, who probably painted more Indians in their own country prior to the perfection of photography than any other artist, was not uniformly successful or always accurate in every detail. Catlin's portrait of the Assiniboin leader The Light (whom he called The Pigeon's Egg Head), executed in St. Louis during the fall of 1831, while that Indian was en route to Washington, appears to me to be exceedingly accurate down to the minor details of the "three-row" quill-worked designs on his skin shirt (Figure 12). On the other hand, Catlin's better-known portrait of his Indian hero Four Bears, the second chief of the Mandan, painted during the artist's brief residence in the Mandan villages during the summer of 1832, is less correct in detail (Figure 13). When we compare this painting with the actual garment preserved in the U.S. National Museum, we see that Catlin exaggerated both the size of the quilled rosette in the center of the wearer's chest and the total length of the garment.[18] We know that Catlin's works exhibit a wide range of accuracy in detail. But there is still need for more precise studies of his representations of the peoples and cultures of different tribes by experienced students of the tribes he pictured. There are also persistent questions regarding where and when he executed some of his drawings and paintings which his own voluminous writings fail to answer.

Many hundreds of portraits, purporting to show western Indians, were executed before 1890. However, they vary greatly in the preciseness of their documentation. Many of the works of the talented Swiss artist Karl Bodmer, who accompanied the German scientist Maximilian, Prince of Wied-Neuwied, to the upper Missouri in 1833-34, are almost ideally documented. Not only are the original water colors named and dated, but the subjects are further identified, and the places and conditions under which these pictures were created are described in Prince Maximilian's text. For example, we know that on May 26, 1833, at the Sioux agency of Fort Lookout, Bodmer executed a full-length portrait of the Sioux warrior Big Soldier (Figure 14). The name and date appear on Bodmer's original water color in the Joslyn Art Museum in Omaha. Prince Maximilian tells us that this Indian "remained the whole day in the position required" while Bodmer unhurriedly completed his portrait. And when the portrait was finished Maximilian pronounced it a "very capital likeness."[19]

Unfortunately, few of the hundreds of artists who interpreted the Old West traveled with a journal-keeping companion who carefully noted their day-to-day accomplishments. However, some artists kept journals. Noteworthy among them was Rudolph Friederich Kurz, active in the same upper Missouri region as Catlin and Bodmer, but two decades later. Not only are most of the revealing sketches in his sketchbooks titled and dated, but many of the subjects are well described in the artist's own *Journal*.[20]

---

[18] John C. Ewers, "George Catlin, Painter of Indians and the West," *Smithsonian Report for 1955* (Washington, D.C., 1956), 497-498 and Plate 10.

[19] Maximilian, Prince of Wied-Neuwied, *Travels in the Interior of North America*, H. Evans Lloyd, tr. (London, 1843), 151-153.

[20] J. N. B. Hewitt, ed., *Journal of Rudolph Friederich Kurz* . . . (Bureau of American Ethnology Bulletin 115, Washington, D.C., 1937).

Gustavus Sohon's movements were described in much less detail in the official records of the northernmost of the Pacific Railway surveys. But Sohon himself commonly dated his many pencil portraits of northwestern Indians, and included on the drawing papers themselves the names and brief but informative identifications of his subjects. Thus Sohon's portrait of Pelchimo is not only a well-drawn likeness of a Flathead chief, but it is dated May 12, 1854, and bears the penciled notation, "Koilt-koi-imp-ty (Indian name). Spoken of by Father De Smet as 'Pelchimo', (by which name he is generally known,) as a good and brave Indian. He is a great favorite of all the whites who know him, for his honesty and good sense"[21] (Figure 15). Unfortunately few artists of the West were as considerate in leaving a precise historical record of each of their works for posterity.

At the other end of the scale we find Jules Émile Saintin's pencil and sanguine drawing entitled "Indian Warrior" (Figure 16). This is a superb example of draftsmanship. But from internal evidence—within the picture itself—we can ascertain that it is almost worthless for the historical record. The artist's model is surely a white man who is too small for his Indian breeches (or rather, leggings). Not knowing quite what to do with the tops of the bulky leggings, the artist has overlapped them in front, conveniently covering the model's privates without the need for a breechcloth, and has supported them by tightly drawing a commercial leather belt around the fellow's waist. The footgear resembles a pair of carpet slippers more closely than it does any Indian moccasins I have seen. We know that the very talented French artist Saintin spent some years in America. But this ersatz "Indian Warrior" is almost certainly a studio portrait of a white man. The only things Indian about it appear to be the leggings, the necklace, the quiver, and the title.

The great majority of pictures of the Old West fall somewhere between the well-documented and faithful works of Bodmer, Kurz, and Sohon, and this obviously false Indian portrait by Saintin. Many of them are not easy to evaluate ethnologically or historically—even by the expert. He may ask: Was the artist ever in the West? Did he really witness the scene he tries to portray? If he did, did he exercise some artistic license in recording what he saw? If he did not, is the picture based upon some story he was told, upon literary references, the works of other artists, or his own imagination—or a combination of several of these factors? Sometimes it is much easier to ask these questions than it is to find their answers.

[21] Ewers, "Gustavus Sohon's Portraits," 42.

In my opinion each picture must be evaluated on its own merits. It is dangerous to appraise individual works upon the basis of the general reputation of the artist who created them—as I have tried to illustrate in the cases of Wimar and Nahl. No masters of western painting produced pictures of uniform value to the historical record—much as dealers would like to have us think that they did. We should remember that it is far easier to sell paintings on the strength of the artist's reputation than upon the merits of a particular work. And sometimes little-known or even amateur artists happened to be in the right place at the right time to produce drawings or paintings which are of unique value to the historical record because they are the only extant on-the-spot representations of a particular person, action, or scene. Such an artist was the missionary priest Father Nicholas Point. His mission among the Flathead, Coeur d'Alene, and Blackfoot Indians of the Northwest in the 1840's was to save souls, but at the same time he created a goodly number of drawings of Indians and Indian life, traders, and trading posts which are the only extant pictorial records of those people, places, or scenes. They add greatly to the rather extensive written records of the Northwest of the 1840's.[22]

I know that few of my readers can join me in the time-consuming search for historical truth in the pictorial record of the Old West. But I hope that those of you who write or edit illustrated books or articles in the field of western history will be as careful in selecting the pictures you use as illustrations as you are in choosing the facts you present in your written texts.

May I suggest a few criteria for selection which may help you to avoid some of the pitfalls that have plagued historians and their publishers in making their choices of pictures in the past:

1. Don't select a picture just because it is new to you and has not been reproduced before. It is far better to reaffirm pictorial truth through reproduction of a well-known, appropriate illustration than to introduce pictorial error.

2. Don't select a picture just because it is clearly and realistically rendered and will reproduce well.

3. Don't select a picture just because it was executed by a famous artist whose works appeal to the public.

[22] John Francis McDermott, "De Smet's Illustrator: Father Nicolas Point," *Nebraska History*, XXXIII (1952), 35-40, 9 plates. Father Point's own profusely illustrated narrative of his experiences in the West, 1841-47, has been translated and edited for publication by Father Joseph P. Donnelly, S.J., of Marquette University.

4. Don't select a picture because it is the only representation of a particular subject—unless you are convinced that it is a truthful representation of that subject.

5. Don't reproduce any illustration which has been checked for historical accuracy and has been found inaccurate. If for some reason you feel you must do this, point out its failings just as you would clear up inaccurate statements by previous writers in your text.

As historians we should recognize that there is no truth to the old adage about a picture being worth a thousand words—unless that picture is truthful. A fictitious picture can do more harm than a false statement, for it may be retained in the viewer's memory long after the written words are forgotten.

Territorial Government and the Records of Its Administration

OLIVER W. HOLMES

NATIONAL HISTORICAL PUBLICATIONS COMMISSION

Other papers in this collection are concerned with some of the more exciting and picturesque aspects of the American frontier: its exploration, its Indians, the fur trade, frontier transportation, its cowboys, its art, and its literature. I have a feeling that, midway through this book, I am interjecting the dullest subject in the curriculum—government. Of course, if I could treat it in terms of outlaws, vigilantes, and peace officers, maybe I could get by, but I have chosen to treat it in terms of territorial governments per se and the territorial process, and the records that treat of these matters. A better understanding of these might, incidentally, provide a framework for that great book, entitled "Law on the Frontier," which would put the outlaws, vigilantes, and peace officers all in their places, but which no one, to my knowledge, has ever written. Most other great themes of frontier history would also be better understood if the governmental framework within which they were operative were better understood. We have been so fascinated by the branches, which form the more colorful manifestations, that we have ignored the importance of the trunk to which all were related.

But the study of territorial government and the territorial process is also important purely for its own sake—as a theme in itself. Why? I would answer, it is because it is a study over nearly two centuries of a new way for a sovereign country to handle subject territory. The Continental Congress passed the Ordinance of 1787 fixing the territorial system in the same year as another congress that the Continental Congress had called into being drafted our Constitution. Thus, almost simultaneously, the revolutionary fathers found what were to be surprisingly satisfactory answers to two great problems: how to govern themselves as a nation and how to manage that nation's empire democratically. For we must realize the thirteen states had inherited and had now to manage a large and most valuable part of the empires of England and France, and were later to take over almost as large and important a part of that of Spain. We could have bungled it. There was in the new nation not nearly the unity of interests that exists today. There were already incipient separatist movements. Transportation and communication, which bind today, were then problems that separated. What did bind the country then? More than anything, it was the Ordinance of 1787, as re-enacted by our First Federal Congress and thus tied into the Constitution. The two great documents fortunately "not only proved compatible" but "reconciled liberty with order to a degree of success never before achieved in government."[1]

Why has the Ordinance of 1787 always been considered one of the happier and more successful policy innovations of our history? "By this peaceful process of colonization," wrote Frederick Jackson Turner, "a whole continent has been filled with free and orderly commonwealths so quietly, so naturally, that we can only appreciate the profound significance of the process by contrasting it with the spread of European nations through conquest and oppression."[2] Well, it was not all peaceful. There was some shooting in the course of our expansion. And, as we think over this somewhat smug-sounding quotation, we cannot help observing that this nation did not find the process working so easily and

---

[1] These are the words of Howard R. Lamar in his *Dakota Territory 1861-1889* (New Haven, 1956), 5. I find his introductory chapter, entitled "Territory Policy of the United States: 1789-1889," one of the more thoughtful summary treatments of the territorial government theme. For background and many suggestions that have been incorporated into this paper, I am indebted to the following articles by Clarence E. Carter: "The Territorial Papers of the United States: A Review and a Commentary," *Mississippi Valley Historical Review*, XLII (1955), 510-524; "Colonialism in Continental United States," *South Atlantic Quarterly*, XLVII (1948), 17-28; and "Apprenticeship for American Statehood," *Department of State Bulletin*, XII (1945), 1109-14. See also Earl Pomeroy, "Toward a Reorientation of Western History: Continuity and Environment," *Mississippi Valley Historical Review*, XLI (1955), 579-600. Pomeroy's *The Territories and the United States, 1861-1890* (Philadelphia, 1947) remains the one best attempt to summarize territorial administration topically, with chapters on "Territorial Finances," "Territorial Justice," and the like, but it covers only certain far western territories in the later territorial period. There are few good treatments of individual territories other than Lamar's *Dakota Territory*, already mentioned, and Lonnie J. White's *Politics on the Southwestern Frontier: Arkansas Territory, 1819-1836* (Memphis, 1964), and territorial administration as such is not the main emphasis in these works. As late as 1955, Dr. Carter could still refer to the territorial period as a " 'dark age' in American historiography."

[2] From the address "The Ohio Valley in American History" (1909), as republished in *The Frontier in American History* (New York, 1920), 171.

naturally for its later overseas territories. These subsequent difficulties, however, perhaps but emphasize the more the system's success upon the continent proper and help to isolate the differences presented by non-contiguous territories.

Within our continental limits, which was all that Turner had in mind, it may be doubted that our pioneers would have struck out so boldly and optimistically to plant new settlements upon frontier after frontier were it not for the great promises contained in this ordinance and later territorial legislation stemming from it—promises of individual rights and citizenship, of early self-government, and of eventual admission to the Union upon the same high basis as the original states. These promises represented in effect a compact between the nation and its advancing frontiersmen, keeping them loyal and buoying up their spirits. These promises tied subtle bonds of common interest around both states and territories. The inherited empire became not an empire but a constituent part of a young nation boundless in its potential, and gave to that nation uncommon strength and unity because of inherent promises for the future—of power, and plenty, and peace—none of which the frontier normally knew, but which its inhabitants wanted desperately for their children. The successful completion of this territorial process for the contiguous territory of this continent, and even a little beyond in recent years, can ever be a lasting source of pride and unity. It is one of the grand themes in our history, and it may be not without broader meaning in political relationships generally.

Of course the process did not always work perfectly, but neither did it on the continent ever fail. As a leading Illinois historian, Theodore Pease, once told the Mississippi Valley Historical Association in a paper on the Ordinance of 1787, "The devil's advocate may be allowed to say everything that can be said in its disfavor, and when he has done his worst, its sanctity will still prevail beyond all doubt."[3] It may be important to know when and why it did not always work perfectly. Were there built-in frictions that became manifest over and over in the territories, which represented weaknesses in the system itself? Or were there special situations—geographical, cultural, historical—which appeared in special places or at special times that caused strains, as, for example, the effects of the slavery controversy on territorial expansion, or of religious and social complications as in Utah, or of an alien language and culture as in New Mexico and Arizona, two of the longest existing territories?

[3] Theodore C. Pease, "The Ordinance of 1787," *Mississippi Valley Historical Review*, XXV (1938), 168.

Although its basic principles remained unchanged from those fixed in the Ordinance of 1787, the territorial process itself was not without change. The earlier years were inevitably years of experiment, and the seemingly good precedents that were established were mostly summed up in the organic act establishing the Territory of Wisconsin in 1836. This became the pattern for subsequent organic acts, which perhaps became in turn too standardized in that they discouraged experiments and innovations that may have been desirable. This seems especially true after the Civil War. Perhaps it was the too-increasing rigidity of the pattern in these postwar years that made it appear difficult, if not impossible, to adapt or adjust it for use for overseas territory, and that led our nation at the turn of the century to fall back on the more conventional methods of governing subject territory employed by the monarchial governments of Europe. One is tempted to ask the whys and wherefores of these later changes for better or for worse.

There are topics of more limited character within this over-all territorial process that are deserving of study, some for their own sake, some for the light they throw on broader subjects. One is tempted to divide examples into executive, judicial, and legislative areas, listing these three branches of government in the order perhaps of their importance in territorial government. The appointed governor, representing the federal governments's control, came first because there was no elected legislature in the first stage of a territory's government and because throughout the life of a territory the governor really represented two governments, the federal and the territorial. He was always the main link with the administration in power in Washington. Some topics that deserve more study than they have received are (1) the appointment of territorial governors and territorial secretaries and their continuing responsibilities to the appointing powers, leading so often to built-in conflicts with territorial legislatures and frontier inhabitants; (2) the role of the governor as commander-in-chief of the territorial militia; (3) the governor as ex officio Superintendent of Indian Affairs in the territory, a study in the coordination of federal and territorial interests in an administrative area of great importance: (4) the governor's influence within his territory on the survey and sale of public lands, one of the major functions to be retained by the federal government; and (5) the governor's relations with the territorial judges, who were also independently appointed by the federal administration, and who in the first stages of a territory, before the territorial legislatures came into existence, formed with the governor a ruling council that could write a code of laws, and who shared with him throughout the territorial period the enforcement of both federal and territorial law.

Turning to these judges and the judicial branch, we might suggest studies of their influence, because of their independent position, on the governor and on the territorial legislature, and on the law and the practice of law in the territories. The dual jurisdiction of territorial courts in that territorial judges enforced both federal and territorial law is a topic of interest in view of the fact that federal and state courts became so completely separate as soon as the territory achieved statehood. In enforcing federal law, what was the relation of territorial judges to the U.S. marshals and attorneys and to the various enforcement agencies of the federal government controlled directly from Washington?[4]

Turning finally to the territorial legislatures, there certainly could be more study of election campaigns and processes as conducted on the sparsely settled frontiers in order to try to ascertain how representative these legislative bodies were. What was the effect over the territorial legislative body of the legislative supremacy of Congress and how and when was the congressional veto used? What were the main purposes of both legislative and popular petitions to Congress and how effective were they? What were the supposed functions of the territorial delegate to Congress, and how effective was he? What were his achievements and frustrations? Although the papers of many territorial delegates can be found here and there in western historical societies and libraries, there are few good studies of this interesting official representing the American frontier at the nation's capital.

One can study topics that cut across all three branches of territorial government, such as, for example, (1) tax legislation and its enforcement in the territories, the use of tax money, and financial administration generally; (2) provisions for public education in the territories and their influence generally on the history of American education; (3) territorial control over the creation of counties and cities and lesser units of government and the delegations of authority to them; (4) territorial efforts to stimulate and regulate business, such as mining enterprises, stockmen's interests, transportation facilities, and the like. Were there

[4] The best studies of law and justice in territorial administration are a series by William Wirt Blume in Vols. LVI-LXI of the *Michigan Law Review*. Blume has also edited a number of volumes of court records of the Michigan Territory Supreme Court. These studies all deal, however, with the earlier territorial period. Comparative studies are badly needed for the later territories of the trans-Mississippi West.

differences in handling these matters when the territories were arms of the federal government, and governors and judges possessed the powers of both governments, from later when the territories had become states and a jealous and rigid separation of powers was in effect?

The naming of such topics is almost endless. One could study them in a single territory, in certain geographical combinations, in certain chronological periods, or in certain political administrations.

We have been thinking of the territorial governments themselves in asking these questions. But we might think too of the over-all responsibilities of the federal government for these territories as represented in the work of the committees on the territories in both House and Senate, where many of the principles and problems of territorial administration were considered and bills drafted to deal with them. Or we might think of these responsibilities as represented by the executive departments charged with the over-all administration of territorial affairs, that is, the State Department until 1873, and the Interior Department afterwards except when still later the War and Navy departments were given responsibility for certain overseas territories. There are no separate monographs, based on a study of the records, as to how these responsibilities were met. And how did the existence of these territorial governments and the territorial system affect and modify the central government's administration of Indian affairs, public lands, frontier defense, and even foreign relations, to name but the main strands in the federal pattern.

It may be that administrative history like this is not popular anymore. It is closely related to the institutional history that was considered important toward the end of the nineteenth century in our pioneer graduate schools of history. But at that time the records for the study of territorial institutions and government were not generally available, and I would like to suggest that the subject has always been handicapped by the fact that part of the records were in Washington and the rest scattered in many territories that had become states; and in both the nation's capital and in the states, these records were usually stored in forgotten places. No major professor early in the twentieth century ever brought them together into a model study that stimulated others and established something of a school of study and interpretation. Conceivably such a school might then have influenced our administration of overseas territory for the better. Are the records at last being made available too late for any but academic use? One cannot know.

First, let us consider the archives in Washington relating to the territories. These are in many ways the equivalent, and continuation, of the archives in England that relate to the thirteen original colonies. The official records that came naturally into existence on this side of the Atlantic may be referred to as the "archives of the colonies," whereas those created in England are "archives relating to the colonies." Our colonial history was rather thin and biased until our historians of the colonial period begin to tap the "archives relating to the colonies" in the mother country, which archives provided a broader framework for the whole and threw new light on the details. Permanent reputations were made by Osgood, Andrews, Beers, and others from their exploitation of these records found logically across the Atlantic. Our colonial history—from monograph to textbook—was rewritten because of their discoveries, and the rewriting is not yet over in its details.

As our colonial history has had thus to be rewritten, so also much of the early history of our western states, including Alaska and Hawaii, will have to be rewritten after archives of the federal government relating to the territories have been made more broadly available. The main difference in theme lies in the fact that whereas the records relating to the colonies chronicle the road to independence, those relating to our territories chronicle the road to union and the building of a greater nation.

Early histories of western states, such as those of Hubert Howe Bancroft, were written without consulting unpublished federal records relating to the territories. Many historians of later date contented themselves with utilizing the printed federal documents, and some still do. It must be admitted that once one crosses the Mississippi in considering the territories, the mass of published government documentation becomes formidable, and few historians have ever mastered it. Others, however, came to realize that still more of the story was buried in unpublished documents in Washington attics and basements, and that often after exhausting printed documents the real key to events was still hidden. Leland and Van Tyne's *Guide to the Archives of the Government of the United States in Washington* (2nd ed., Washington, D.C., 1907) gave them the first systematic picture of some of these unworked veins, although it could not go into sufficient detail to reveal the full extent of the riches. David W. Parker's *Calendar of Papers in Washington Archives Relating to the Territories of the United States,* published in 1911 by the Carnegie Institution, whetted more appetites, although Parker too worked but a few of the richer veins and his calendar came down only to 1873, when the State Department relinquished control of the territories to the Interior Department.

Many early workers in the field of western history sought information or transcripts of records through their congressmen or directly from the agencies, but they sooner or later learned that for adequate results it was necessary that they go to Washington themselves. Some began going, armed with as potent introductions to higher officials as they could command, and then learned that they still needed to ingratiate themselves with chief clerks and lesser officials in order to be turned loose in freedom to explore attics and basements. Our colonial historians in going to Europe had found the records they sought gathered together in archival establishments for the most part, but our earlier historians of the West arriving in Washington found no such institution to serve them. They found it frustrating to follow trails that led from one agency's records to another. Their appetites were whetted but they could not tarry to master the masses of material. Microfilm had not yet come to their aid.

It was to meet this impasse that seven of the more active midwestern societies—Ohio, Indiana, Illinois, Michigan, Wisconsin, Minnesota, and Iowa—decided to combine to employ an agent to calendar pertinent material in Washington for them on cards. Then they could review the cards, order photostat copies of the documents as and when they desired, and scrutinize them at their leisure. The United States and Canada, it may be noticed, were similarly employing agents in European archives to perform a like function. The agent employed for this early consortium undertaking was Dr. Newton D. Mereness, who thereupon spent approximately twenty years of his life hunting through the accumulated old files of federal agencies for pertinent series of records and calendaring from them those documents that related to the upper Mississippi and Great Lakes regions. There resulted what is usually known as the "Mereness Calendar," numbering over 270,000 cards, which cost the cooperating societies over $100,000. The most complete set was kept at the University of Illinois, the participating societies only ordering such portions of the whole as they felt were worth having.

The Mereness Calendar, however, was never completed. The records of the Commerce Department, the Treasury Department, the Justice Department, the General Accounting Office, the federal courts, and the House of Representative files were never touched at all. Work in other departments and offices was often incomplete, and Mereness missed a few lesser series even where he thought he had covered the waterfront.

The major shortcoming of the enterprise from the national point of view was, of course, that it related only to the Midwest. Neither the southern territories nor those of the far West were included. The Mereness project served to indicate the importance of these records, but also made clear the vastness of the undertaking if it were to be extended to cover the same sources for all territories.

Unquestionably Mereness in his day was the person best informed on territorial records in Washington agencies, and it was logical that he should be appointed to select and prepare the more important of these records for publication after Senator Ralston's act of March 3, 1925, authorized the project that came to be called the *Territorial Papers.* On July 1, 1926, an appropriation having been secured to implement the authorizing act, Mereness and a staff began work in the Division of Publications in the Department of State. They produced thousands of new cards. By 1929, however, the project was bogged down. Dr. Clarence E. Carter took over in 1931, after it was resurrected, and carried it on doggedly and according to a consistent pattern until his sudden death in 1961.

It is curious that this notable documentary publication of the National Archives appears under the broadest possible title, *The Territorial Papers,* whereas, strictly speaking, its contents are limited to archives of the central government relating to its territories. The publication does not begin to include the archives of the territories themselves. This project was begun in a day when no one worried very much about semantic distinctions and all unpublished documents were generally labeled "papers," which they unquestionably were. With such a broad title, a lesser archivist than Dr. Clarence Carter might have become confused, or, perhaps, have stepped off the reservation deliberately; but Dr. Carter from the beginning through the first twenty-six volumes of this monumental work hewed exactly to the line by publishing only archives of the central government "relating to" the territories. Strictly speaking, his objective was much narrower than that. He was concerned, as is his successor, Dr. John Porter Bloom, with the documents in the archives of the federal government that relate to the government of the territories, that is, to territorial administration per se and not to all phases of territorial history that federal records might help to elucidate. Even within the narrower objective there is still such an enormous quantity of material that the editor is forced to be very selective.

Even the published *Territorial Papers* series has not, however, satisfied the western historians. Those in the far West are understandably too impatient to wait for the volumes pertaining to their states. They are aware also that the few volumes to be allocated to each of their states will, when they do appear, contain but a small fraction of the documentation they consider to be of importance. The National Archives has tried to meet some of their demands with its supplementary microfilm publication projects. For a time there was, as most of you realize, a real question as to whether it might not be desirable to abandon the published series completely, and put more time and money into microfilm. A special committee of the American Historical Association was appointed to study and report on the situation. Their report might have been forecast. They wanted both publication and supplementary microfilm. Trying to do both with inadequate funds will not help us to get along any faster with either. But John Porter Bloom is at work carrying on where Dr. Carter left off with the published series, and copy for part of his first Wisconsin volume has been sent to the printer. And we are continuing to make available each year on microfilm, in our microfilm publication program, more and more of the basic record series that contain the correspondence and other documents of offices and officials that were concerned with various aspects of the history of the territories.

We have sketched these events hurriedly and superficially chiefly to indicate the insistent and increasing demands of the West for the records of what might be called its colonial period, and the steps that have been taken to meet these demands. Since practically all the records involved are now in the National Archives, the finding of the solution or solutions rests squarely on the shoulders of this agency, and the financing of the necessary activities would seem to be a federal obligation.

I could wish for time and space to describe in more detail the many series of records in the National Archives that relate to the territories, for I feel these series are too little known and understood even by our experts in frontier history. It has been estimated that for the brief period 1836-48, when Wisconsin was a territory, no less than 150 series in the National Archives can contribute documents of importance to the history of the territory. We perhaps need a special little manual to guide students in this important area of federal administration just as we have been preparing special guides to the records relating to the Civil War.[5] It is my wish for the remainder of this paper, however, to

[5] K. W. Munden and H. P. Beers, *Guide to Federal Archives Relating to the Civil War* (Washington, D.C., 1962), 721 pp. A guide to the Confederate archives, being compiled by H. P. Beers, is nearing completion.

turn briefly to the archives that were created in the territories as complementary to those created and maintained at the seat of the federal government.

Two very different categories of archives created in the territories exist. The first is represented by the records of field offices of federal agencies supervised from Washington that operated in the territory, which field offices continued for the most part to operate without change in the succeeding states and continued to hold and add to the records they had created during the territorial years. The second category is represented by the records of the territorial government itself, and includes the records of the governor and secretary and of all offices dependent from them, the records of the territorial legislature, and the records of the territorial courts. To all of these—functions, offices, and records—the states succeeded.

To return briefly to the records of federal agencies that operated in the territories independently of the territorial government just as they later operated in the successor states independently of the state government, these agencies included the U.S. Army, the U.S. Postal Service, the General Land Office, the Office of Indian Affairs (which admittedly operated through the territorial governor when he served in ex officio capacity also as Superintendent of Indian Affairs, but his records in the latter capacity were federal records and remained in federal custody), the U.S. marshals and attorneys, and the federal courts. Later in the nineteenth century a host of other agencies of bureau level entered the field, many of them of scientific character, as for example the Weather Bureau and the U.S. Geological Survey. The records of the field offices of these agencies are of great importance in studying the territories, but they represent a vast body of material that cannot be described in a few minutes. A complicating factor is that jurisdictional boundaries of these field offices did not usually conform to the boundaries of territories. Archives of field offices of these agencies reaching back into the territorial years should still be in federal custody unless they (1) were mistakenly left with "archives of the territories" to the states, which sometimes happened, (2) carelessly or improperly fell into private possession, or (3) have been destroyed or lost. Some of the more important older ones were brought to Washington as field offices were closed and are now in the National Archives. Those that remained down to recent times in federal offices in the states have for the most part been rounded up and centralized in the regional records centers of the National Archives and Records Service, where they are being organized, inventoried, and made available to scholars.

It is the second category of records found outside the nation's capital, the archives created in territorial offices and by territorial officials, which, when the territories ceased to exist, came into the custody of successor states, to which I would turn our final attention. State officials, when the functions continued without important changes, often continued to add to the same files and make entries in the same books. Records of the territorial offices often still remain today in the successor state offices, especially if the territorial period ended in the late nineteenth century or in the twentieth century. Sometimes they, or some of them, may have been gathered into state archival agencies or historical societies. Some doubtless have been lost but probably more appear to be missing than actually are, because often they have become scattered among frequently reorganized state offices or forgotten in infrequently visited storage areas. They are usually in poor physical condition. They should be sought out and brought together by states having archival agencies so that they can be studied along with federal records for the same period, and the staff in the National Archives should know roughly what archives of territorial officials exist, where they are, and who has custody, so that they can refer historians and attorneys to them for purposes of supplementing their researches in the National Archives.

I would like to propose that each state that was once a territory make a survey and inventory of records created by officials of its territorial government, whether those records are now to be found in the custody of present agencies of state government, including a state archival agency or historical society, or, as has sometimes happened, have found their way into the custody of private libraries or private families. A few states may already have considerable knowledge of the nature and whereabouts of this archival material of their territorial period, but all states could improve this knowledge, and, so far, no state has published a systematic description of it. Normally, a survey such as I propose should be made by a state's archival agency, but if there is none, or if it is not professionally qualified for such an assignment, let the historical departments of the state universities step in and take responsibility, because this is research material that should represent grist for their mills.

There should be some effort to establish a common pattern for the inventory of these records in state after state, for the pattern of territorial government was similar and the resulting series of records created by territorial officials were similar, and a comparison of holdings between territories would be facilitated if such a pattern could be agreed upon. Let us hope that two or three or four of the more advanced archival agencies in as many of our states will decide to make such a survey and get togther to agree on the pattern of their reports. Other states will then almost certainly follow the example set for them.

If the states expect the federal government to continue to publish for them the archives in Washington relating to the territories, both in printed form and on microfilm, each state should feel that it has an obligation in return to survey and describe such records as it still possesses or can locate of the territorial government that preceded statehood. It may find many records that are deserving of publication, both by letterpress and by microfilm. Once we can see the pattern of what exists in all states, we can perhaps work out, with the help of some central agency, such as the National Historical Publications Commission, an intelligent cooperative publication program for these neglected records, thus supplementing the federal program. With such a planned program, the raising of the necessary funds should be easier and, with such a program agreed upon, the National Historical Publications Commission could put its shoulder to the wheel and help find funds. It has already recommended small grants to help some states to publish certain territorial records on microfilm, but it is not desirable to go far in this direction without a decision as to the desirable over-all program to which all states should be making their respective contributions.

In summary, no comprehensive and lasting history of either territorial government as a whole or territorial government in specific territories, or, for that matter, of general histories of the territorial period in most of our western states, can be written without putting together both the records to be found in Washington and those to be found in the states. The trouble has been that in the past it has been impossible to get them together. We are working at it in Washington, but there is still a long, long way to go. And it will also have to be worked at from the other direction. The states too have a long way to go. Illinois and Indiana once made a good beginning, but others have not followed their example, and the example seems all but forgotten now. It is time all our western states accepted their responsibility and began making inventories of these elusive and disappearing records in which is chronicled their own heroic age.

The
Fur Trade
as Business

RICHARD E. OGLESBY

UNIVERSITY OF CALIFORNIA, SANTA BARBARA

When Frederick Jackson Turner stood before the meeting of the American Historical Association in Chicago in 1893 and exhorted his colleagues to look to the frontier for the secrets of American history, not only was he legitimizing inquiry into a relatively neglected field, he was issuing a call to lofty drama. "The wilderness masters the colonist," he affirmed: "It strips off the garments of civilization and arrays him in the hunting shirt and the moccasin. It puts him in the log cabin of the Cherokee and Iroquois and runs an Indian palisade around him. Before long he has gone to planting Indian corn and plowing with a sharp stick; he shouts the war cry and takes the scalp in orthodox Indian fashion."[1] This was the substance of high adventure, and stuffy scientific types opened wide their eyes in contemplation of the dramatic possibilities inherent in this new area of investigation. And when the master rose to poetic heights, calling for man to "Stand at the Cumberland Gap and watch the procession of civilization, marching single file—the buffalo, following the trail to the salt springs, the Indian, the fur trader and hunter, the cattle-raiser, the pioneer farmer—and the frontier has passed by,"[2] he captured a generation of historians, and further stimulated the already avid interest of the reading public in America's frontier past.

Much of the light, rather than the heat, generated by Turner's clarion call has centered on the first white man to appear through the Cumberland Gap, the fur trader and hunter. He set up his trading posts on the Kennebec in the 1620's, pushed pack-horse trains, bells tinkling, into the Alleghenies from South Carolina and Pennsylvania a century or so later, and eventually led the way into Kentucky, Tennes-

[1] Frederick Jackson Turner, *The Frontier in American History* (New York, 1962), 4.
[2] *Ibid.*, 12.

see, and Ohio, activities which, though important, have attracted little in the way of historical inquiry. But when this vanguard of civilization crossed the Mississippi, reaching for the Rocky Mountains and beyond, he not only became the Mountain Man, highest evolution of the fur hunter, he won the hearts of historians and popularizers alike, insuring his undying fame as the most noted, if not the most noteworthy, of frontiersmen. Biographies by the brigade have marched from pen and press, and, as a consequence, few phases of our history are as well chronicled as the advance of Americans from mid-continent to the Pacific.

The significance of the Mountain Man is, of course, undeniable, and probably cannot be overemphasized. He poured tens of thousands of dollars worth of furs down the Missouri and into the American economy, carried the flag to the Pacific, bringing the United States into confrontation with the British in the Northwest and the Spanish and Mexicans in the Southwest, discovered the mountain passes which would enable the movement of population to the West Coast, ferreted out the fertile river valleys and parks that would lure the pioneer farmer across the "Great American Desert," and usually filled out a full life of adventure as an Army scout or emigrant guide. This story has been well told, but not always for the best of reasons. The Mountain Man lived a fantastic life, replete with Indian massacres, starving times, and grizzly bears, and too many authors have been content just to tell a good story.

But while this has been done, a most significant phase of the fur trade has been largely ignored. The fur hunter as a personality is quite familiar, but what of the man or men behind him? Very little has been done to illuminate the fur companies in St. Louis and eastward which provided the wherewithal permitting the Mountain Man to be who he was, where he was, and when he was. Under what conditions did these companies operate? What was their significance to the local economy of St. Louis, western entrepot of the fur trade? What was their importance to the economy of the frontier in general, or the nation as a whole? Did their operations contribute anything to the development of commercial institutions or business ethics in the United States? What happened to the tens of thousands of dollars the sale of western furs produced? These and a host of similar questions have never been answered satisfactorily, and when they are, new dimensions may be added to the significance of the fur trade in America. To demonstrate the neglect this aspect of the fur trade has suffered, let us examine one small segment of the fur trade in St. Louis between the years 1820 and 1823. It is an almost blank period in the annals of fur commerce, a transition between the end of one era, marked by the death of Manuel Lisa in 1820, and the advent of another, represented by the successes of William Ashley in 1824 and 1825. The usual explanation for this gap is that it coincides with the panic and depression of 1819, and therefore there was little economic activity of any kind during those years. The evidence, I think, shows quite the opposite.

The fur trade in St. Louis was as old as the town itself, and what little prosperity had come to the hamlet on the west bank of the Mississippi had been the result of that traffic. Originally founded as a trading post for the firm of Maxent, Laclède and Company in 1764, and populated mostly by Frenchmen from the Illinois country, the Mound City had been slow to develop. Under Spanish domination, and inhibited by the monopolistic system of trading rights they employed, St. Louisans did little to expand commerce beyond local limits. The only notable exceptions were Auguste and Pierre Chouteau, who enjoyed the lucrative trade with the Osage Indians,[3] and Jacques Clamorgan, whose Company of the Discoverers and Explorers of the Missouri launched three abortive attempts to open trade with the mountain tribes of the Northwest.[4] But not until after the United States came into possession of Louisiana did the fur trade of the Missouri valley begin to enrich the economy of the West.

Indeed, not until 1807, when Manuel Lisa, in partnership with Pierre Menard and William Morrison, sent an organized expedition to the mountains, was the fur trade put on a solid commercial footing.[5] From that successful beginning, which opened trade with the river Indians, established mountain posts, and made contact with the Crow, Arapaho, and other plains and mountain tribes, the fur trade dominated the economy of St. Louis and the whole trans-Mississippi West, and was in turn dominated by Manuel Lisa. The stimulation of that first voyage, and the promise of great profits brought back by Lisa the following year, caused the creation of the Missouri Fur Company over the winter of 1808-09, a corporation which included some of the most prominent citizens of St. Louis, but which was motivated by the personality of the fiery Spaniard. Beset by typical frontier money and credit problems,

[3] Richard E. Oglesby, *Manuel Lisa and the Opening of the Missouri Fur Trade* (Norman, 1963), 16.

[4] The most recent summary of the activities of this extraordinary man is A. P. Nasatir, "Jacques Clamorgan," in LeRoy R. Hafen, ed., *Mountain Men and the Fur Trade* (Glendale, Calif., 1965), II, 81-94.

[5] The most complete story of Lisa's enterprises is told in Oglesby, *Manuel Lisa.*

difficulties with the Indians, and internal dissensions, to say nothing of one complete reorganization, the Missouri Fur Company struggled on until 1814 before succumbing to the War of 1812.

Driven from the mountains by the hostility of the Blackfeet Indians, and prevented from returning to that area by the lack of financial support, Lisa nonetheless kept in the trade. Though he found new partners, first Theodore Hunt, a new arrival from Kentucky, and later Cabanné and Company, neither proved the vehicle for achieving the dream he had envisioned: a thriving St. Louis as the capital of a vast fur empire in the Northwest, and Manuel Lisa as the leading figure in that commerce. Finally, however, in 1819, Lisa was able to reorganize the Missouri Fur Company with entirely new personnel and a reasonably adequate capitalization, some $70,000.[6] This still was not enough, but it was better than the paltry sums he had had previously. Breaking with traditional avenues of commerce, Lisa applied to David Stone and Company of Boston and the Great Lakes to supply him with the necessary merchandise, and prepared to seek his goals. Unfortunately, death intervened.

While neither Lisa nor any of the others engaged in the fur trade during this early period made any great fortune, the thousands of dollars worth of furs which coursed down the Missouri spurred the economy of the city to greater heights, brought some fluid capital west of the Mississippi, and laid a solid economic base for future development. But if he had been relatively unsuccessful prior to 1820, I think Lisa looked forward with great anticipation to the next few years, feeling that perhaps the fur trade was about to emerge from its primitive fetters to become a highly profitable large-scale industry.

Lisa's death not only deprived the Missouri Fur Company of his dynamic leadership, but also brought into the open one of the strangest manifestations of the fur trade, the method of operating the business. During his lifetime, the talented trader had carried the entire burden of administration on his own shoulders. He knew all the employees, did the hiring and firing, all the personnel work (not all of it happy—as evidenced by the acidulous comments of Thomas James),[7] and kept the

[6] Lewis C. Beck, *A Gazetteer of the States of Illinois and Missouri; Containing a General View of Each State—a General View of Their Counties—and a Particular Description of Their Towns, Villages, Rivers, etc., etc.* (Albany, 1823), 329-330. Thomas Biddle said that the company had a capital of $17,000, but he was counting only the goods and equipment upstream left over from Lisa's prior companies. Joshua Pilcher valued the company's capital goods at $50,000 in 1822. *House Executive Document No. 7,* 18th Cong., 1st Sess., Serial 93.

[7] Thomas James, *Three Years Among the Indians and Mexicans* (Waterloo, Ill., 1846).

accounts of the company on paper and in his head.[8] In addition, he selected the seasonal outfit, decided what goods were needed where, drawing on his own experience to know the types and quantities of goods to order, and actually procured most of them during the winter months, making trips eastward when necessary. He also had the responsibility of delivering those goods upriver safely and on time, a trust in which he never failed. His knowledge was so great, his judgments so valid, that the Missouri Fur Company had outstripped all of its rivals on the Missouri, and maintained a practical monopoly of river trade. Unfortunately, no one else had been trained to perform these functions.

Without him, vital operations devolved upon two relative greenhorns, Thomas Hempstead and Joshua Pilcher. While they did amazingly well considering their inexperience and the circumstances which they faced, the absurdities inherent in the fur trade, and in all large-scale frontier enterprise in those years, proved insuperable. What makes their failure so difficult to comprehend is that what was impossible in 1820 is commonplace, even necessary, today.

No one takes notice of a business that might have its main office in St. Louis, with branches on either coast, and offices in London, Hong Kong, or Timbuctoo. In this age of instant communication to anywhere, and rapid transportation of personnel, merchandise, and equipment by train, plane, truck, and boat, it is natural, even desirable, for a business to have such an organization. Credit for large-scale operations is readily available from banks, insurance companies, lending institutions of all kinds, and even the federal government. Competition, while severe, is sophisticated, and the market is usually broad enough for everyone to have a profitable share. This kind of situation makes it difficult to understand how a money-making enterprise with a monopoly in a certain area could possibly fail. But consider the situation of Thomas Hempstead, acting partner for the Missouri Fur Company in St. Louis. His was a large-scale corporation, by frontier standards, with headquarters in St. Louis. David Stone and Company was his eastern representative, importing trade goods from Europe to the company's order, and shipping them to St. Louis to meet certain transportation deadlines. Stone and Company also marketed a quantity of the company's furs in eastern and European markets. The merchandise brought in by Stone and Company was retailed a thousand or so miles up the

[8] Missouri Fur Company Ledger Book, April 1812–July 1813; 1817, in Lisa's hand, is Vol. XXX, William Clark Collection, Kansas State Historical Society, Topeka.

Missouri, with payment taken in peltries. These furs and skins were brought down to St. Louis for sale or transshipment elsewhere to more favorable markets. This was a strikingly modern enterprise, and it would seem that Hempstead, in St. Louis, would have command of all phases of the business.

Unhappily, many modern improvements were not available in 1820. Communications, for example, were something less than instantaneous. As trade goods for the upper posts had to be on the river in late April or early May at the latest to take advantage of the fall season, orders for those goods had to be in Boston the previous November.[9] This meant that Pilcher, in charge of upstream activities, had to have his list of required articles completed by early October. Mail communication by company express on the river was far swifter than U.S. Mail between St. Louis and Boston, but all mail movement was subject to loss or delay, so precautions had to be taken to send several copies of orders to make sure that one reached its destination.

Even if the requisition for merchandise reached Boston in good time, many of the articles would have to be imported from London. Then the whole was sent by ship, usually to New Orleans, transferred to steamboat for St. Louis, and then hauled by keelboat up the Missouri. Thus Pilcher and Hempstead were forced to estimate a year in advance the goods they would need, and, as Stone and Company invariably was late in delivery, they sometimes were estimating two years in advance without the intervening year's goods on hand. No order ever was filled exactly, so Hempstead and Pilcher were guessing at best.

Then, too, credit was a baneful influence. There was only one bank in St. Louis in 1820, and though it managed to withstand the assault of the Panic of 1819 for some months, largely because it was made a depository for federal funds,[10] that depression rocked the financial structure of the entire country, and particularly the frontier. The federal government was not in the credit business, and other lending institutions were nonexistent. There was little cash money, and when it was noted that the Missouri Fur Company had a capitalization of $70,000, that only meant that the combined credit ratings of the board of directors added up to that figure. There probably was not that much cash in all St. Louis. Therefore, all goods purchased by the company were on credit advanced from David Stone and Company. The terms were deceptively simple and enticingly easy. The entire order was advanced on credit,

[9] This was Stone and Company's deadline, and even it was a bit optimistic.
[10] John Ray Cable, *The Bank of the State of Missouri* (New York, 1923), 64-65.

payment due twelve months after delivery. The charge was usually 6 per cent, with an additional 6 per cent per year for late payment. Theoretically, the company could order a complete outfit with no money down, and, by the time the note was due, have enough returns from the trade to pay off the original debt, hopefully with enough left over to put the company on a cash basis. This would not only save the 6 per cent, but would put the company in a position to bargain with several prospective suppliers to help keep costs down to a minimum.

Lisa had hoped to do even better than that. When he contracted with Stone and Company in 1819 for $25,910.98 worth of trade goods,[11] the Missouri Fur Company already had merchandise, traders, and trappers upstream, the remnants of Lisa's previous organizations, and he hoped that by the time Oliver Bostwick, Stone and Company's agent in St. Louis, delivered the goods in the spring of 1820, there would be enough in the treasury to pay for most, if not all, of the order, and so put the company on a cash basis for the first time in its hectic career. So confident was Lisa of success that he mortgaged his entire property in St. Louis as security.[12] It did not quite work out that way, but within a brief period the Missouri Fur Company was on the verge of getting out from under the crushing burden of continuing credit.

But while communication and transportation were difficult, and credit restrictions nearly impossible, the real debilitating force in the fur trade was excessive cutthroat competition, and never was that better evidenced than during the period under consideration, when the Missouri Fur Company was the dominant element in the trade and other groups were trying to force an entrance onto the Missouri. The business community has never been known for its high moral standards, except, of course, verbally, but it is utterly impossible to characterize the competition of this era in a word or phrase. It can only be described.

The fur trade, rather than declining, underwent a new burst of activity after 1819, due primarily to the panic and ensuing depression. St. Louis was thrown back onto a frontier-type economy, and, as the fur trade had always supported the frontier, it was natural for men to turn to it as a means of sustenance. It was still the easiest business to enter with a small amount of capital, and the vitality of the trade in the face of the depression caused others, who normally would not have done so,

[11] Deposition of Thomas Hempstead in the case of David Stone, Josiah Bellows, & Oliver Bostwick *vs.* Mary Lisa, Executrix, & Charles S. Hempstead, Executor, of Manuel Lisa, Nov. 9, 1824, St. Louis Records, Book I, p. 447, Office of Recorder of Deeds, City Hall, St. Louis. Hereafter cited as Hempstead I.

[12] *Ibid.*

to throw in their lot. Besides, the pot of gold at the end of Lisa's rainbow was out there somewhere, and men inevitably were available to seek it. The depression stimulated them to do it at that time. As a further incentive to the adventurous, the American military establishment, the hangover of the ill-fated Yellowstone expedition, remained on the Missouri, and traders felt that some advantage was to be gained by the simple presence of federal troops. All of these factors led men at loose ends to try the trade, making things more complicated for Hempstead and Pilcher.

An example of the chaos this milieu produced was the situation of the Kansa Indian trade. The Missouri Fur Company had had a post with that tribe for some time. Over the years it had deteriorated gradually as the company had concentrated efforts elsewhere, and by 1820 most of the Kansa trade was going to the post run by Francis and Cerré Chouteau, members of the oldest commercial family west of the Mississippi. In addition, two other firms, Legarc, Chouteau and Brothers, and the U.S. Indian Factory at Fort Osage did business with the Kansa.[13] The Missouri Fur Company determined to regain a profitable portion of the Kansa trade, and sent Michael Eley and Cyrus Woods to the area to establish a new post, while independent traders fell heir to the old one. Eley and Woods took their charge seriously, built a sturdy fort, stocked it with a large assortment of merchandise, and prepared to offer stiff competition to all rivals. Their advent caused Pierre Chouteau, Jr., who soon would be supplying the Missouri Fur Company with goods, to write to Cerré on August 30, warning of the impending competition, and suggesting a move northward, hopefully to greener pastures.[14] Thomas Hempstead was always careful to keep good men in charge of his new post, even sending his brother up there in 1821, so the struggle for pelts was in deadly earnest, but such were the conditions of trade that three posts, four groups, and an unknown number of legal and illegal independents contended for a business which could support only one. William Hempstead lamented in 1823 that his Kansa post was doing nothing,[15] and no one else was doing any better. The Indians en-

[13] Thomas Biddle to Henry Atkinson, *American State Papers, Indian Affairs,* II, 201.

[14] Pierre Chouteau, Jr., to Cerré Chouteau, Aug. 30, 1820, Chouteau Collection. Missouri Historical Society, St. Louis.

[15] William Hempstead to Stephen Hempstead, April 8, 1823. This letter is now in the Hempstead Collection of the Missouri Historical Society, but was loaned to the author by Mr. Robert K. Black of Upper Montclair, N.J., while the latter had possession of it.

joyed it, however, for the main staple of trade, laws notwithstanding, was alcohol.

Conditions were little better in St. Louis. Thomas Biddle noted in 1819 that besides the Missouri Fur Company, there were five other groups licensed to trade on the Missouri, supplemented, of course, by the government factory.[16] None were very large, but all were active, the list constituting a greater number of organizations than the river had seen in some years. The old-line trading firm of Berthold and Chouteau, heretofore content with supplying traders who operated only on the lower river, was now threatening to enter the upriver trade in force. This firm had been dickering with John Jacob Astor's American Fur Company, but had yet to make any commitment to the New York colossus.[17] Still, their direct competition would be a serious blow to Hempstead, for Pierre Chouteau, Jr., was an experienced river trader, and his firm had substantial backing. Not only that, but rumors flew throughout 1820 and 1821 that Wilson Price Hunt, the former Astorian, who had resided in St. Louis after his great exploit, was to lead the Berthold and Chouteau party up the Missouri. Everyone knew that Hunt maintained a connection with Astor, and that the American Fur Company often had availed itself of his services in St. Louis.[18] As it turned out, Hunt declined the assignment, and Berthold and Chouteau hired Joseph Brazeau, Jr., to follow Missouri Fur Company men and build posts wherever they did, a harassing tactic calculated to undermine Missouri Fur Company influence with the Indians.[19]

More serious was the possibility that instead of operating through one of the established St. Louis houses, Astor, or, more properly, his energetic field partner, Ramsay Crooks, would move directly onto the St. Louis scene, throwing the entire weight of the American Fur Company into the struggle for the Missouri trade. Fortunately for the St. Louis traders, although they did not know it at the time, Astor seems to have preferred to keep out of St. Louis. His American Fur Company had yet to show a profit by 1820, showed very little by 1823, and the old

[16] Biddle to Atkinson (see note 13).

[17] Astor and the Chouteaus had been talking merger as early as 1800. The correspondence on the subject over the years is contained in the Charles Gratiot Letterbooks, the Chouteau Collection, and other scattered references in the Missouri Historical Society.

[18] There are several references to Hunt's continuing connection with the American Fur Company in the Chouteau Collection.

[19] David Lavender, *The Fist in the Wilderness* (New York, 1964), 333.

skinflint wanted no more to worry about than he already had.[20] As late as 1823, Crooks was lamenting to his friend, partner, and confidant, Robert Stuart, "Mr. Astor is so fervently opposed to *extension* that he considered it wrong in me to make even the bargain I did last summer with Berthold and Chouteau to import their goods for 1823."[21] Personally, however, Crooks was anxious to get back on the Missouri, and would utilize the first opportunity to do so. His efforts in that direction were somewhat hampered by the American Fur Company's deliberate drive to have the government abolish the factory system, which effort was rewarded with success in 1822.

From the north came a new disturbance in the form of the Columbia Fur Company, formed in 1821 by Joseph Renville, and containing such prominent Canadians as Kenneth McKenzie, William Laidlaw, and Daniel Lamont.[22] Renville, who had been interpreter for the British trader Robert Dickson on American soil during the War of 1812, and who had recognized the potentialities of the Missouri trade during time spent with the Sioux, took advantage of the consolidation of the Hudson's Bay and Northwest companies to pick up recruits for his adventure. He hoped to develop the trade of the upper Mississippi valley and then move over onto the Missouri. As British subjects could not be licensed to trade on American soil, two American citizens, William Tilton and S. S. Dudley, were nominally in charge, but Renville was its guiding spirit, and McKenzie, Laidlaw, and Lamont its active agents.[23] Competition was commencing from all directions.

Also in the Mound City were the stirrings of yet another company interested in the upper river, a new partnership instigated by the lieutenant governor of the new state of Missouri, William H. Ashley. Ashley, "a person of credit," somewhere had picked up considerable financial backing, and had joined with Andrew Henry, former partner of Manuel Lisa in the old Missouri Fur Company, and first man west of the Continental Divide with traders and trappers. They were gathering their forces over the summer of 1821 preparatory to launching an expe-

[20] Lavender clearly shows how Crooks utilized every opportunity to open trade on the Missouri while Astor held him back. *Ibid.*, x.

[21] Quoted in *ibid.*, 341.

[22] These individuals lost their jobs with the Hudson's Bay Company due to its consolidation with the Northwest Company.

[23] Hiram M. Chittenden, *The American Fur Trade of the Far West* (Stanford, 1954), I, 323 ff. Although he mixes up the nationalities of some of the principals, Chittenden plainly shows the effective competition put up by the Columbia Fur Company.

dition the following spring.[24] So things were considerably crowded in the Missouri fur trade during this period, and an outside observer scarcely would know that a depression existed.

With all these people in competition for a fairly limited supply of furs and skins, to say nothing of merchandise, credit, and a fluctuating supply-and-demand situation, the fun began. The Missouri Fur Company was allied with David Stone and Company of Boston, and, as Stone was in violent competition with Astor on the Great Lakes,[25] Thomas Hempstead thought he could count on Stone's constant support on the Missouri. Being honest, and somewhat naive, Hempstead thought this for entirely too long. The handwriting appeared on the wall as early as the fall of 1820, when Hempstead negotiated with Oliver Bostwick for the 1821 outfit. Bostwick drove a hard bargain, a little arrogantly, considering how late he had been with the previous order, and demanded that half the new purchase be paid in cash.[26] This only indicated to Hempstead that Stone and Company were "honorable men, but very scary."[27] They turned out to be neither.

Stone had been giving the American Fur Company a very difficult time in the Great Lakes region, and Crooks finally hammered out an agreement whereby Stone would leave the Lakes, and Crooks would buy up his merchandise at a premium. Stone pulled out, but continued to maintain a northern outlet through James Lockwood in Green Bay, who was operating mainly west of the Lakes. Crooks thought this a violation of their accord and screamed a protest which echoed in New York and Washington, but Stone held on. Yet even while they were at each other's throats in Wisconsin, Crooks and Bostwick combined in St. Louis to sell goods to James Baird for the Santa Fe trade.[28]

What Stone and Bostwick seemed to be looking for was a combination with the American Fur Company for a massive effort on the Missouri, and this they eventually achieved. The Missouri Fur Company

[24] The story of Ashley's activities is told in Dale L. Morgan, *Jedediah Smith and the Opening of the West* (Indianapolis, 1953), and the documents provided in Dale L. Morgan, *The West of William H. Ashley* (Denver, 1964).

[25] Lavender, *The Fist in the Wilderness*, 267-268.

[26] Deposition of Thomas Hempstead, St. Louis Circuit Court File, Oct. Term, 1824, No. 35, Office of Clerk of Circuit Court, Civil Courts Building, St. Louis, reprinted in Charles E. Peterson, "Manuel Lisa's Warehouse," *Missouri Historical Society Bulletin*, IV (1948), 81-84. Hereafter cited as Hempstead II.

[27] Hempstead to Pilcher, Oct. 22, 1820, Fur Trade Papers, Missouri Historical Society, St. Louis.

[28] Lavender, *The Fist in the Wilderness*, 334-335.

had no place in such an arrangement, but until it could be con-
summated, Stone was not averse to making a dollar by supplying
Hempstead, and, if worse came to worse, he might permanently join
the Missouri Fur Company. But by tying the Missouri Fur Company to
them by credit, Stone and Bostwick held the power of life and death. If
it should become necessary to eliminate the Missouri Fur Company, it
could be done easily and effectively by withholding supplies. Mean-
time, it was not difficult to see that the Missouri Fur Company did not
make enough to get out from under simply by delaying delivery of merchandise until well into the summer instead of meeting the spring sail-
ings up the Missouri from St. Louis. This may be a cynical view of
Stone and Company, and perhaps it does them a grave injustice, but the
circumstantial evidence is pretty damning.

Bostwick never lived up to his agreements to deliver goods to St.
Louis in the spring. Lisa's original order did not arrive until well into
the summer of 1820.[29] When Hempstead made the agreement for the
following year in the fall of 1821, an order amounting to $27,815.65,[30]
Bostwick promised to have the merchandise in St. Louis by May, or
June at the latest. June 1 came and went without the appearance of either Oliver Bostwick or the goods, and Hempstead was forced to get an
advance from the Bank of Missouri to enable him to purchase a few
supplies locally, and hire a few men to move them upstream.[31] The
bank itself was about to go under, but, as Hempstead was one of the di-
rectors, he procured the loan.[32] Bostwick arrived in St. Louis on June
23, profuse in his apologies for being late. He graciously took care of
the small bank loan, and proceeded to paint a glowing picture of future
prospects, pointing out the great improvement in the fur market, and
the fall in prices of trade goods, in some cases from 50 to 100 per cent.[33]
But it mattered little to Hempstead what the price of goods was if they
were not available.

At the time, Hempstead was busily preparing the expedition of Mi-

[29] The mortgage was made during the summer of 1820, prior to the delivery of the
goods.
[30] Hempstead I.
[31] Oglesby, *Manuel Lisa*, 180.
[32] Brackenridge Jones, "One Hundred Years of Banking in Missouri," *Missouri
Historical Review*, XV (1921), 345-392, lists Hempstead as a director, p. 381. The
bank ceased operations on August 14. James M. Primm, *Economic Policy in the Development of a Western State: Missouri, 1820-1860* (Cambridge, Mass., 1954), 2.
[33] Hempstead to Pilcher, June 27, 1821, Thomas Hempstead Letterbook, June 27,
1821–Feb. 12, 1823, William Robertson Coe Collection, MS 345, Yale University
Library, New Haven. Hereafter cited as Hempstead Letterbook.

chael Immel and Robert Jones for the Rocky Mountains, the first party to head back there since the War of 1812, and he finally got them on the river on July 10.[34] Bostwick's goods arrived on July 22, long after they should have been on their way upstream. Even so, Hempstead was able to turn over to Bostwick $31,875.65, paying off the remainder of the original outfit and the one-half payment in cash for the 1821 merchandise.[35] The head of the Missouri Fur Company in St. Louis was almost exultant as he wrote to his partner, Joshua Pilcher, "I think this year will establish the credit and standing of the Missouri Fur Company to the great mortification of some people in this country."[36] His joy was of short duration, however, as "some people" were not so easily daunted.

The company boat, "a new boat that never had made a trip," and was, moreover, "completely rigged and she did not leak one drop," was quickly loaded for the voyage northward. The night after loading was completed, "the boat was cut loose by some friend of ours." At the end of a six-mile chase, the boat was recovered, unharmed, hauled back to St. Louis, inspected, and immediately sent on its way. On the night of August 13, a scant two miles above Bellefontaine, the craft sank, soaking all the goods on board, and at a cost that would approach $10,000.00.[37] The competition was becoming quite spirited.

Then Bostwick, who had agreed in his contract with the Missouri Fur Company not to sell goods to anyone trading above the Grand River, proceeded to sell to William Ashley $6,000 worth of trade goods. There was no doubt of Ashley's destination, and Hempstead finally began to have some second thoughts about Stone and Company. Joshua Pilcher, upstream, could only lament, "too late, too late, too late."[38]

Too late for a lot of things. Bostwick had promised a shipload of barleycorn and beads that summer which had a great deal of difficulty in reaching St. Louis. Through a whole series of delays, in which more than fate had a hand, the vitally needed corn and beads did not reach Hempstead's hands until November 18, and he was forced to take them overland by pack-horse train to the upper posts.[39] The costs were immense.

[34] *Ibid.*, July 10, 1823.
[35] Hempstead I.
[36] Hempstead to Pilcher, July 27, 1821, Hempstead Letterbook.
[37] *Ibid.*, Aug. 13, 1821.
[38] *Ibid.*, Sept. 7, 1821.
[39] The Hempstead Letterbook chronicles the long, sad tale of the barleycorn and beads over the summer and fall of 1821.

But caught in the web of ever-expanding debt, Hempstead was forced to make another agreement with Stone and Company for his 1822 outfit. The Bostonian promised faithfully that the merchandise would be in St. Louis by April 15. Bostwick himself arrived in St. Louis on March 25, and no doubt suffered mixed feelings as Hempstead turned over to him $30,472.30,[40] but he again brought tidings that the goods could not be expected before June 1. This was an extremely bad year to be behind, as Ashley was completely organized, and had purchased everything that floated in and around St. Louis. Hempstead was forced as far south as Ste. Genevieve in search of a river-worthy craft.[41] But time was running out for the Missouri Fur Company, and soon the Blackfeet would terminate their major effort.

Aside from the exasperating difficulties with Bostwick, Hempstead was encouraged by his position. As head of the largest and strongest company on the river, Hempstead suddenly found himself wooed by his most serious competitors. Both Berthold and Chouteau and the American Fur Company approached him, desirous, they claimed, of making an agreement either to share the trade, or consolidate to better reach the mountains.[42] Hempstead was flattered, but drove a hard bargain, or rather, tried to. No one was really interested. Those offers seem to have been merely cover-ups for the real deals being made behind closed doors. Crooks had sent Samuel Abbott to St. Louis to look over the situation in the summer of 1821, and wrote Astor later that year informing him that he planned to move into St. Louis. An arrangement had been made with Berthold and Chouteau, but only for the importation of their goods for the next year, nothing more binding than that. Abbott was instructed by Crooks to "keep things pretty quiet about our establishing at St. Louis and perhaps I may be able to go there in the course of the winter to arrange matters finally."[43] So while he was making overtures to Hempstead, Crooks was planning his own establishment.

Held back by Astor, at least as far as bringing the American Fur Company to St. Louis, Crooks tried another approach to the problem of the Missouri Fur Company by attempting to lure Joshua Pilcher away

[40] Hempstead I.

[41] Hempstead to Pilcher, April 3, 1822, Hempstead Letterbook.

[42] Oglesby, *Manuel Lisa*, 185-186.

[43] Crooks to Abbott, Aug. 16, 1821, Chouteau Collection. Crooks also wrote to Astor later that autumn, "Preliminary arrangements are made for prosecuting the trade of the Missouri & St. Louis next season. . . ." Quoted in Kenneth W. Porter, *John Jacob Astor, Business Man* (Cambridge, Mass., 1931), II, 717.

from the company's service. Knowing Pilcher to be an excellent trader, Crooks inquired if he might be free to join another concern, say the American Fur Company. Pilcher refused, with a candor worthy of Lisa: ". . . there are several young gentlemen who have been ingaged in the service of the Company, and some of them are now interested in it; their fortunes have become identified with my own; they look to me with confidence as a head as a leader; and my confidince in and attachment for them is unlimited; for in them is united with all the ordinary quallifications for this business; integrity, pride, inteligence spirit and interprise rarely surpassed; and in prosecuting a business of such enormous weight, I should feel much at a loss without the aid of such persons."[44] Apparently Pilcher and Hempstead were the only traders interested in such things as integrity, but it is refreshing to note that at least someone was. Perhaps that was the reason Hempstead did not seem particularly concerned over Ashley's competition. With Andrew Henry in charge of Ashley's operations in the mountains, the Missouri Fur Company would not have to worry about any double-dealing from that direction, as Henry was one of the most respected gentlemen in the trade.[45]

Astor tired of all the machinations in and around St. Louis, and decided to end them in the most effective way. He called Oliver Bostwick to New York in early 1823 to incorporate that individual and the firm he represented into the American Fur Company.[46] But while Bostwick returned to St. Louis after making the preliminary arrangement, Astor himself was not above getting in a few licks at his partner-to-be as he wrote Samuel Abbott in St. Louis:

Mr. Bostwicks object in going to St. Louis is to purchas Deer & other skins, I wish you to anticipate him   could you get some Promise from the Missourie Fur company to give you an oppertunity to purchas their Skins   Say the whole of them except Boffolo, and you might except Beaver—or in other words get the Deer & Beare & if they wish the otter & fishers with them—if you think well consult with Mr. Hunt & if taught best perhaps Hunt can approach them better   if so let him do it—you will of course not raise the price only when & where it is necessary—If you can do no better than get Bostwick to give you an interest in the purchase say ½ or ⅓ or even if you cannot get more than ¼ for our interest in the purchase of the Deer & otter furrs & skins they buy of the Missourie Fur Company.[47]

[44] Pilcher to Crooks, June 16, 1822, Chouteau Collection.
[45] Too little is known of Andrew Henry, but he was held in high esteem by partners and competitors alike.
[46] Lavender, *The Fist in the Wilderness*, 341.
[47] Astor to Abbott, March 13, 1823, Chouteau Collection.

Ashley's magnificent success after the disastrous year of 1823, which witnessed the Immel-Jones massacre, a mortal wound for the Missouri Fur Company, the attack of the Arikara on Ashley's party, and the farcical campaign against the Indians conducted by Henry Leavenworth, reduced the trade to a less complicated competition between large companies, making the business look almost orderly after the chaotic years between 1820 and 1823, when everyone was attempting, by fair means and foul, to achieve the advantage.

But it had been quite a rat race while it lasted. Ashley apparently had, or readily could obtain, enough money to act independently of all the others, adding to the confusion only by competing for men and supplies, and although he acted outside the law in moving upriver before being granted a license,[48] he did nothing else untoward. The Missouri Fur Company, dependent as it was on Bostwick, struggled forward under dire handicaps. Bostwick, although committed to the Missouri Fur Company, pursued his particular interest whether or not it hurt Hempstead and Pilcher. Berthold and Chouteau followed their own specific policies, negotiating with the American Fur Company, the Missouri Fur Company, and even Bostwick when it suited them, and threatened serious competition to all. The Columbia Fur Company was moving in from the north, draining off wealth that normally would have gone to St. Louis. And hanging over the entire situation like the sword of Damocles was the American Fur Company, with its highly ambivalent policy. Ramsay Crooks was vitally interested in the Missouri, while Astor was holding him back. Crooks was dealing with Berthold and Chouteau, Bostwick, Hempstead, and anyone else from whom he thought he could wring a profit. Interests clashed, deals and counterdeals were made and broken, the net result being that everyone suffered. Confusing to be sure, but the point is clear.

It is easy to see why these years have been almost a total blank in the annals of the fur trade. They simply are too confused and confusing to submit to the usual historical generalization. But the activities of those years, while sketchy in outline, were nonetheless vigorous in application, with perhaps more animation than at any other period, and call for a new look at the fur trade in general. The ferocity of competition for credit, merchandise, Indian favors, and advantages over rivals was demonstrably present, but perhaps only more dramatically than at

[48] Ashley's license came through nearly two weeks after he set sail. He seems to have harbored no doubts that it would be forthcoming.

other times, and certainly this cutthroat competition was a continuing factor throughout the years of the trade, largely determining the profits or losses of the firms involved. The difficulties of operation under such a severe shortage of credit have never been explored adequately, though the power of the creditor is amply shown here. There is also, I think, another reassessment in order.

Historians long have made much of the fortunes of John Jacob Astor and William H. Ashley, about the only real examples of men who made a great deal of money from the fur trade, and have marveled that there were so few of these individuals. After all, millions of dollars worth of fur moved through St. Louis. Where are the great fortunes? I think that even this brief survey of the period between 1820 and 1823 clearly demonstrates that the wonder is not that there were so few fortunes derived from the fur trade, but that there were any at all.

The Fur Trade
as Seen from the
Indian Point of View

PRESTON HOLDER

UNIVERSITY OF NEBRASKA

The major concern of this presentation is the European fur trade and the fur trader as seen from the viewpoint of the Indians on the frontier of the Missouri River in what is now the Dakotas. Strictly speaking there is no Indian point of view, only the viewpoint of Indians. This will depend on the kind of Indians, which were many and diverse in historical origins, and the nature of their major interests.

The communities or so-called tribes which the Europeans met in North America can be conveniently classified into two main types. Most familiar to us were the wandering groups of hunters who occupied vast reaches of the country. As archeological work is completed in the Mississippi basin it becomes clear that roving groups had only recently replaced more sedentary peoples. At the time of the *entradas* of De Soto and Coronado stable village life was spread along the main rivers of the entire Mississippi drainage. This way of life was at least 1,000 years old in this region. The villagers were hoe farmers. Women cultivated maize, beans, squash, sunflowers, amaranth. They gathered such wild products as pecans, walnuts, hickory and hazel nuts, as well as roots and soft fruits. Stores of food were laid up as much as two years in advance in baskets and well-made ceramic containers. Fundamentally, the men were hunters who furnished the meat portion of the diet along with furs and hides for clothing. Processing of the foods and clothing was the work of the women. Trade was largely in luxury items and raw materials. Sea shells from the Gulf were traded north to the Great Lakes. Copper from the Lakes was traded south to the Gulf. Obsidian found its way from the Rocky Mountains east to the Mississippi. De Soto noted that bison hides moved east out of the plains to the peoples along the main river. Sea shells from the Pacific littoral appeared far east in the Missouri drainage. After its introduction by the Spaniards the domes-

ticated horse spread over most of the continent along these old channels
of native communication.

The Spanish *entradas* of the sixteenth century disrupted this old sub-
sistence pattern along the Mississippi and its easterly affluents, although
it continued to survive along the middle reaches of the Missouri River.
Recent extensive archeological researches indicate that these villages
were present as early as the thirteenth century. The sequence continues
unbroken into eighteenth-century times. Our concern here begins with
these latter people. Archeological reconstructions show the early eighteenth-century settlements as tiny secure hamlets of some fifteen to
twenty earthlodges scattered along the lower terraces of the river. Fields
were in the convenient bottoms where trees furnished essential fire-
wood and building materials. This mode of existence was ancient and
indigenous, as were trade links south into central Nebraska and Kansas,
and east into the Mississippi valley.

The French fur traders who penetrated these fastnesses after 1700
were not really official representatives of government or of trade. The
Indians seldom if ever met such remote figures as the *bourgeois,* the
factor, and other officers of the trade in their administrative centers. It
seems unlikely that the close connection between the various government officials and the interests of the trade was clearly understood. The
first visitors operated essentially as free agents far in advance of the "establishment" of the fur trade as such. These *coureurs de bois, voyageurs, hivernants, mangeurs du lard,* as they were called in their various
capacities, formed the backbone of the labor force of the trade. Re-
cruited mainly from French or *métis* families in the St. Lawrence valley,
they formed a distinct group, only nominally French.[1]

Such *coureurs de bois* surely possessed much unofficial knowledge of
the hinterland, kept as trade secrets quite independent of the official
notices of the Missouri country. There was little reason for them to
share such information with their superiors. It was advantageous to
hide routes and contacts even from those in the same station in life.
Tribal lists brought back by Joliet suggest that *coureurs de bois* knew
of and probably had been into the Missouri River country by the late
1680's—some two decades before official notices appear. There is no
specific information regarding the nature of the terrain and its people
on this frontier until 1714. In that year Étienne Véniard de Bourgmont ascended the river, apparently as far as the mouth of the

[1] Marcel Giraud, *Le métis canadien* (Paris, 1945), 324-331.

Niobrara.[2] He had been a commandant at Detroit who left his post there to follow the life of a *coureur de bois* more than a decade earlier. He mentions that the Arikara had seen the French and knew them. They were then settled just upriver in some forty villages scattered along the shores. Bourgmont married an Indian woman and continued the life of *coureur de bois,* the object of repeated complaints from both the religious and the military. By his own account in 1724 he had spent twelve years with the Missouri Indians. It can be safely assumed that he furthered his knowledge of the upriver country.

Again in 1734 Bienville mentions *voyageurs* who had visited the Arikara.[3] These contacts must have continued. When the la Vérendrye expedition visited the Mandan villages to the north in the early 1740's it learned of a French national who lived with the Arikara. One resident of the Arikara village had been to the Southwest where he had learned Spanish.[4]

During this period the visitors whom the Indians saw dressed like Indians, traveled and lived like and with them, speaking the native languages and marrying into the native communities. They worked in the same fashion as the Indian hunters. Judging from archeological and scattered documentary evidence this trading newcomer was just another foreign peddler in a long list of such intruders, albeit one with novel and in some cases exotic goods. The fur trade commenced as just one more episode in an ancient story of aboriginal economic and cultural interchange. This continuity is striking in the Mississippi-Missouri valleys, whose waterways were vitally important to the Indians long before Europeans appeared.

Most of the early trade was carried out in native terms of gift exchange. In one sense or another the trader was always a guest in the village. It is not clear whether the early *coureur de bois* based himself in such a village and trapped in the surrounding country or whether he bought furs from Indian producers elsewhere, returning to his base village until he accumulated sufficient pack to justify the long journey back down the river to the post, where he would replenish his supply of goods.

[2] Marcel Giraud, "L'exacte description de la Louisianne de Veniard de Bourgmont," *Revue historique,* CCXVII (1957), 29-41; also in *Missouri Historical Society Bulletin,* XV (1958), 3-19.
[3] Pierre Margry, ed., *Mémoires et documents pour servir l'histoire . . . des . . . Français . . . l'Amérique septentrional (1614-1754)* (Paris, 1888), VI, 455.
[4] L. J. Burpee, ed., *The Journals of Pierre Gaultier de Varennes, Sieur de la Vérendrye and His Sons* (Toronto, 1927), 424-427.

In any event the trade placed the Indians in a position to enrich themselves in two principal ways: there was the advantage of direct barter with the visitors, and they were in a good position to act as middlemen between such visitors and other native producers of furs. Judging from the Indians' alacrity in performing this role throughout the fur trade, they must have tried to hold the *coureur de bois* in their own village by making it unnecessary for him to search further for his furs. It may be true that the elements of the trade were not essential for the Indians' livelihood: iron knives, axes, needles, brass kettles, textiles to replace hide robes and enhance the prestige of the wearer, glass beads to serve instead of porcupine quills, copper bangles and bells, vermilion, perhaps gunpowder. It seems most unlikely that the new peddler appeared to be the avant-garde of any "establishment." The *hivernant*, himself, did not live in a world in which a "fur trade" existed that was destined to engulf his hosts. Even the wealthy men who controlled this commerce in faraway centers, and who, in turn, were controlled by it, saw little coherent structure in this sprawling unkempt enterprise. Their field representatives had even less understanding of the complete monster. The Indians saw only these individuals, with certain peculiar interests in a few items of produce.

The villagers were offered every incentive to become Europeanized: to become eager to join in the commerce and to adjust their customary existence to the new elements. During this century the Arikara learned from a Spanish captive how to crush glass and cast their own beads.[5] In the village debris a growing proportion of iron and glass arrowheads fashioned on old flint patterns signify this change.

In their social relations these villages were homogeneous only on the surface. Among the Arikara there were actually two very different social levels. The member of a chiefly or high-ranking family was clearly pictured in the official records. His relations to the fur trade representatives were those of an equal or, in some instances, a superior. In addition there were common families of inconsiderable social position or those whose fortunes of life had not yet allowed them secure social status. These troublesome individuals appear most often in the records as villains or pests. Their constant demands and threatening behavior exasperated or frightened the trader, leading to allegations of savage and unreasoning performances far beyond the limits of human actions.

Economic life in the villages differed qualitatively from that of Eu-

[5] Anna H. Abel, ed., *Tabeau's Narrative of Loisel's Expedition to the Upper Missouri* (Norman, 1939), 149.

rope. Village production was fundamentally for use, never for profit as such. There were no wages. Labor was strictly devoted to the maintenance of life. Goods were in the possession of the actual family or household producing them. There was an effective redistribution and communal sharing of many essentials, since reciprocal gift-giving was the rule. Ties of kith and kin formed a network across the whole community. The only wealth accumulated was in nonessentials or luxuries: elements of decoration and costume, specially prepared hides, and, as time went on, horses and objects from the trade.

Horses formed an important new source of wealth for gaining and enhancing high-status positions. For some Indians of the plains this wealth seems to have brought extensive changes in the social structure of the community.[6] Some of the village dwellers left a sedentary way of life to become unsettled bison hunters. The Cheyenne changed thus in the latter half of the eighteenth century. On the eastern edge of the plains the pattern was more complex. The acquisition of the new tool intensified existing patterns. The intermittent communal bison hunts took the Pawnee away from their villages more frequently and longer so that their homes were abandoned for much of the year. The Osage and Kansa simply traveled longer distances. The Arikara and Mandan were able to bring more meat back to a village which remained much the same as it had been for hundreds of years. There new wealth solidified old advantages. The Arikara chiefly families were honored by gifts of horses from the commoners. In turn, the favored ones maintained the ancient status quo, which gave religious sanction to the permanent village and the cultivation of corn. Their stable hamlets were headquarters for native trade fairs. There the fur trade representatives could best establish a secure base.

This differential accumulation of prized goods was on a very limited scale. Those who enjoyed high status were honored by those lower in rank. Frequently the honoring took the form of presents. The finest horse from a successful raid went to the chief or the priest, as an offering of respect either to the person or to the supernatural symbol. The lofty validated their position by redistributing goods. The tightfisted would not be esteemed. Yet in the exchange those high in rank were not slighted. They received the best because they were of the best.

---

[6] Oscar Lewis, *The Effects of White Contact upon Blackfoot Culture* (Memoirs of the American Ethnological Society, VI, New York, 1942); see also John C. Ewers, *The Horse in Blackfoot Indian Culture* (Bureau of American Ethnology Bulletin 159, Washington, D.C., 1955).

Something of this Indian attitude penetrates the complaints of the French trader Antoine Tabeau early in the nineteenth century:

That is what I found among the Ricaras. This nation, having already wasted great quantities, is accustomed to receive gratuitously. It looks upon the whites as beneficent spirits who ought, since they can, to supply all its needs and it looks upon the merchandise, brought to the village, as if destined for it and belonging to it. Furthermore, the great notion that they [the Arikara] have of their buffalo robes, founded upon the price that they foolishly give the Sioux for them and still more upon the fatigue and dangers that we face in order to produce them, causes them always to imagine that they lose in the trade. Besides, their minds not grasping our ideas of interest and acquisition beyond what is necessary, it is a principle with them that he who has divides with him who has not. "You are foolish," said one of the most intelligent seriously to me. "Why do you wish to make all this powder and these balls since you do not hunt? Of what use are all these knives to you? Is not one enough with which to cut the meat? It is only your wicked heart that prevents you from giving them to us. Do you not see that the village has none? I will give you a robe myself, when you want it, but you already have more robes than are necessary to cover you." All the logic and all the rhetoric in the world are thrown away against these arguments, and how hope for success in a nation imbued with these principles and always destitute of everything.

. . . Thus the announcement of the prices I wished to charge estranged the people at first. But the necessity of not conforming to some abusive and ruinous customs contributed more to this estrangement. I made few presents beyond the ordinary and I even aspired to free myself from making them to villages that had nothing to offer in return. I refused to establish in my lodge a public smoking-room, an abuse consecrated by its age and expensive as it is tiresome. I did not pay back invitations with feasts, still less the dishes brought with interested designs. I did not keep twenty persons in the lodge of my host and I did not divide my daily fare with twenty parasites. Finally, my profits did not permit me to accept the parties and the alliances that were offered me.[7]

The Arikara were bound to see Tabeau as one who cared so little for his position that he would not validate it with gifts. A serious charge, indeed, since he placed himself in a position of authority at the trading sessions, setting exorbitant prices with a dictatorial hand. For his part he continued to complain that the Arikara would not *buy* from him. This clearly unequal sort of exchange was totally incomprehensible to them. They continued to think in terms of the ancient honorable system of gift exchange. Tabeau accepted the hospitality and shared the house of Kakawita for many months. He owed his life and his extrica-

[7] Abel, *Tabeau's Narrative,* 134-136.

tion from a mortally serious contretemps to his host's efforts. There is no doubt that he never did repay in a fashion befitting a man of high status. Within the lodge, in the very heart of the family, Tabeau reported,

I separated myself from my hosts by a partition of upright stakes, in which I left only a single opening for a door which was always locked on the inside. Having then made a chimney in my apartment, I ate alone there every day, and, refusing all the presents of meat, except those of Kakawita, I had no longer anything in common with the others. This innovation at first caused murmuring. I was a miser, a hard man, a glutton; but time caused their claims gradually to be forgotten. It is true that the correction of this ruinous abuse was noticeable. I could scarcely help inviting Kakawita and sending pieces of meat to his wife, who, in her turn, gave me regularly a share of the largest parts of the best pieces of all the hunt of her husband.[8]

Tabeau was no tightfisted monster lacking in moral sensibilities. He was caught up in the requirements of his own system, trying desperately to extricate himself without serious loss. He, too, had those to whom he was beholden for monies and profits in their turn. Nevertheless, we could agree with the Indians that he behaved very strangely for a human being.

In this setting Tabeau was a harbinger of maturing changes. The fur trade of the Missouri had expanded greatly in the last three decades of the eighteenth century. Within twelve years after they gained hegemony over Louisiana, Spanish authorities in St. Louis were prepared by 1775 to outfit official trading expeditions to the Arikara in amounts involving 1,000 pounds of trade goods.[9] Twelve years later Joseph Garreau was dispatched to become a hunter on the upper river, where he married into the Arikara village.[10] He appears repeatedly in the records. By the time of Lewis and Clark's visit he was well known for his ability to speak the difficult language. He became a kind of native ambassador and official representative who translated and mediated foreign contacts for the villagers.[11] About the same time as Garreau's departure the British sent James Mackay on an overland visit to the Mandan villages.[12] In 1790 he was followed there by an expedition from St.

---

[8] *Ibid.*, 145.

[9] Lawrence Kinnaird, ed., *Spain in the Mississippi Valley* (Washington, D.C., 1949), I, 228.

[10] A. P. Nasatir, ed., *Before Lewis and Clark . . . 1785-1804* (St. Louis, 1952), I, 82.

[11] Elliott Coues, ed., *History of the Expedition Under the Command of Lewis and Clark* (New York, 1893), I, 245.

[12] A. P. Nasatir, "Anglo-Spanish Rivalries on the Upper Missouri," *Mississippi Valley Historical Review*, XVI (1929-30), 366.

Louis under Jacques d'Eglise, who reports that Pierre Menard had already been settled among these people for some fourteen years. In 1794-95 Jean Baptiste Trudeau (Truteau) visited the Arikara villages near the mouth of the Cheyenne River.[13] Within ten years Antoine Tabeau had established himself as a trader in the new Arikara villages near the mouth of the Grand River.

By the closing decade of the eighteenth century the ancient native frontier was invested by Europeans from the confluence with the Mississippi to the headwaters along the easterly flanks of the Rockies. The native economy was now closely dependent upon the vagaries of the developing Industrial Revolution. The region became an arena for political rivalries which had no roots whatsoever in the native traditions. This change was crucial and devastating for the village peoples. Beginning around the middle of the eighteenth century new diseases such as smallpox and cholera began to take their toll. In the 1770's and 1780's terrible epidemics reduced the Arikara to a mere three villages, and continued with mounting virulence into the next century.[14]

Simultaneously the severity of Dakota raids increased. This threat appeared in the mid-eighteenth century when various groups of Dakota Sioux moved southwestward into contact with the villagers along the river after some 150 years of intercourse with the French and years of warfare with the Ojibway. With their close relatives, the Assiniboin, the Sioux found easy access to horses and riding skills, creating still another native adaptation of a European complex. In something less than two generations, by the close of the eighteenth century, they had transformed themselves from miserable weak bands of foot nomads into highly successful bison hunters who could raid the villages at will. The dependence of the villagers upon horticulture limited their use of the horse, but their middleman advantage in trade rewarded their continuance of a stable village existence even when it placed them constantly at the mercy of raiders. Along with their many horses the Dakota now possessed ample stores of firearms and ammunition. The entire period of U.S. hegemony on the Missouri is marked by the progressive disintegration of the villages, while the Dakota nomadic bands grew in size and power.

There had been permanently attached traders or trading posts in the native hamlets since the opening of the nineteenth century. Regardless

---

[13] Doane Robinson, ed., *Journal of Jean Baptiste Truteau* (South Dakota Historical Collection, VII, Bismarck, 1914), 429.
[14] *Ibid.;* see also Abel, *Tabeau's Narrative,* 124.

of the relationship or attitude of the Indians with individual traders, they clearly began to view the fur trade and its agents as a threatening force. The Ashley incident at the Arikara village in 1823 involved a set battle with traders and trappers which culminated in the burning of a village. The subsequent shelling of the same village by official U.S. armed forces under Leavenworth and the final pillage and burning merely continues this new note of desperation in the relations of the Indians with the whites.[15]

Chittenden designates this campaign "the first ever conducted by the Army against Indians west of the Mississippi and it was the precursor of that long series of operations . . . which culminated in the conquest of the West."[16] The involvement of the U.S. government in the fur trade anticipated in Lewis and Clark's original visit was further implemented by Lieutenant Pryor's return in 1807, reinforced by the visit of the Astorian party in 1811, and now permanently and forcibly established with the threat of extermination.

The chiefs and leading families still maintained at least the appearance of a friendly attitude in their dealings with the traders and official representatives of the U.S. government. There is no doubt of the hostility on the part of the people at large. Increasingly the once friendly Arikara were now reported to be dangerous enemies.

Nevertheless, the Arikara were inextricably linked to the trade. In their frantic efforts to resolve the dilemma of this period they abandoned village life entirely and became wanderers for some years in the 1830's. Ironically, their decision to settle down again brought them to Fort Clark to face the horror of the smallpox epidemic of 1837, which in a few weeks reduced the Mandan to some thirty-one broken survivors.[17]

The nineteenth-century journals of such traders as Charles Larpenteur and F. A. Chardon,[18] who had long contact with the Arikara, convey the impression that these men were irascible, unpleasant, and domineering, with little or no appreciation of the human qualities of the

[15] Harrison C. Dale, *The Ashley-Smith Explorations . . . 1822-1829* (Glendale, Calif., 1918), 70-84.

[16] Hiram M. Chittenden, *The American Fur Trade of the Far West* (New York, 1902), II, 588.

[17] Henry R. Schoolcraft, *Historical and Statistical Information Respecting the . . . Indian Tribes of the United States* (Philadelphia, 1851-57), I, 257.

[18] Charles Larpenteur, *Forty Years a Fur Trader on the Upper Missouri*, Elliott Coues, ed. (New York, 1898); Anna H. Abel, ed., *Chardon's Journal at Fort Clark, 1834-1839* (Pierre, 1932).

Arikara. The Indian view of the trade and fur trader in the nineteenth century must have grown increasingly jaundiced.

Boller's description from the 1850's gives the final atmosphere at Fort Clark on the eve of the Arikara removal upstream to Fort Berthold:

Both the forts [trading posts] as well as the village itself were completely infested with rats, to the discomfort and annoyance of all the inhabitants, both white and red. These pests had been an importation from one of the Company's steamboats years before, and had multiplied to such an alarming extent that the Indians, who had first felt themselves favored above their neighbors by the acquisition had abundant reason to change their opinion.

The Riccarees were savage-looking Indians and more insolent than any we had yet met. The men had villainous countenances, which in many cases were disfigured by the loss of an eye, either from accident or disease. Sore and inflamed eyes are very common among them owing to their filthy habits and smoky lodges.

We found, upon reaching the landing, that the Indians had attempted to come on board in numbers and upon being repulsed fired their guns into the air in token of their anger and sullenly retired to the village. The Agent, having some business at Fort Clark, was proceeding thither alone and unarmed when a well-known rascal—the Whiteface Bear—ran up to him and discharged his gun into the ground close by his feet.[19]

The records from mid-century are replete with these episodes. The Indian view of the fur trade and trader had completely reversed in the span of a century or so. Small wonder that these people began to speak of their lost Golden Age. It must have seemed very real to them in the chaos of a disintegrating world. The fur trade began with the promise of a bright future and grew into a curse or incubus which assisted in the destruction of the Indians. It is not really valid, of course, to visualize the history of the fur trade in this way. In the earliest time there must have simply been individuals from two vastly different worlds who met in their common humanity to exchange gifts and ideas. In the process Europeans became more than half Indian sometimes. Certainly the Indians took on many European ways.

For the Indian this process began as a new elaboration of old elements: new people appeared in familiar contexts bringing novelties which led to change. From these changes new weaknesses formed. The large expeditions brought terrible epidemics, followed by the resident trader with his demands, and finally there were the mounted hunters and their continual raids. It was too late to abandon the villages by the time the new situation was more fully grasped. The attempt failed and

[19] Henry A. Boller, *Among the Indians Eight Years in the Far West, 1858-1866* (Chicago, 1959), 28-30.

the people stayed on until ultimate detribalization. In the closing days of this epoch there is little doubt that the Indians recognized the role unwittingly played by the fur trader, further implemented by the armed forces of the United States. They also realized their helplessness.

Things went along quite differently from the trader's point of view. At first he was a guest in a secure Indian town. On intermittent visits he was at the beck and call of his hosts. For him this was not an important period. When the villages were disintegrating his position was more secure, his control was established, returns were predictable. The establishment was permanent. Only the extinction of the game animals threatened his trade. His views are almost a mirror image of the Indian's vision.

Often, as in this reversal, the same period of time holds different values and meaning, not only for the Indian vis-à-vis the trader, but frequently for the ethnologist in contrast to the historian proper. This shift is not distortion. It merely reflects differences in outlook which should be combined to improve our understanding of the intricacies, and fundamental principles as well, which are involved in such human interaction and change. For the ethnologist the matter is further complicated by the two kinds of Indians which appear here. One Indian was actually present when the interaction with the Europeans took place. Unfortunately this man has to be pieced together from the fragmentary and distorted glimpses reflected in the uncomprehending mirror of his observer. The other, later, Indian wistfully looks backward away from the final times of horror to the glories of an earlier time, seeing the trade in a light that it never possessed.

It is difficult for the ethnohistorian to bridge this gulf in views, to extricate something of the truth from such contrasting, incomplete lines of evidence. To him the early dimmest time is important for glimpses into the Indians' situation when it was relatively undisturbed. The ethnohistorian becomes a specialist in minutiae, a kind of microhistorian trying with sparse, fragmentary records to correlate these glimpses with ethnographic information which has been obtained at a much later date. This period and place may be insignificant and unrewarding for the historian who wants to define the economic and political meaning of the fur trade in the development of various nations. For this very reason, perhaps, some such small details may add a new dimension to the historian's over-all grasp of the trade. Increasingly there is archeological illumination of some of these unclear corners of time. We can actually look forward to a much sharper, richer delineation of these transitions in the future.

The Frontiersman
in Popular Fiction,
1820-60

JULES ZANGER

SOUTHERN ILLINOIS UNIVERSITY, EDWARDSVILLE

Though the actual character of the American frontier has been from its beginnings problematical and subject to a wide variety of descriptions and interpretations, the character of the American frontiersman was to become fixed in the popular imagination relatively early. In less than half a century, from about 1820 to about 1860, the image of the frontiersman in popular writing was to change from one which combined, in proportions determined by the shifting lights of the observer, savage simplicity and primitive depravity to one which projected the frontiersman as representative American: independent, self-made, democratic, and heroic.

The problem of his relationship to civilization—as exemplified by the ambiguity of Daniel Boone's motives: was he advancing civilization, or was he retreating from it?—was, if not resolved, at least effectively by-passed by predicating the frontier itself as the seat of native American virtues and institutions, and the civilized East as European, aristocratic, and effete. In this regard, the creators of popular fiction may be said to have anticipated certain American historians by approximately half a century.

The emergence of the frontiersman as a heroic figure in American fiction came in response to a number of influences.

Of major importance was the extreme popularity in the United States of Sir Walter Scott's Waverly novels. These romantic novels, with their depictions of rugged Scottish Highlanders and equally rugged scenery, created a taste here both for local-color writing and for a body of historical fiction celebrating patriotic subjects and native scenes. In their search for an American yeomanry, a number of writers were to select the frontiersman, a choice dictated in part by Scott himself, who frequently compared the Highlands-Lowlands border culture to the

American frontier, and the Highlanders to its Indians. In part, too, the choice was determined by the public acclaim won by Jackson's Kentucky riflemen at New Orleans, and by Jackson's subsequent political campaigns. Though for an earlier generation Royall Tyler's Brother Jonathan had served as a symbol of native American virtue and shrewdness, the Yankee farmer was neither distant enough nor sufficiently heroic for nineteenth-century romantic taste. The frontiersman appeared to be satisfactory on both counts.

The frontier romance which resulted from this selection was a relatively short-lived and minor popular literary form, lasting only until the late 1840's, when it was largely replaced in the public esteem by sentimental and genteel novels, and by novels which exploited the slavery question. During the fifties, the frontier romance was in eclipse, except for the novels of such prolific hardy annuals as Mayne Reid and Emerson Bennett. Later, however, in 1860, when the first of the "dime novels," *Malaeska, the Indian Wife of the White Hunter,* was published, the frontier romance was reborn, and with it the frontier hero; both have flourished continuously ever since.

It is with the first major appearance of the frontiersman that I am most concerned, since it was here, in the period before 1860, that he acquired those characteristics which, with very little alteration, were to mark most of his subsequent appearances in fiction.

Of primary importance in shaping the image of the frontiersman in popular fiction were the historical and pseudo-historical figures of Daniel Boone and Davy Crockett as created by a spate of popular biographies, almanacs, and, in Crockett's case, political broadsides. Unlike Boone, Crockett was not an original figure, but rather the most highly developed version of an American popular type that extended back at least as far as 1804. Each of these men was, in his own lifetime, to pass from history into myth, to become a kind of legendary American hero. To trace the transformation of these men, to examine in detail the ways in which historical fact was made indistinguishable from fictive embellishment, is not the purpose of this paper. It is enough to note that the process involved the linking of a group of classic and conventional heroic attributes—courage, fortitude, loyalty to one's comrades—with certain characteristics peculiarly appropriate to the local and contemporary American frontier, i.e. the ability to move soundlessly through the forest, to outshoot and outwit the Indians, to track game through the trackless wild.

In an absolute sense, we perhaps might say that the fictional frontiersman had not two but only one archetypal original—that Crockett is merely a vulgar, comic, and debased version of Boone—a kind of vaudeville turn which transforms the unapproachable, elusive, and incomprehensible Boone into a garrulous and accessible social lion. They are, however, significantly different. It is important to recall that while Boone's characteristic act is one of withdrawal, moving ever farther into the wilderness until he disappears from before our eyes, Crockett is characteristically a backtrailer, moving from the canebrakes to the state legislature, from the legislature to the national capitol, from the capitol to his grand eastern tour, moving from obscurity into the public eye.

The figures of Boone and Crockett not only differed in regard to this general relationship to society. Each was to acquire from this relationship to civilization a set of identifying characteristics which further distinguished him from the other. Boone, for example, forever shunning the settlements and seeking solitude, is characteristically both laconic, letting his actions speak for him, and alone, suddenly appearing when he is needed like some beneficent spirit of the frontier, then disappearing again. Crockett, on the other hand, is, above all things, a creature created by public speech—a figure whom we never actually see act, except through the shaping medium of his own account of himself. That is, Boone is most often presented in the third person, in a dramatic present; Crockett in the first person, in a recollected past. Further, Crockett is conventionally presented in a public and social situation—matching boasts with a bully, making a stump speech, and even in Congress.

Because Boone in the solitude has as his foils the savages, the wild beasts, and the wilderness itself, because his crises are always mortal crises, he possesses a great dignity, a native nobility appropriate either to his role as man against Nature or as Natural man. Crockett's crises, however, are essentially verbal; his triumphs are victories of wit or picturesque metaphor or hyperbole. It was not necessary, we remember, for Crockett actually to shoot the coon; he merely told him his name, and the coon came tamely down from the tree. It is above all Crockett's speaking voice that most fully characterizes the man. It is densely dialectal, that is to say, American, and filled with a high-sounding rhetoric and exaggeration that is clearly intended to amuse rather than to convince. It is a speech that contrives to embody all the characteristics attributed to the frontiersman by the patronizing East: coarse, picturesque, full of brag, it is a speech that celebrates the joys of indolence and waste, of corn liquor and the hunt, and of brutal hand-to-hand combat. In short, it supports perfectly the traditional picture of the frontier as a place where civilized men are turned into savages. Consequently, it serves simultaneously to mock the frontiersman and to disarm his eastern critic. It is this aspect of Crockett which places him very close to the head of that long line of American humorists whose humor comes close to being subversive of popular American ideals, for one cannot but suspect that the ultimate frontiersman mocked by Crockett's speech is Daniel Boone himself.

To sum up, Boone and Crockett oppose each other in a number of significant ways. Where Boone is the man in Nature, solitary and independent, Crockett is the man in Society, and a creature of faction; where Boone is silent and elusive, Crockett is the noisy braggart of the canebrakes who would "crow like a rooster and neigh like a stallion"; where Boone is serious, noble, and heroic, Crockett is humorous, mocking, and picaresque. Seen in this light, the mythic Crockett appears as a brutal inversion of the mythic Boone—an anti-Boone. It remains one of the major ironies of American history that the actual Boone should have died in Missouri, a garrulous old man of eighty-six, and the actual Crockett should have died heroically defending the Alamo.

For the purposes of the creators of the frontier romance, then, both Boone and Crockett functioned to establish the limits of the popular image of the frontiersman.

And this itself, I should like to suggest, is particularly worthy of notice, since the range of possible characterizations defined by the Boone-Crockett spectrum is extraordinarily narrow. That is, for the writers of popular fiction, the frontiersman could be presented as heroic and dignified or heroic and vulgar, as virtuous and noble or virtuous and comic. Making this narrowly positive range of characterization particularly surprising and noteworthy is the fact that there had existed almost from the beginning of colonization here a long, continuing tradition of anti-frontiersman sentiment in American writing about the frontier. William Byrd in his *History of the Dividing Line,* written in 1728, comments upon the North Carolina frontier as a "lubber-land" where the inhabitants "loiter away their capital lives, like Solomons Sluggard, with their Arms across, and at the Winding up of the Year Scarcely have Bread to Eat." And of other dwellers on the frontier he remarked, "Thus did these Wretches live in a dirty State of Nature, and were mere Adamites, Innocence only excepted." For Byrd, the easiness of living on the frontier was itself a barbarizing influence. Almost half a century later, Crèvecoeur, in his *Letters from an American Farmer,* was to comment even more stringently on the frontier and the frontiersman: "Now we arrive near the great woods, near the last inhabited districts; there men seem to be placed still farther beyond the reach of government, which in some measure leaves them to themselves. . . . The few magistrates they have, are in general little better than the rest; they are often in a perfect state of war; that of man against man, sometimes decided by blows, sometimes by means of the law; that of man against every wild inhabitant of these venerable woods, of which they are come to dispossess them. There men appear to be no better than carnivorous animals of a superior rank, living on the flesh of wild animals when they can catch them; and when they are not able, they subsist upon the grain." In the early part of the nineteenth century, this antagonism toward the frontiersman perhaps best reveals itself in Timothy Dwight's famous account of the inhabitants of the frontier: "A considerable part of all those who begin the cultivation of the wilderness may be denominated foresters, or pioneers. . . . These men cannot live in regular society. They are too idle, too talkative, too passionate, too prodigal, and too shiftless to acquire either property or character. They are impatient of the restraints of law, religion, and morality." Dr. Dwight, like Byrd and Crèvecoeur before him, comments on the barbarizing influence of life on the frontier, and describes in detail the process by which the pioneer "becomes less and less a civilized man." Such views can be described, of course, as the views of easterners, yet it must be pointed out that until well into the second half of the nineteenth century practically all writing about the West was written by easterners.

Despite this continuing anti-frontier tradition, and the whole influence of sectional bias, the frontiersman of fiction remained within the narrow and virtuous limits of the Boone-Crockett range of characterization. Nor can it be said in explaining this phenomenon that the frontier itself had failed to throw up sufficient villains to provide actual prototypes for the writers of popular romance. For Boone there was Simon Girty, the renegade; for Crockett there were Murrell, all the ill-famed ruffians of the Natchez Trace, the notorious outlaws of Ogle County in Illinois, and the Harpes. Nevertheless, there were remarkably few villainous frontiersmen in the popular fiction of the first half of the nineteenth century.

That this was so can be accounted for by the tendency of the creators of frontier romance to identify the frontier with American virtue and American institutions. Where the commenters and diarists and critics saw the frontier as the place where men forgot the civilization that made them human and learned to live like animals, the writers of fiction saw the frontier as the place where men forgot the artificialities that made them mere effete, Europeanized puppets, and learned to live like true men. Such frontier villains as do appear—Big Harpe in James Hall's *Harpe-s Head,* Simon Girty in Emerson Bennett's *Ella Barnwell*—are invariably presented as speaking without any trace of frontier dialect, and are denied, as well, the buckskins, the long rifle, even the sun-tanned face. The very faults in the frontier character pointed out by men like Byrd, Crèvecoeur, and Dwight are presented by the writers of fiction as virtues: prodigality becomes generosity, impatience of restraint becomes independence, dependence upon the chase becomes closeness to nature, the "dirty state of nature" becomes less dirty and more natural as Innocence is restored to the Adamites, and even idleness becomes, if not positively virtuous, at least quaint and attractive. As for the tendency to be too talkative, that, as we all know, becomes, with Crockett himself, a transcendent gift for storytelling, while the inability to live in regular society becomes, with Boone, the mysterious call of the unpeopled wilderness.

Though both Boone and Crockett helped to define the image of the frontiersman, an additional factor of incalculable influence in shaping his fictional character was the Leatherstocking Tales of James Fenimore Cooper. In the course of these five novels Cooper was to shift Natty Bumppo from a relatively peripheral role to the very center of the dramatic action in response to the tremendous enthusiasm of the public for the character. In *Virgin Land,* Henry Nash Smith has analyzed the literary and social problems Cooper faced in attempting to transform the illiterate, lower-class, old hunter of *The Pioneers* (1823) to the romatic figure of the following novels. Perhaps another way in which the successive versions of Bumppo might be regarded is to recognize them as a series of points shifting along the Boone-Crockett axis.

Seen this way, Natty Bumppo appears to be moving from a position closer to Crockett, in *The Pioneers* where he is a garrulous, toothless, withered, old man living on the fringes of settlement, and in *The Last of the Mohicans* where he is a soldier of the king and a methodical killer of Indians, to a position closer to Boone, in *The Prairie* where he achieves the dignity of an epic or mythic figure, in *The Pathfinder* where he comes as close as it is possible for him to being the romantic lover, and in *The Deerslayer* where he is the embodiment of the American Adam living freely and harmoniously in nature.

Leatherstocking is an admixture, then, of Boone and Crockett characteristics; there can be no question, however, that Boone dominates even from the beginning, and grows stronger in the later novels as Cooper himself grows increasingly alienated from and less sympathetic to American democracy. Natty Bumppo, Cooper insists, is not a representative American frontiersman, but rather a *beau ideal,* and Cooper, as if to emphasize the distinction, carefully provides such Crockett characters as Hurry Harry and Ishmael Bush to illustrate the difference. These men are vulgar, wantonly wasteful, crude, without any of the higher sensibility, the ethical fineness that distinguish the Leatherstocking of the later novels. As he is patterned on the Boone model, so they are clearly cast in the Crockett mold. If Boone and Leatherstocking are "Nature's Noblemen," Crockett and his followers must be nature's plebeians.

The image of the frontiersman, then, was to impress itself upon the popular consciousness in the first quarter of the nineteenth century from a variety of sources: the press, the theater, history and pseudo-history, and forthright fiction, and to assume a trinity of forms: Boone, Crockett, and Leatherstocking.

Of the three, Boone was, of course, the oldest and the most continuously influential image of the frontier hero, and Leatherstocking, in most characteristics, was his avatar. Leatherstocking, in turn, has been identified as the prototype of the fictional frontiersman of the first half of the nineteenth century. Henry Nash Smith describes them in *Virgin Land* as the "Sons of Leatherstocking," and traces in convincing detail the persistence of such stigmata as Leatherstocking's speech, dress, and long rifle in the frontier romances written after 1825.

Nevertheless, I should like to suggest that a number of the characteristics of the frontiersmen who follow Leatherstocking indicate that their lineage is not nearly so clear as Professor Smith's enveloping title states, and that it might profit us to look at those qualities of the fictional frontiersman which do not fit into and even run directly counter to the Leatherstocking pattern.

One of the earliest of these "Sons of Leatherstocking" was Earthquake, of James French's *Elkswatawa, or The Prophet of the West.* Earthquake is especially interesting in this regard because *Elkswatawa* appeared in 1836, nine years after *The Last of the Mohicans* and two years after the *Narrative of the Life of Colonel David Crockett.*

Earthquake has Bumppo's general appearance, his woodcraft, his knowledge of Indian language, his buckskins, his long rifle, his tendency toward high-falutin' speech in moments of crisis. He has, like

Leatherstocking, a young aristocratic friend, a "high-toned and chival-rous Virginian" named Richard Rolfe; when he is rescuing Rolfe, or Rolfe's fair sweetheart, from the Shawnees, he is an imitation of—even an exaggeration of—Leatherstocking. For instance, after a long and very lofty speech in which he reveals his intention of rescuing Rolfe's sweetheart, Earthquake bursts into such copious tears that they "flow in a stream down his rugged and weatherbeaten face." The author comments: "It was a lovely sight to see a rough hunter of the west, whose appearance indicated him a stranger to feeling, thus overcome by sym-pathy for the distressed."

So far, Earthquake is indeed Leatherstocking's son. But he has an-other side. As his very name suggests, he is as much a son of Crockett, the alligator-horse, as he is of Bumppo. He is an especially interesting figure because his creator lacked the skill to blend the two influences, so that Earthquake alternates schizophrenically between imitating Leatherstocking and imitating Davy Crockett. Significantly, it is Earth-quake in his Crockett moods that prefigures the later frontiersmen of fiction, not Earthquake in his Leatherstocking moods.

One of Earthquake's outstanding habits, not shared by Leatherstock-ing but common to most of the fictional frontiersmen of the forties and fifties, is the habit of telling long, exaggerated, densely dialectal stories in the first person. These stories are perfectly self-contained; that is, each would be just as complete if it were lifted out of the novel altogether and told separately, or dropped into another novel: they are set-pieces. In *Elkswatawa*, as in Emerson Bennett's many far western stories, in E. Willett's *The Hunted Life*, and others, the ac-tion is suspended at regular intervals while the old frontiersman enter-tains an audience with a lengthy tall tale. Sometimes a more or less log-ical pretext for introducing a story is provided by the author; more often, the story is introduced in the manner of the old Roy Rogers joke: "I've got to dash off and save Dale from the Indians, capture the bank robbers, and head off the rustlers at the pass—but first I think I'll sing a little song." In some later books, such as Mayne Reid's *The Hunters' Feast*, or D. P. Thompson's *Gaut Gurley*, Leatherstocking dis-appears without a trace: the sole function of the frontiersman is to pro-vide a first-person speaker to tell stories.

Neither is the typical frontiersman's relationship to the young eastern-er he guides the same as Bumppo's relationship to the genteel heroes of the Leatherstocking tales. The mountain men of Emerson Bennett, Mayne Reid, and others lack that class humility that characterizes

Bumppo. It is instructive in this connection to look again at Earthquake and his "high-toned and chivalrous young Virginian." Earthquake, like Leatherstocking, is leader and mentor in the woods; unlike Leatherstocking, he is mentor in worldly affairs as well. Rolfe, arguing his first case at law, presents an airtight, flawless case, a credit to his education, his reasoning ability, and his class. Though law and evidence are on his side, Rolfe loses the case, but Earthquake, like Crockett before him a native politician, is not discouraged: "Rolfe is a larning," he says. ". . . He don't rare and pitch enough. I must tell him, and I think I can make him come to it, artur a while."

The attitude of the unlettered, primitive, and plebeian frontiersman toward the education, the conventional dress and manners, and the gentility of the easterner, then, also helps to identify his place in the Boone-Leatherstocking-Crockett spectrum. The mythic Boone is too aloof, too monumental to take notice; Boone opens the way, never looking back at those who follow. He is above class. Leatherstocking, though unlettered, respects the educated; though primitive in dress and manner, he displays a natural refinement and fastidiousness himself and defers to the conventionally ladylike or gentlemanly in his eastern companions; though plebeian, he is content to keep his place. Leatherstocking, of course, is a snob. His vision of society is rigidly hierarchical, and much of his speech is concerned with defining himself in terms of that hierarchy. He repeats interminably that he is "a man without a cross," he is continually concerned with distinguishing acts appropriate to his and others' "gifts" and "nature," he disqualifies himself from his one love affair on the grounds of his own social unsuitability, and when he is old he bemoans his having fallen from the hunter's to the trapper's estate. The typical frontiersman of later fiction, however, follows the ebulliently democratic Crockett rather than the elusive Boone or the servile Leatherstocking. He is not only illiterate but openly contemptuous of learning: "Edicated—augh!" says Black George, the old trapper in Emerson Bennett's *Prairie Flower*. "Heyar's what never did that; never had no need on't; know how to shoot and trap, but cant make pot hooks . . . couldn't live no longer for't." He is not only unconventional and primitive, but despises the conventional dress and manner of the easterner; "When I sees a feller rigged out in sich —— silky, black, preacher toggery as you've got on," says One-Eyed Sam, the old trapper of Bennett's *The Border Rover*, "I ginerally puts him down as sp'ilt meat—jest fit for turkey buzzards." And as for class deference, the typical old trapper is prone to address his aristocratic young eastern companion as "hoss," and Black George of *The Prairie Flower* habitually lumps the upper-class young Bostonian hero and his lower-class Boston Irish servant together as "young Bossoners."

Another respect in which the fictional frontiersmen of the thirties, forties, and fifties resemble Crockett more than Boone and Leatherstocking is in their attitude toward the Indians.

An important part of the Boone legend has always been Boone's ability to win the respect of the Indians, his adoption into an Indian tribe; he is traditionally seen as peacemaker as much as Indian fighter. Leatherstocking's relationship with the Indians is, of course, chiefly marked by his loyal alliance with one tribe and inveterate hatred of another; some of his best friends are Indians.

Typically, however, the fictional frontiersman's attitude toward the Indians is one of indiscriminate enmity; again, he follows Crockett, whose career began when he fought under Jackson in the Creek war, a war that can only be described as genocidal. It must be remembered that the wars of Boone's time and of Cooper's youth were not wars of white men against the Indians, but of white men with Indian allies against other white men with Indian allies. By the time that Crockett went to the Creek war, Indian wars had become wars of extermination or removal.

On the other hand, Leatherstocking, though he has Indian friends and allies, is always conscious of and articulate about the differences between his ways and the ways of the Indians, going no further in adopting Indian ways than to perfect his woodcraft. The later frontiersmen, haters of the Indians, imitate those whom they hate, taking scalps and boasting savagely of their kills.

A particular characteristic of the fictional frontiersman which distinguishes him from the Leatherstocking model is the manner in which he speaks. In *Virgin Land,* Professor Smith observes that Leatherstocking's speech is dialectal and functions as a conventionalized means of indicating his low social status, relative to the officers and gentlemen with whom he consorts, all of whom speak norm or elevated speech. Mark Twain, however, in "Fenimore Cooper's Literary Offenses," observed of Leatherstocking's speech that its outstanding characteristic was its unevenness:

Cooper was certainly not a master in the construction of dialogue. . . . In the *Deerslayer* story he lets Deerslayer talk the showiest kind of book-talk sometimes, and at other times the basest of base dialects. For instance, when someone asks him if he has a sweetheart, and if so, where she abides, this is his majestic answer:

"She's in the forest—hanging from the boughs of the trees, in a soft rain—in the dew on the open grass—the clouds that float about in the blue heavens—the birds that sing in the woods—the sweet springs where I slake my thirst—and in all the other glorious gifts that come from God's Providence!"
And he preceded that, a little before, with this:
"It consarns me as all things that touches a fri'nd consarns a fri'nd."
And this is another of his remarks:
"If I was Injin born, now, I might tell of this, or carry in the scalp and boast of the expl'ite afore the whole tribe; or if my inimy had only been a bear"—and so on.

Twain, writing from the point of view of a man who prided himself on his ability to reproduce dialect accurately, views Leatherstocking's shifting modes of speech as evidence of Cooper's incompetence as a writer. Actually, examination reveals that Leatherstocking's speech patterns are not expressions of *who* he is (as a realist would demand) as much as they are an expression of *what* he is saying. That is, when Leatherstocking speaks of the hunt, or of war, or when he utters commonplaces, his speech is appropriately dialectal; when, on the other hand, he expresses the sentimental or mystical side of his nature, his speech becomes elevated and loses its dialectal characteristics; it approximates, that is, the speech of the aristocratic characters in the novels.

Seen this way, the disjunctions in Leatherstocking's speech can be understood as evidences of the disjunction in his character, of the uneasy combination of sententious, sentimental moralist and illiterate backwoodsman. Crockett's speech is without such stylistic fluctuations and on the occasions that he essays elevated speech it is with the clear intention of mocking it. His speech has a stylistic integrity that corresponds to the integrity of his characterization. Those romancers who followed Cooper and Crockett had then two alternative models of speech to imitate: Cooper's style, which shifts incredibly from dense dialect to what Twain called "the showiest kind of book-talk," or that of Crockett, who consistently talks what is conventionally understood as an illiterate dialect.

As the fictional frontiersman became increasingly unidealized and realistic, his speech followed the Crockett pattern. In part this can be seen as an attempt at verisimilitude, in part as a recognition of the intrinsic entertainment value of dialect speech, in part as the crystallization of the fictional frontiersman's character into the nativist mold.

From this conception of the frontiersman as aggressively democratic, contemptuous of class distinctions, formal education, and civilization itself was to come the basic configuration of the frontier romance in the relationship of the frontiersman and the young easterner.

The model for this relationship appeared first in the Leatherstocking series, where Natty Bumppo and Oliver Effingham represented respectively the frontiersman and the easterner, the plebeian and the aristocrat. Here Effingham is presented first in the guise of a younger Leatherstocking, buckskins, long rifle, and all; subsequently, it is revealed that Leatherstocking has taught young Effingham to shoot, to track, and all the skills of woodcraft. In this tutorial relationship was prefigured the basic confrontation of frontiersman and easterner in dozens of novels to follow.

The democratic and desentimentalized old frontiersman of the Crockett type who dominated the later novels, however, was a teacher of a different discipline. If the young eastern gentleman learns any woodcraft at all, it is the least of what he learns. The lessons the easterner learns from his frontier mentor are lessons of democracy, of manliness, and of tough-mindedness. The easterner is introduced as an inept greenhorn, and in the course of the novel must prove that he is worthy of the old frontiersman's respect. This is an inversion of the classic pattern in which the uneducated countryman goes to town, where he is an object of amusement and derision. If the easterner is amused by the appearance and speech of the old frontiersman, the frontiersman is at least as amused by the greenhorn. The older man does not attempt to modify his own nature to meet the standards of the educated young easterner; it is the young easterner who must win the grudging approval of the old frontiersman.

It has been suggested that the reason for the gray hairs of the fictional frontiersman is that he must be old in order to disqualify as a romantic hero. Seen in terms of this tutorial relationship between frontiersman and easterner, however, the gray hairs of the frontiersman appear symbolic of the older, manlier virtues of democratic comradeship, endurance, and simplicity which the young easterner must exchange for his newfangled and aristocratic education before he can be truly an American. The process whereby the easterner loses the marks of civilization and exchanges them for those of the frontiersman becomes not a barbarizing one but an educative one; the westward journey becomes a journey of initiation into the essential American experience.

In summation, at the time when Jacksonian democracy and national expansion had thrust the frontiersman and the West favorably into the public consciousness, the writers of popular romance sought for a symbol to embody the new ideas of the frontier. Cooper's Leatherstocking provided a popular literary image, embodying as he did many of the characteristic virtues of the mythic Boone. But Leatherstocking possessed as well a number of qualities which made him unsuitable as a model: in a period of exuberant, expansive democracy, he was both servile and snobbish; in a period when national policy and popular feeling had set its face against the Indian, Leatherstocking was too closely allied in attitudes and sympathies with the Indian. In addition, the sentimental and philosophical aspects of his character failed to correspond to the image of the frontiersman with which the public had become familiar in the persons of Colonel Crockett, General Jackson, and the various backtrailers who had made the frontiersman a recognizable type. In Crockett himself the writers of popular fiction were to find a literary model which both embodied the idea of the West held by most easterners, and provided an image of the heroic, democratic American suitable for the age.

The American Frontier in German Fiction

GEORGE R. BROOKS

MISSOURI HISTORICAL SOCIETY

When the young German, Gert Goebel, arrived in Balti-more en route to a new life on the western frontier of the United States during the summer of 1834, he inquired about the conditions he might expect to find in his new home. The answers must have been quite a shock, for he later wrote: "The few Germans in Baltimore with whom we became casually acquainted shook their heads when we told them that we were going to Missouri. There, they told us, you are liable to be scalped by Indians, the white people are robbers and murderers and you cannot leave the house without being exposed to the dangers of wild animals and poison snakes. How little people knew about the west. . . ."[1] The Germans on the other side of the Atlantic then knew perhaps just as little about our West (which at that time meant generally the lands bordering the Mississippi River), but they were soon to be told a great deal—or so they were led to believe—by numerous romantic novels with an American setting that captured their imaginations and fired a desire for emigration on the part of many of their countrymen. Since the image of pioneer life projected in these books represented a principal source of information about America for the nineteenth-century German and as such tied directly into the story of the settlement of much of the Midwest, it might be well worth the effort to return—after slightly more than a hundred years—and reconstruct the edge of American civilization as it was depicted by the more important of the German authors who used the frontier as a subject for their works.

The appearance of an American background in German fiction came about originally out of purely literary considerations, but eventually

[1] From a manuscript translation by M. Heinrichsmeyer of Gert Goebel, *Länger als ein Menscheleben in Missouri* (St. Louis, 1877), in the possession of the Missouri Historical Society, St. Louis. In the original edition this excerpt appears on p. 18.

took on deeper social and political implications. German writers in the early part of the last century barely had time to absorb the influence of the immensely popular romances of Sir Walter Scott before their attentions were drawn across the Atlantic by the works of James Fenimore Cooper; translations of *The Pioneer* and *The Spy* scored instant successes in 1824 and *The Last of the Mohicans* appeared two years later. German readers, thanks to the introduction of Cooper, could satisfy their *Drang in die Ferne* by retreating not in time to the historic past of medieval chivalries, but in distance to the verdant remoteness of the American wilderness with its exotic inhabitants. Even the aged Goethe, who one might suspect was by then above the whim of catering to the rising popular demand, suggested to younger writers the desirability of American themes and laid out the framework for an American novel in 1827.[2]

Gradually, however, the American locale came to mean something more than just a means of vicarious escape for the German reader. Ernst Willkomm's emigration novel, *Die Europamüden* (which appeared in 1837 and followed closely Goethe's suggested formula) gives in its very title indication of the new approach, and if we add that the characters in the story embarked for a home in the New World on the American brig *Hope,* the symbolism becomes almost embarrassingly evident. The extent of the exact influence the novels had on emigration to America has yet to be examined, and even if it were, it might prove to be one of those intangibles which is difficult to assess completely. Possibly the fiction did not have the impact of direct factual reports, such as Gottfried Duden's,[3] but to a people restless, discontent through political oppression, and yearning for a new life, the books held forth some hope of a different and better world, an assumption substantiated somewhat by the fact that in no other country during the nineteenth century were American-based novels as popular as they were in Germany.

The didactic purpose to which some fiction was put is perhaps most concisely summed up in the dedication of Charles Sealsfield's *The Courtship of George Howard* (1843):[4] "To the German nation, roused to the consciousness of its power and dignity, these pictures of the do-

[2] For a discussion of this see Preston A. Barba, "Balduin Möllhausen, The German Cooper," *Americana Germanica,* XVII (1914), 21-22.

[3] Gottfried Duden, *Bericht über eine Reise nach den westlichen Staaten Nordamerikas* (Elberfeld, 1829).

[4] Originally published separately as *George Howard's Esq. Brautfahrt* (Metzler, 1843), it was later incorporated into editions of *Lebensbilder aus der westlichen Hemisphäre.*

mestic and public life of the free citizens of a free state, destined to historical greatness, are respectfully dedicated, as a mirror for self-examination, by the author."[5]

Uprisings and subsequent reprisals growing out of the *Bundestag Ordinnanzen* of 1831 drove some 150,000 Germans to our shores in the decade of the 1830's, transforming the character of many frontier towns such as Cincinnati and St. Louis, and creating whole new villages and farms on the midwestern landscape. As a result there arose a very direct personal involvement for many in the homeland with the interior of our country, and because they purported to tell what America was like, the novels enjoyed also a popularity among the families left behind by those who had already gone to make their home across the sea. Thus for one reason or another the Germans became curious or concerned about the nature of America; but what was the image they received, the image upon which they could base their opinions?

For this we will turn directly to selections from the works of four prominent early nineteenth-century German writers, all of whom spent some portion of their lives on the American frontier. Charles Sealsfield (whose true identity as a Moravian-born former monk, Karl Postl, was only revealed after his death) made two extended trips to America between 1823 and 1830; Friedrich Armand Strubberg (who used his middle name as a nom de plume) was here from 1826 to 1829 and then returned to the Texas area for about fifteen years prior to 1854; Friedrich Gerstäcker's American odyssey occurred between 1837 and 1843; and Balduin Möllhausen achieved some prominence as a figure in the story of western exploration in the 1850's. All, therefore, had a firsthand acquaintance with the American frontier, and their descriptions of the land, the inhabitants, and the social customs of America deserve a second look.

"A farmer's life has been described to me . . . by several friends, as most suitable for a German."

"Oh, ah! Yes I dare say!" growled Dr. Wisslock, nodding his head, significantly; "I dare say, picturesque landscape—hanging woods and rocks—creepers and wild vines—bleating herds, and bear's flesh—the usual dream. You'll find out your mistake."[6]

---

[5] Charles Sealsfield, *Life in the New World or Sketches of American Society* (New York, 1844). Sealsfield's name often appears as Seatsfield on the title pages of English-language editions.

[6] Friedrich Gerstäcker, *The Wanderings and Fortunes of Some German Emigrants* (London, 1848), 294.

This mistake, which was pointed out to one of the characters in Gerstäcker's novel, *The Wanderings and Fortunes of Some German Emigrants,* if it was a mistake, was come by honestly. For what the wise old doctor was ridiculing—the hanging woods, creepers, and bleating herds—was extremely close to the image of the American frontier being presented to the Germans by their writers.

Gottfried Duden had reported back from Missouri in the 1820's that "the splendor of the forests . . . baffles all description,"[7] but this did not prevent his literary contemporaries from carrying on idyllically over the beauties of the landscape. For them the midwestern valleys presented an endless panorama of primeval forests, tangled vines, and crystal streams in a profusion to fire the imagination of any romantic. Sealsfield, for one, delighted in creating word pictures of his favorite frontier, the Texas-Louisiana countryside, where "Sycamores and afterwards pecans arched themselves on both sides over the river, and a band of deer and a flock of turkeys added to the beauty of the landscape."[8]

In the new-found land of plenty the forests teemed with game, which once in a while attacked with an intense ferocity, but more often was present only to be sacrificed to the insatiable demands of the hunters' guns. Comments like this one were frequent: "I was now in Arkansas. Game seemed to abound. Flocks of wild turkeys filled the forests as thick as partridges in Germany, and deer were equally plentiful; in one day I saw several herds of ten or twelve each."[9] Practically nothing on four legs was overlooked by the writers. Strubberg depicted a zoological wonderland in his *Amerikanische Jagd- und Reiseabenteuer*[10] as he enthralled his public with visions of buffalo moving over the prairies in herds of thousands, and described in detail the various species of bear, deer, antelope, panther, jaguar, Mexican pig, wolf, and beaver to be found on the frontier.

Periodically the rich forests gave way to a small settlement or plantation, and again the authors found attractive vistas such as this to describe to their eager public:

At the left, there were about two hundred acres extending towards the Jacinto, which formed here a large bend; the plantation thus was situated alto-

[7] William G. Bek, tr., *Gottfried Duden's Report, 1824-1827* (Columbia, Mo., 1919), 61.

[8] Charles Sealsfield, *The Cabin Book, or Sketches of Life in Texas* (New York), 1844), 7.

[9] Friedrich Gerstäcker, *Wild Sports in the Far West* (Boston, 1859), 83.

[10] Armand (Friedrich Strubberg), *Amerikanische Jagd- und Reiseabenteuer aus meinem Leben in den westlichen Indianergebieten* (Stuttgart, 1858).

gether in a peninsula, exceedingly attractive, a real idyl. Before the house the immeasureable prairie, extending perhaps twenty, perhaps fifty, nay a hundred miles toward the west, presenting here and there an archipelago of islands trembling and shining in the transparent atmosphere—between these the heads of grazing cattle and mustangs, and to the left and right cotton-fields and islands.[11]

Now and then voices were raised to indicate the frontier's unpleasant aspects, hinting that it might not be another Eden and allaying, perhaps, Duden's apprehensions that "if only the agreeable things are mentioned this region will appear a veritable paradise to every German."[12] Gerstäcker, in one novel which involved the plight of some colonizing Germans who were bilked into buying part of a Kentucky swamp on the idea that it was highly suitable for settlement, took a somewhat different view of America. The forests became dark traps; the vines crept like reptiles. Strange horrible noises disturbed the night, and mosquitoes feasted on Teutonic flesh during the day:

. . . they came to the banks of a muddy brook with a rather wide bed, but which now appeared nearly dried up, and poured its muddy water in a narrow thread only into the Mississippi . . . immense cotton-wood and cypress trees lay, wildly thrown together . . . whilst some broken branches and stems stuck in the mud of the brook in all directions, and appeared sufficient of themselves to prevent navigation, even with a light boat . . . gigantic stems which rose, smooth and faultless, to a height which they had never before contemplated, produced a strange, almost uneasy impression upon the wanderers; then again the vines and creepers which wound themselves from stem to stem, the wild and desert-looking fallen masses of wood, often half rotten, the enormous withered trunks which here and there, as if stifled by the creeping plants, madly stretched their naked giant arms towards heaven, as if supplicating help, gave the whole such a gloomy forbidding aspect, that the little tailor, after a minute's pause of astonishment, drew a long breath . . . and said—"Well, I had imagined the thing quite different from this. . . ."[13]

But for those who were not led astray, the American frontier was generally depicted as the land of promise. Because many of the Germans would sooner or later try their hands at farming, the soil itself was of more than passing interest, and happily the writers were able to report in this respect a virtually inexhaustible supply of virgin loam: ". . . as we proceeded upwards, the vegetable soil increased in thickness, reaching from one to four, eight, twelve, and at last fifteen feet . . . there was no lack of timber for building houses, or making fences, and

[11] Sealsfield, *The Cabin Book*, 31.
[12] Bek, *Duden's Report*, 80.
[13] Gerstäcker, *Wanderers*, 143-145.

this discovery tranquilized us."[14] That was Texas; Ohio was even better: "Its soil is inexhaustible; its fertility, especially in the northern and southern parts, being truly astonishing; and though some portions have been cultivated upwards of thirty years without being manured, the land still yields the same quantity of produce."[15] The American Bottoms land was the best of all, but with a slight drawback: ". . . it is considered the most productive land in the United States. The vegetable mould must be fifty to sixty feet deep; but it is low, and in consequence wet, and therefore unhealthy."[16]

Of course the land had to be cleared before it could be used, and the methods employed by the novelists' fictional characters were close to those suggested in Duden's factual *Report*. It was hard work, to be sure, but the effort was compensated for by the fact that so much necessary building material was acquired incidentally in the process:

When about to make a clearing, the American looks out for the largest and straightest oaks, which he fells and splits into poles, from ten to twelve feet long, for fencing. When he thinks he has enough for this purpose, the rest is cut up and piled; next, the trees which have a diameter of eighteen inches and under are felled, at about a half a yard from the ground, and cut into lengths, while the larger trees are girdled all round with the axe, and very soon die. The shrubs and bushes are then rooted up with a heavy hoe. . . .[17]

Its underbrush having thus been dispatched, the land gave rise to the settlers' small farms which, again, were usually shown in a way so innocent and pleasant, that nothing appeared to mar the vision of an earthly paradise:

Indeed, Stevenson's family seemed to be a pattern of American domestic life;—the interior of the house, simple, it is true, and even poor, was as bright and clean as one could have wished it; the utensils shone and glittered again, and the mother with her two grown-up daughters, clad in the homespun grey of the western forests, looked like the ideal of a worthy matron, surrounded and supported by youth and beauty. . . . Cows and horses stood in peaceful agreement, side by side, and licked the salt which a little fair-haired boy strewed for them, upon troughs hollowed out and fixed for the purpose, with an eagerness and enjoyment. . . . A small flock of sheep, with the leader, a stately ram, also approached. . . .[18]

[14] Sealsfield, *The Cabin Book*, 7.

[15] [Charles Sealsfield], *The Americans as They Are: Described in a Tour Through the Valley of the Mississippi by the Author of "Austria as It Is"* (London, 1828), 11.

[16] Gerstäcker, *Wild Sports*, 77.

[17] *Ibid.*, 165.

[18] Gerstäcker, 213.

Again in some cases—in this next instance a description of the more settled aspects of the older frontier in Ohio—the homes began to take on the character of European estates: "The farms and country houses are elegant; I saw hundreds of them, which no English nobleman would be ashamed of."[19]

But there was more to America than the natural wildness of the abundant forest or the ideal tranquility of a newly settled farm. The exotic inhabitants of the frontier paraded through the German novels: Yankee backwoodsmen and trappers; French, Spanish, and Creoles; that strange breed, the Kentuckians; and not the least by any means, the original Indians. All played important roles and each group emerged almost type-cast with its own set characteristics.

The most curious individuals to the German mind were the wiry backwoodsmen. Skin thick as leather, steely-eyed, slow in speech but quick in action, those pioneers were the unique characters on the frontier and appeared in the novels as apostles of a strange yet simple code of ethics:

A daring consciousness of inherent power is one of the chief peculiarities of the backwoodsman's character. Nor is it strange that a man who is in daily and hourly danger of being either choked in a swamp or drowned in a bayou—of being devoured by an alligator, or torn to pieces by a bear—should at length acquire that familiarity with what is generally called danger, which naturally produces a change in their manners, language, and whole existence. Their phrases are original and practical; often rough and uncouth, it is true—but rarely, if ever, vulgar. . . . Their manners display a recklessness, which at one moment makes your hair stand on end—and the next provokes a roar of laughter. Strange beings are these children of the west, and little understood by the civilized world. They are a vast community of separate existences—each, in a sense, independent of every other thing, except God![20]

Much of the attraction to these independent citizens of the frontier lay in the fact that they were free men, unshackled by either custom or political restraint, to come and go as they saw fit. Their spirit grew from the land itself, which Sealsfield found in "such magnificent contrast . . . to the old world—to all artificial splendor and the mere works of man."[21] The same writer, in another work, noted:

There is something peculiar in these boundless prairies that exalts the

[19] Sealsfield, *Americans as They Are*, 15.
[20] Charles Sealsfield, "The Squatter Chief; or The First American in Texas," in *Life in the New World*, 269.
[21] *Ibid.*

spirit, rendering it, we might say, as well as the body, energetic and firm. There are to be found the wild horses, the bison, the wolf, the bear, and innumerable serpents, and the trapper excelling all in wildness—not the old trappers of Cooper, who never saw a trapper in his life—but the real one, who could furnish matter for novels, which would inspire with a wild enthusiasm, even the most phlegmatic.[22]

Not all was pure and heroic about them, however, for we discover that "the trappers are generally outcasts or outlaws, who have escaped from the arm of the law,"[23] and their actions were not always the results of the highest motivations: "Avarice is a mighty incitement to bloody deeds; and generally, one of two trappers who chance to meet, has to fall by the other's hand. He hates his white rival much more, on account of the valuable beaver-skins, than he hates an Indian."[24] Some of the more unfortunate attributes, we are told, were due to extenuating circumstances. Even diet, it seems, played a part in forming a trapper's personality: "The fact, that for years he lives on the strongest possible food, the meat of the bison, and without bread or anything else, contributes much to this inhuman wildness."[25]

But on the whole the trapper or backwoodsman was illuminated in the novels in a most sympathetic light; he was the real man of the frontier. Perhaps he had a rough exterior, but usually he was blessed inwardly with a liberal humanity that came from being a free man living an unfettered existence in nature:

We met several of these trappers, among others an old fellow, so thoroughly tanned and hardened by storm, privation and tempests, that his skin resembled more the shell of a turtle than the cuticle of a man.[26]

These trappers are wonderful psychological phenomena, thrown into wild, boundless nature, their reason often developing itself in a manner so ingenious, nay grand, that among some I have observed a genius which would have done honor to the greatest philosophers of ancient or modern times.[27]

For some reason, of all the backwoods characters, the Kentuckians were singled out as the least desirable—generally put down as a headstrong and rough lot at best. Gerstäcker, as we mentioned earlier, chose Kentucky as the location for all that was wrong with the American landscape, and Sealsfield, for another, imbued the Kentuckians with every disagreeable trait of personality that came into his mind, con-

[22] Sealsfield, *The Courtship of George Howard*, 42.
[23] *Ibid.*
[24] *Ibid.*, 43.
[25] *Ibid.*
[26] *Ibid.*
[27] *Ibid.*, 42.

cluding that "Louisville is not a pleasant town to reside in, owing to the character of the majority of its inhabitants, the Kentuckians."[28] And if he did find something nice to say about the state, his comments were tempered by remarks about its residents: " . . . it would be difficult to quit this country, did not the character of the inhabitants lessen one's regret at leaving it."[29] Kentuckians were a "proud, fierce, and overbearing set of people,"[30] and although the men were "of an athletic form, and there may be found amongst them many models of truly masculine beauty,"[31] they were imbued "with genuine Kentuckian, half-horse, half-alligator profile, and the proper addition of thunder, lightning and earthquake."[32]

But if the Kentuckians were on the lowest rung of the Anglo-American ladder as individuals, they were still infinitely superior to the French, Spaniards, and—by association—the Creoles, all of whom suffer, one suspects, as much because they were the representatives of established European empires as for what they were themselves. "The French and Spaniards put their spurs into our sides and tyrannize over us, because we defend our rights,"[33] moaned one character, but the more typical complaint was aimed at their laziness and easygoing existence, something difficult for the Teutonic mind to comprehend: "St. Louis is a sort of New Orleans on a smaller scale; in both places are to be found a number of coffee-houses and dancing rooms. The French are seen engaged in the same amusements and passions that formerly characterized the Creoles of Louisiana, with the exception, that the trade with the Indians has given to the French backwoods-men of St. Louis, a rather malicious and dishonest turn—a fault from which the Creoles of Louisiana are free. . . ."[34] As a matter of course, one German summed up his contempt of these people by saying, "If the French (and) Spanish . . . had succeeded in this country, and placed themselves on an equality with the wealthiest in the land, surely I could do the same."[35]

In view of the many derogatory comments about other nationalities on the frontier, one might anticipate encountering an idealized image

[28] Sealsfield, *Americans as They Are,* 47.
[29] *Ibid.,* 49.
[30] *Ibid.,* 50.
[31] *Ibid.*
[32] Sealsfield, *The Cabin Book,* 57.
[33] Sealsfield, "The Squatter Chief," 283.
[34] Sealsfield, *Americans as They Are,* 94.
[35] Sealsfield, "The Squatter Chief," 327.

of the Germans themselves; but, strangely, the German immigrants in America did not always receive flattering treatment in novels by their countrymen. Sealsfield had little use for them, in fact; and while Strubberg, Gerstäcker, and Möllhausen proved to be more kindly disposed, these three authors were extremely objective in their portrayals, pointing out the shortcomings and human frailties in the Germans' struggles to overcome the difficulties of relocation in America.

Strubberg's *Bis in die Wildnis*,[36] for example, told the unfortunate story of a group of German peasants who arrived in New York under the leadership of their village schoolmaster. They were barely ashore before they met up with bogus land agents who fleeced them of all their money; for the author, the fault lay with the gullible, naive Germans, rather than with those who did them in. Gerstäcker's *The Wanderings and Fortunes of Some German Emigrants* offered much the same tale, as we have mentioned, taking the colonists into the swamps of Kentucky, their promised paradise. Möllhausen, a bit more humane in his views, nevertheless dwelt extensively on the sufferings of his countrymen in the new world and their yearning for the homeland.

There was, of course, a natural amount of pity for the German immigrant in an alien land, and typical of this feeling is Gerstäcker's description of a young German who has just missed a St. Louis–bound packet boat:

It is a poor German, who arrived only three days before from his fatherland, who intends to go up to Missouri, and his whole family—a wife, three young children, and an aged mother, who would not be left alone in the old home—are on the vessel that is gradually disappearing in the misty distance. Many ask him what is the matter, many laugh at him, some pity him—he himself sits unsympathizing, and consequently, does not comprehend their questions, their ridicule, or their pity; but all he understands is, that he is alone, destitute, in a foreign city, and will never, never again see those who belong to him. . . .[37]

His wife, incidentally, cannot be expected to fare much better: "Poor woman! 'tis the first time she has travelled in an American steamer; and the belief that anything would be done to her out of *charity* may be forgiven her—she knows no better!"[38]

The pity was sometimes supplanted by scorn and a disgust at the way the Germans conducted themselves in the New World. The large Ger-

[36] Armand (Friedrich Strubberg), *Bis in die Wildnis* (Breslau, 1858).
[37] Friedrich Gerstäcker, *Western Lands and Western Waters* (London, 1864), 10.
[38] *Ibid.*

man community in Cincinnati was not completely possessed of those
fine Nordic virtues one so often hears about, as this passage from Gerstäcker suggests:

> Unfortunately, my beloved countrymen are not celebrated for cleanliness
> and good conduct, and the degree of estimation in which they are everywhere
> held does not all accord with the accounts I had read in a number of works
> on America concerning the way in which they were treated there; and al-
> though the well-behaved are respected there as elsewhere, yet it is painful to
> hear the word Dutchman, as the Americans always call us, used as a term of
> reproach, even when you yourself are excepted. Everywhere in America, and
> particularly in Cincinnati, there are people who, having gained a few dollars,
> look down with contempt on their poorer countrymen, and even join with
> the Americans in abusing them, showing how little they care about the
> esteem in which the German is held. . . .[39]

Finally we must turn to consider the Indians, the original inhabitants of the frontier, for whom, as for the German immigrants, we are
asked to hold alternative feelings of pity or scorn, despite occasional
idealizations of them as the noble savages.

Sealsfield's first novel, *Tokeah, or The White Rose* (which was first
published in Philadelphia in 1829 and did not appear in Germany,
slightly altered and retitled *Der Legitime und die Republikaner,* until
four years later), championed the cause of the red man. Following the
romantic traditions of Chateaubriand and the elegiac heritage of Cooper, Sealsfield decried the injustice of the Indians' plight as the legiti-
mate owners of the land, engaged in a final struggle with the white intruders; but never having had much direct contact with any Indians, he
was forced to rely on earlier literature for his impressions and conclusions, which were more romantic than realistic.

However, the other three authors we have been discussing had considerable contact with Indians, and their firsthand acquaintance with
the subject led them to somewhat different points of view. Strubberg,
although he often idealzed *his* Indians,[40] was more usually factual, and
at one point even went so far as to describe the red men as "pronounced *Lumpe.*"[41] In Gerstäcker's works the Indian appeared as he
was found, with few editorial laments on his unfortunate situation: "A
tall, powerful Indian, decked out with glass beads and silver ornaments,
came staggering towards me, with an empty bottle in his left hand and

[39] Gerstäcker, *Wild Sports,* 120-121.
[40] For a discussion of Strubberg's treatment of the Indians, see Preston A. Barba,
"Friedrich Armand Strubberg," *German American Annals,* XI (1913), 28 ff.
[41] *Ibid.,* 9.

a handsome rifle in his right, and holding them both towards me, gave me to understand that he would give me the rifle if I would fill his bottle. . . . The poor Indians have fallen so low. . . ."[42] Möllhausen, who perhaps had more contact than any of the others through his various expeditions into the West, preferred to depict the isolated types he found on the borders of civilization: the lazy brave loitering before a frontier store or trading post, the lone trapper or fisherman who chose to remain among the whites rather than move farther into the West, the savage converted by missionaries, or the government ward on a reservation. In these later novels the descendants of Chief Uncas vanish from the frontier, leaving in their place a few solitary figures who were apparently more frequently encountered in fiction than in flesh—if we can judge the case from Duden's account: "No doubt you are surprised that I have hardly uttered a syllable about the Indians. Who in Germany would believe that a person could live a whole year on the far-away Missouri, without having been visited a single time by Indians. After having read the various books concerning these people, I myself was greatly concerned in this regard. It is probable, however, that in my neighborhood no Indian has been seen for ten years. . . ."[43]

As the Indians moved farther into the land of the setting sun, there appeared in their stead the first outposts of organized American society. This, too, fell under the eyes of the German writers, and if perhaps we have been entertained and amused by some of their impressions of the land or those who dwelt upon it, we must not forget a more serious note: that ultimately it was the character and the symbol of liberty on our continent which held out the great hope for the future to the *Europamüden,* the oppressed and poor of the old world.

The feeling of hope can be derived from the very nature of the novelists' descriptions of frontier towns and cities, where polyglot crowds moved freely in a vigorous, occasionally boisterous, and often vulgar way. If the Germans were frequently depicted as bewildered innocents arriving in the midst of this confusion, they soon found themselves— and the confusion, an indication of the relaxed social structure of the frontier, became an attraction in itself to those who had known strict regimentation on the other side of the Atlantic.

Some of the criticisms of American life which appeared in the novels are worth mentioning, if only because they ring an uncomfortably true note today. One German complained that "the American seeks, in all

---

[42] Gerstäcker, *Wild Sports,* 92.
[43] Bek, *Duden's Report,* 62.

his undertakings and labours, to earn the largest possible sum in the shortest possible time; and, starting on this principle, arranges everything accordingly";[44] a Yankee in one book was made to exclaim: "It is our American calamity, that we bring down to our coarse democratic level everything that comes within our reach";[45] and it is hard to overlook the following in view of the character of modern suburbia: "The very wandering spirit of the inhabitants seems still to contend with the principle of steadiness in the very construction of their buildings."[46] These few examples are enough to show us that the German novelists possessed a fairly perceptive insight into the American character, especially in the areas which would be difficult for the German mind to understand. But while the Germans may have found it hard to adjust to American society, they never questioned the right of individual liberty which often made the society so incomprehensible to them—but at the same time so attractive.

We may feel, in conclusion, that perhaps the German novelists were too idyllic about the frontier landscape and did exaggerate its natural advantages, or conversely, were too vivid in depicting some of its drawbacks and dangers; perhaps they were too rigid in their characterizations of the inhabitants, or a bit shocked at the free and easy way of life. Despite all these shortcomings, the American frontier as it was described in German fiction offered the picture of a new life to thousands on the continent of Europe and undoubtedly was instrumental in bringing many immigrants to our shores. For what Sealsfield once wrote about Ohio applied as well to the Germans' general impression of America and the opportunities offered on its frontier: "It combines in itself all the elements that tend to make its inhabitants the happiest people on the face of the earth. Nature has done everything in favor of this country."[47]

[44] Gerstäcker, *Western Lands,* 12.
[45] Sealsfield, *The Cabin Book,* 45.
[46] Sealsfield, *Americans as They Are,* 35.
[47] *Ibid.,* 10.

Cowboy Philosophy

A Cold Spoor

JOE B. FRANTZ

UNIVERSITY OF TEXAS

He rode away from the soapy red clay slopes of Georgia, a rebel who had lost his cause and had nowhere to return to. He left the rolling farmland with its crisp cut hedges along West Otter Creek, because, having seen the wide world stretching from his home in Macoupin County, Illinois, all the way to Shiloh or Savannah, those eighty acres no longer seemed large enough. He was a myopic young man of genteel birth sent west to run a family holding on his way up to the presidency of the United States. He was a French monsieur with a feeling of grandeur, building a mansion on the Dakota plains that would be a wonder to behold even among the many wonders of the mid-twentieth century. He was a German baron, writing for credulous readers of the automatic fortune to be made in cattle. He was a Negro, seeking a job where he would be accepted for his cow sense and not rejected because of his color. He was a Mexican drifting north, perhaps, except for the Indian, the first man in the region, ready to have his name corrupted and his broken English hooted at, secure in the knowledge that he brought more natural inheritance to the trade than any of the fairer-skinned hands riding alongside.

He was, of course, the American cowboy, loping out of somewhere to become a continuing object of interest, sometimes affectionate, sometimes derisive, but never unconcerned. In a day of leisurely development he became an instant myth, a legend that endures and enlarges. Often nearly illiterate, he nonetheless wrote more about himself than any other group of grubbers, except possibly for politicians and entertainers. And men looked him over, assayed him—dime novelists, with prose both purple and prolix; serious novelists, too often posing as pseudo-psychiatrists; movie and television scenarists, hard-eyed, hackneyed, and wholesale; and even pedestrian professors, seeking significance amidst their desiccating delving. Serious Swedish magazines search him soberly. "Rawhide" can be seen on television screens throughout the world—in Japanese in Hiroshima, in German in Göttingen, in Spanish in Bogotá—though no longer in Hollywood English in Edwardsville or Austin.

Through all of this spotlighting the American cowboy has ridden on, serene and uncaring. He is the American hero. Now and then, for a spell, he shares his eminence with a soldier, spaceman, ax-swinging woodsman, explorer, miner, or athlete. But these interlopers fade, and our cowboy rides on, confidently ready as always to take on the next one. Some observers have called him the spirit of the United States, and almost all of us have seen ourselves apotheosized in and through him. He is the knight on horseback, undaunted by danger, direct and decisive. He talks little, but his words can sing out like bullets spitting off a tin target. He stands for no nonsense, but he can play hard and rough. He is, in the current term, a tiger when on a tear. And he is gentle to children, chivalrous to womenfolk, and careful of the feelings of everyone except four-flushers. He sees through the complexities of situations, and he exacts a swift, simple, stern justice. He carries his letter of credit in his face, and though he might be fooled once, he can't be fooled—or fooled with—twice.

No need here to re-examine the cowboy. This savant of the sage is unassailable. If he were not, he would have been surmounted and surpassed long before now, for he has been carved every which way by hack after hack. But he remains as tough as rawhide, and as resilient. So let us accept his *aura popularis* and proceed from there.

If he is *the* freeswinging American, then he must speak for his less explicit, mumbling fellow citizens.

That is a conclusion I reached. I reached it not by dry-as-dust research, but intuitively, the way great truths always come flashing in. I accepted it as truth, the way a child accepts the fact that his father leaves for work each morning, without researching to see whether "to work" is actually where father does go. The child, though, comes intuitively nearer the truth than I.

You see, I have now researched my intuition. Months ago an editor asked me whether I would write a chapter on cowboy philosophy for a book on great American declarations. He felt as I did—that with all the cowboy has written and with the thousands of quotations that have been drawn from his picturesque earthy speech, somewhere he must have expressed with powerful pithiness the blessings of being a free man in an ample, uncrowded world. Blithely I agreed, promising the quotation and short accompanying manuscript within a month or so. I haven't delivered it yet.

The cowboy left his tracks everywhere. For a quiet man he spoke all over the place. When he didn't speak, writers put words in his mouth. He is definitely on record.

But too often he talked anecdotally. He remembered. A superb hyperbolist, he elaborated and exaggerated—about danger, about horses, about places, about work, even now and then about women. But every time he seemed to be on the trace of a philosophy, he would suddenly and disappointingly back off. Trying to catch him making *the* statement was about as rewarding as watching a fine preliminary salesman who can't close a deal.

One problem stems from separating the cowboy from the general western frontiersman. Just as the Hollywood stereotype of a cowboy hero may have him panning for gold, running a marshal's office, dodging a posse, or logging in the Cascades—any occupation except farming or sheepherding, so the cowboy fuses like a noonday mirage into the over-all western portrait. Thus when Lewis Garrard reminisces about going west from Cincinnati in 1846, he repeats this advice handed him by an experienced frontiersman: "If you see a man's mule running off, don't stop it—let it go; it isn't yourn. If his possible sack falls off, don't tell him of it; he'll find it out. At camp, help cook—get food and water —make yourself active—get your pipe and smoke it—don't ask too many questions, and you'll pass!"[1] This is good cowboy advice. It has the ring of cowboy truth. It has, as they say in creative writing courses, verisimilitude. But it was spoken, according to Garrard, by a "kindly intentioned . . . old mountaineer."

Considerable importance is attached by armchair philosophers and arm-waving politicians to the fact that the cowboy seldom complained, but accepted the adversities and tedium of his life silently, as American heroes should. Of course, the fallacy here is that Americans as a people do not complain; if you have doubts, visit a Jefferson Barracks' bull session, any faculty meeting anywhere, or even the after-hours hangouts of the St. Louis Cardinals, either horsehide- or pigskin-oriented. Americans are a restless race of complainers, who zealously guard their prerogative to grumble. To most of us, a silent person is a complacent person, and complacent people don't illuminate the altar of progress.

However that may be, the uncomplaining cowboy was uncomplain-

[1] Quoted in Oscar Lewis, *The Autobiography of the West* (New York, 1958), 237.

ing in part because he knew no better, and expected little better. He was like the Tarasco or Otomi in Mexico who feels no envy as his fellow man flashes by in an automobile. The thought of owning one of those vehicles lies beyond his horizon of dreams, never to appear as the remotest possibility of attainment. And like the old man chasing the young blonde, or the dog chasing the car, he wouldn't know what to do with it if he caught it.

So the cowboy is silent and accepting, eating his unvaried and uninspired grub, riding in the rain, drinking dust, and sleeping on the unyielding ground with a saddle for a pillow. But as Teddy Blue points out, "They never kicked, because those boys was raised under just the same conditions as there were on the trail—corn meal and bacon for grub, dirt floors in the houses and no luxuries."[2]

Even if the cowboy dream did come true, and through planning or rustling he managed to get a few head of his own, chances are that his newfangled economic affluence would result in the addition of few material solaces, except that he would give up sleeping two-in-a-bed with other hands when he visited Dodge.

After all, should a strong man, grown beyond tears and fears, grouse when the occasional woman who wandered in could take the privations in stride? Look at the experience of one young girl from Vermont who married Timothy Dwight Hobart, a man of substance and promise. As they worked their way westward, she was struck by the fact that the men seemed to look rougher the farther they rode from Vermont. Kansas turned out to be "a bare desolate looking state, and the Indian Territory . . . a jumping off place."

But then she reached one of their honeymoon hotels, only seventeen miles from their destination. They ascended the outside stairway of the Baldwin House in Miami, Texas—the only hotel in town—to find a room furnished with a "wooden box, standing on end with a tin wash basin, one broken chair, and a bed." The final leg of the journey was made in a "most fearful, genuine dust storm."[3] And only a few weeks back life had consisted of a large two-story home in the Green Mountains, amidst hills, forests, and sparkling streams. If Minnie Warren Hobart could say "Never mind, I was happy," then what could a cowhand do but get out his makin's, roll another smoke, and light it in the wind?

    [2] E. C. ("Teddy Blue") Abbott and Helena Huntington Smith, *We Pointed Them North* (New York, 1939), 7.
    [3] L. F. Sheffy, *The Life and Times of Timothy Dwight Hobart, 1855-1935* (Canyon, Texas, 1950), 10.

Andy Downs, then, was speaking for men and women everywhere, and not just for cowboys, when he said, "The West demands you smile and swallow your personal troubles like your food. Nobody wants to hear about other men's half-digested problems any more than he likes to watch a seasick person working."[4]

If stoic silence is not the cowboy's contribution to the pragmatic philosophy of American living, what is the essence of the cowboy outlook that makes him speak to all of us over the past century? Could it be a generous spirit? Considerateness?

> Let me be easy on the man that's down
>   and make me square and generous with all.
> I'm careless sometimes, Lord, when I'm in town,
> But never let them say I'm mean or small.[5]

Granville Stuart, who suffered something less than total enchantment with the cowboy, would endorse the sentiment of this quatrain. Although he thought that cowboys hardly uplifted culture in the areas they touched, he nonetheless felt constrained to write that despite their operating beyond organized society or law, "they formulated laws of their own that met their requirements. . . . They were reluctant to obey any law but their own and chafed under restraint. They were loyal to their outfit and to one another. A man that was not square could not long remain with an outfit."[6]

Square or not, the cowboy was, in John Clay's words, "a bird of the wilderness, accustomed to freedom, not trained to be interfered with, a child of the frontier handy with his gun, [who] did not understand the changing days west of the one-hundredth Meridian and he died hard."[7]

Before he died hard, however, the cowboy made his impression, a creature of contradictions, now boisterous in the saloon and bawdy-house, now silent and serious and solitary, now openhanded and ample, now squinting and sighting without mercy at some stranger who had wronged him only once. Clay, who could write rapturously, once silhouetted him against a backdrop of infinity:

You saw him move away at the regular fox trot just as the grey dawn lit up the jagged peaks around old Split Rock, the other cowboys following him in pairs. One dropped out after another as he gave the word, and

---

[4] Quoted in Philip Ashton Rollins, *The Cowboy* (New York, 1922), 67.

[5] Oscar Rush, *The Open Range* (Caldwell, Idaho, 1936), 190-191.

[6] Granville Stuart, *Forty Years on the Frontier*, Paul C. Phillips, ed. (Cleveland, 1925), II, 182.

[7] John Clay, *My Life on the Range*, new ed. (Norman, 1962), 106.

then far away in the distance you saw his figure against the horizon as he followed a divide, the furthest point of the morning gather. When the herd was bunched he changed on to one of the cutting horses. . . . Horse and man seemed to be one piece, a centaur on the prairie, moving in unison as the half-wild, excited cattle milled round and round.

Happy days those before the days of barbed wire, the great Wyoming valleys redolent of grass, and the elk still numerous in the timbered mountains. How peaceful it looked as your eye from some vantage point swept the valley, a silver stream winding serpent-like through the great flats of grey sagebrush.[8]

Clay's evocative prose here skirts poetry. The reader's mind begins to churn with ideas of cowboy philosophy. Here is the clue: a cowboy's statement, ringing and clear, about the amplitude of living in those days, of his harmony with his horse, his oneness with his environment, will ensnare the elusive philosophic fragment that illuminates both our heritage and our higher desires.

With sights aimed on the interminate stars, or at the least on the transcendent mountains to the westward, we examine cowboy reminiscences, one after another. A veritable lode lies before our eyes, waiting to be mined. But one day the mining has ended, and only dross has resulted. With your mind and your heart set on spaciousness and the grandeur of a wild, free past, you have dredged only such low-grade veins as this: "You always want to shoot 'em in the right eye because that disturbs their aim";[9] "The cowboy may be classed as an amphibious animal, as he can live in water—diluted with whisky—or out of it";[10] "Whiskey is good, but it doesn't stick to the ribs."[11]

On a slightly higher plane, here is James H. Cook:

The uninitiated are prone to think that the vocation of the cowboy was a continuous experience of excitement, dangers, and lawlessness . . . they were merely incidental to the main process of affairs which was steadily grinding the rough and savage material of the times and localities into the more symmetrical and refined forms of civilized existence.

The sunshine and the winds of the prairie aided . . . in developing men naturally self-reliant. In all classes of men there were drags—"scrubs"—who managed to ride along by some means on the shoulders of the good ones. . . . They were often fair-weather sailors, with no pride when it came to

[8] *Ibid.,* xi-xii.
[9] Abbott and Smith, *We Pointed Them North,* 58.
[10] *Texas Live Stock Journal* (Oct. 21, 1882).
[11] Walker D. Wyman, *Nothing But Prairie and Sky* (Norman, 1954), 113.

doing unpleasant tasks well, however much they had of another sort of pride which would make them die game in a saloon brawl.[12]

Charlie Russell, whose feeling for the art of the West is acknowledged internationally, added a wistful if incidental facet to the philosophic questing: "History and romance died when the plow turned the country grass side down."[13]

No artist, but a man with a sense of succinct artistry, was J. S. Kenyon, a hand on the 3,000,000-acre XIT Ranch in Texas. Mused Kenyon: "It is a grand place to view the stars."[14] That one sentence could sum up the attraction of the frontier. Implicit is the American dreaming, his having Heaven in view, and the possibility of his roping the horns of Heaven and dragging it down within touching distance of men on earth.

Probably the best spokesmen for the cowboys were not the cowboys themselves, who for all their gift of simple speech often fumbled words when they wandered off marked trails into the side paths of abstraction. Instead, the best spokesmen were likely to be fringe men, the poets with their practice in harmonizing words and thoughts. Although these poets are seldom listed in the anthologies of great writers, they were invariably men who had hung around cow camps, who could take a turn as a hand when the crew was short, and who knew the difference between son-of-a-gun stew and alkali.

Let's look at a few of these bards of the outer borders. Their lyrics might be imperfect, but they catch a mood, a feeling—a philosophy perhaps?

> I fancy he saw something in the clouds above the trees,
> Which the gold and glory seeker passes by and never sees;
> And I think he gathered something from the woods and running streams
> Which is just as good as money to the man of many dreams.[15]

Or we could turn to the Bible, which doesn't list cowboys in its concordance, but which in its universality of experience dealt with men who knew in their day that the frontier was a good place to view the stars. Listen to the prophet: "Whose house I have made the wilderness,

---

[12] James H. Cook, *Fifty Years on the Old Frontier*, new ed. (Norman, 1957), 100-101.

[13] Quoted in Ramon F. Adams and Bob Kennon, *From the Pecos to the Powder* (Norman, 1965), 7.

[14] Quoted in Cordia Sloan Duke and Joe B. Frantz, *Six Thousand Miles of Fence* (Austin, 1961), 217.

[15] Rush, *The Open Range*, 20.

and the barren land his dwelling. He scorneth the multitude of the city, neither regardeth he the crying of the driver."[16]

Or Hamlin Garland, whose frontier was more that of Mississippi River country:

> Do you fear the force of the wind,
> The slash of the rain?
> Go face them and fight them!
> Be savage again.[17]

Of course, if you heeded too doggedly the admonition to be savage, you would fall in line with the theological fate reserved for rustling cowboys and buffalo hunters: "when a bad man dies he goes either to hell or the Pecos."

John Young, that old *vaquero* of the brush country, preached the philosophy of chance: "Deserving or undeserving," he observed, "I and they were but creatures of circumstance—the circumstance of an unfenced world."[18]

This idea of an unfenced world remains a compelling and continuing idea, expressed popularly during World War II by Cole Porter, a son of Indiana who knew the range from the halls of Yale, an apartment on New York's East Sixties, or the deck of a lavish yacht cruising in the blue Mediterranean. But when this super-sophisticate, known for his crisp rendering of brittle love songs, wrote a waggish "Don't Fence Me In," he hit a chord that told GIs everywhere—from the prairies of Harlem to the sidewalks of Abilene—what he was fighting for:

> I want to ride to the ridge where the West commences
> Gaze at the moon 'til I lose my senses.

Another sophisticate, this time from the British Isles and writing in the 1880's, a man who spelled ranch with a final *e*, caught this same unfenced feeling. He observed how "portly British squire(s) or smug city merchant(s)" arrived with some disdain to inspect ranch properties, only to be "at once seized with the spirit of adventure."[19]

Owen Wister, who made the cowboy literarily respectable, believed in his hero so long as he could resist Progress. But for whatever philosophical harvest it may yield, Wister observed that with the arrival of

[16] Job 39:6-7.
[17] Hamlin Garland, "Vanishing Trails," in *University* [of Chicago] *Record,* X (1905), 56.
[18] J. Frank Dobie, *A Vaquero of the Brush Country* (New York, 1929), 279.
[19] John Baumann, "On a Western Ranche," *Fortnightly Review* (April, 1887), 516.

Progress the cowboy's "peculiar independence is of necessity dimmed."[20] Does this suggest that the idea of cowboy—i.e., freedom—is incompatible with Progress?

Undoubtedly part of the attraction of the cowboy and the ranch stems from the fact that, like baseball, the rules seldom change. The Mexican *vaquero,* hard on the heels of the *conquistadores,* the pre-American Revolution cow boy of the Carolina Piedmont, or the cattle raiser of the 1830's who utilized the grasslands of Indiana, Illinois, and Missouri to feed the beefeaters from Ohio eastward[21]—all faced the same basic problems of branding, strays, or rustlers as the rancher of the plains generations or even centuries later. In fact, you need not confine yourself to the flat or rolling country. As one pre–Civil War cowboy wrote from San Jose, California, to "The folks at home," "You would laugh now I can tell you if you could see me careering over the mountains after some of these wild Spanish steers."[22]

But let's return to the poets, to see whether they can get away from the cowboy's preoccupation with what he did rather than what he thought. On one occasion Badger Clark likened cowboy quality to the wind:

> So I jumped and sweat for a flat-foot boss
> Till my pocket bulged with pay,
> But my heart it fought like a led bronc' hawse
> Till I flung my drill away.
> For the wind, the wind, the good-free wind,
>   She sang from the pine divide
> That the sky was blue and the young years few
> And the world was big and wide!
>
>   .   .   .   .
>
> Then I watched the gold of sunset bars
> And my camp-sparks glintin' toward the stars
> And laughed at the pay I'd lost.[23]

Ah, there's the key—the wistfulness for the wide, free world of youth, the desire to hold on to youth itself.

---

[20] Owen Wister, "The Evolution of the Cow-Puncher," *Harper's New Monthly Magazine* (Sept., 1895), 617.

[21] Paul Wallace Gates, "Cattle Kings in the Prairies," *Mississippi Valley Historical Review,* XXXV (1948), 379-412.

[22] Gustave E. Genthner to "The folks at home," Sept. 14, 1860, Genthner Papers, Huntington Library, San Marino, Calif.

[23] Badger Clark, *Grass-Grown Trails* (Boston, 1917), 10.

> Loose rein and rowelled heel to spare,
>   The wind our only guide,
> For youth was in the saddle there
>   With half a world to ride.[24]

Youth—and space:

> Oh Lord, I've never lived where churches grow.
>   I love creation better as it stood
> That day You finished it long ago
>
> .   .   .   .
>
> I thank You, Lord, that I am placed so well,
>   That you have made my freedom so complete
> That I'm no slave of whistle, clock or bell,
>   Nor weak-eyed prisoner of wall and street.[25]

Or again, in a bewildering, constricting world:

> 'Twas good to live when all the sod,
>   Without no fence nor fuss,
> Belonged in pardnership to God,
>   The Gover'ment and us.
> With skyline bound from east to west
>   And room to go and come,
> I loved my fellow man the best
>   When he was scattered some.[26]

And then the plaintive look backward:

> These ain't the plains of God no more,
>   They're only real estate.[27]

It's a teasing trail, this path to a cowboy philosophy. Every time it promises a firm grasp, it slips away like Brazos quicksand or a new meander along the Musselshell. But somewhere a cowboy must have said the right words, must for a moment have held terse truth in his hand. When I find it, I know it will speak of the wind: "I've courted the wind and I've followed her free";[28] and of freedom: ". . . Then / Sweep away, wild with sheer life, and free, free, free—/ Free of all confines of time and flesh";[29] and of joy in the job: "This is the life I

[24] *Ibid.*, 58.
[25] Badger Clark, *Sun and Saddle Leather* (Boston, 1920), 55.
[26] *Ibid.*, 88.
[27] *Ibid.*
[28] *Ibid.*, 86.
[29] J. Frank Dobie, *The Mustangs* (Boston, 1952), 331.

love to lead";[30] and of solitude: "But I must follow the lonely way";[31] and of his special place among the heroes of eternity:

Harp and flute and violin, throbbing through the night,
Merry eyes and tender eyes, dark head and bright;
Moon shadow on the sundial to mark the moments fleet,
The magic and enchanted hours where moonlight lovers meet;
And the harp notes come all brokenly by night winds stirred—
But the hired man on horseback is singing to the herd!

      .   .   .   .

If to his dreams a face may come? Ah, turn your eyes away,
Nor guess what face may come by dream that never comes by day.
Red dawn breaking through the desert murk;
The hired man on horseback goes laughing to his work.

The broker's in his office before the stroke of ten,
He buys and smiles and he sells and smiles at the word of other men;
But he gets his little commission flat, whether they buy or sell,
So be it drouth or storm or flood, the broker's crops do well.
They are short of Katy Common, they are long on Zinc Preferred—
But the hired man on horseback is swimming with the herd!

      .   .   .   .

A little midnight supper when the play is done,
Glancing lights and sparkling eyes—the night is just begun.
Beauteous night, O night of love!—Youth and joy are met.
Shine on our enchantment still! 'Sweet, your eyes are wet.'
'Dear, they sing for us alone!' Such the lover's creed.
—But the hired man on horseback is off with the stampede!

There is no star in the pit-black night, there is none to know or blame,
And a hundred yards to left or right, there is safety there—and shame!
A stone throw out on either side, with none to guess or tell—
But the hired man on horseback has raised the rebel yell!
He has turned to loosen his saddle strings, he has fumbled his slicker free,
He whirls it high and he snaps it wide wherever the foremost be.
He slaps it into a longhorn's eyes till he falters in his stride—
An oath and a shot, a laugh and a shot, and his wild mates race beside;
A pony stumbles—no, he is up, unhurt and running still;
'Turn 'em, turn 'em, turn 'em, Charlie! Good boy, Bill!'

      .   .   .   .

The proud Young Intellectuals—a cultured folk are these,
They scorn the lowly Babbitts and their hearts are overseas;
They turn their backs upon us, and if we ask them why
They smile like jesting Pilate, and they stay for no reply;

---

[30] Rose Davidson, *Breeze over Texas* (Dallas, 1940), 15.
[31] Arthur Chapman, *Cactus Center* (Boston, 1921), 14.

They smile at faith and honor, and they smile at shame and crime—
But the old Palo Pinto man is calling for his time.

For he heard old voices and he heard hoofs beat,
Songs that long ago were gay to time with drumming feet;
Bent back straightens and dim eyes grow bright—
The last man on horseback rides on into the night!
Cossack and Saracen
Shout their wild welcome then,
Ragged proud Conquistadores claim him kind and kin,
And the wild Beggars of the Sea leap up to swell the din;
And Hector leans upon the wall, and David bends to scan
This new brown comrade for the old brown clan,
The great-hearted gentlemen who guard the outer wall,
Black with sin and stained with blood—and faithful through it all;
Still wearing for all ornament the scars they won below—
And the Lord God Out-of-Doors, He cannot let them go!
They have halted the hired horseman beyond the outer gate,
But the gentlemen adventurers cry shame that he should wait;
And the sour saints soften, with a puzzled grin,
As Esau and Ishmael press to let their brother in.
Hat tip-tilted and his head held high,
Brave spurs jingling as he passes by—
Gray hair tousled and his lips a-quirk—
To the Master of the Workmen, with the tally of his work![32]

So where are we? The *feel* for the cowboy is everywhere; the symbol of the cowboy is just as pervasive. We know what he stands for. But he remains the man of action, terse and pithy perhaps, but without that ability to wrap up the aspirations of his fellow men in one pointed, pregnant phrase. Maybe because he is *of* the wild, free, danger-studded life instead of being the intense but peripheral observer, he can never speak for those others of us who feel ineffable calls that evoke feeble, frustrated answers. The philosophy of the cowboy is not spoken, but tacit. It must remain what he was, not what he said.

[32] Eugene Manlove Rhodes, "The Hired Man on Horseback," *Adventure* (Feb., 1928). The poem later appeared in various works, including May Davison Rhodes, *The Hired Man on Horseback* (Boston, 1938), ix-xiii.

Contributors

George R. Brooks, Director of the Missouri Historical Society in his native St. Louis, graduated *summa cum laude* from Williams College in 1951, where he majored in History of Art and German Literature. After serving for four years in the U.S. Navy (on combat duty in Korea at first and later on the staff of the Chief of Naval Operations in Washington) he earned an M.A. in Archaeology at Washington University in 1958, was Curator of the Missouri Historical Society 1959-60, Assistant on Conservation at the Fogg Museum 1960-62, and has filled his present position since that year. He has contributed articles to the *Gazette des Beaux Arts* and the *Missouri Historical Society Bulletin*.

John C. Ewers' many papers and books have been concentrated on the Indians of the West. He entered the National Park Service in 1935, was Curator of the Museum of the Plains Indians at Browning, Montana, 1941-44, became Associate Curator of Anthropology in the U.S. National Museum (Smithsonian Institution) in 1946, was named Planning Officer for the new Museum of History and Technology in 1956, Assistant Director of that museum in 1959, Director in 1964, and since 1965 has been devoting all his time to research and writing as Senior Ethnologist in the Smithsonian Institution. He has given much attention to painters and paintings of the Indian in books ranging from his *Plains Indian Painting* published in 1939 through *Artists of the Old West* in 1965 as well as in many invaluable papers in the *Smithsonian Institution Annual Reports* and historical journals. He has now in press an edition of Catlin's *Okeepa*.

Joe B. Frantz, Professor of History at the University of Texas, is well known as a western historian, author, and swapper of campfire stories. Holding three degrees from his university, he has also been a Fellow in Business History at Harvard University, a Ford Foundation Fellow, a Social Science Research Council Fellow, and a Fulbright Lecturer at the University of Chile. He has filled a number of responsible positions in the Mississippi Valley Historical Association (now the Organization of American Historians), the Western History Association, and the Texas State Historical Association, of which he has recently been named Director. He has written or co-authored a number of books about the Southwest—among them *The American Cowboy: The Myth and the Reality*—and is now at work on a history of the western cattle industry.

Herman R. Friis left teaching at the University of Southern Illinois to become Geographer-Archivist in the National Archives. In 1952 he became Chief of the Cartographic Records Division, in 1959 Chief of the Technical Records Division, and in 1962 was named Senior Specialist in Cartographic Archives, which is equivalent to a research professorship. He is a fellow of the American Geographical Society and the Society of American Archivists. Since 1946 he has been a member and a chairman of committees in the National Academy of Sciences–National Research Council, in the federal government, and in professional organizations. He recently received the Outstanding Achievement Award of the Association of American Geographers. His most recent (March, 1967) publication is *The Pacific Basin: A History of Its Geographical Exploration,* which he edited.

Preston Holder, Chairman of the Department of Anthropology at the University of Nebraska, has explored the ancient hunting complexes of the plains, the middle ceramic periods of the Southeast and the Mississippi valley, and the village periods of the Missouri valley. This latter work has included the exploration of the first historic Arikara village at the confluence of the Grand and Missouri rivers, the Leavenworth village where many outbound explorers and traders stopped in the early nineteenth century. In ethnohistory Holder's major interest has been the rise and growth of the village peoples of the eastern plains. He has published papers in the *American Anthropologist,* the *Journal of the Washington Academy of Sciences,* and other scholarly quarterlies, and has in final preparation ethnological analyses of plains culture history with special emphasis on the fur trade period along the Missouri River.

Oliver W. Holmes, Executive Director of the National Historical Publications Commission since 1961, originally of Minnesota, was awarded his doctorate in American History at Columbia. He joined the staff of the National Archives in 1936, where he served as Chief of the Division of Interior Department Archives, Director of the Office of Natural Resources Records, and Chief Archivist of the Social and Economics Records Division prior to his present appointment. A founding member of the Society of American Archivists, he was President of that society in 1958-59 and has contributed many articles to its journal, *The American Archivist.* His special interests are archives, manuscripts, and their administration, the editing and publishing of historical materials, the American frontier, and the history of American transportation.

Donald Jackson since 1948 has been in charge of the book-publishing program of the University of Illinois Press. After an early interest in the writing of fiction, he turned to the history of trans-Mississippi exploration. Among other books he has edited *The Letters of the Lewis and Clark Expedition* (University of Illinois Press, 1962), and the two-volume *Journals of Zebulon Montgomery Pike* (University of Oklahoma Press, 1966). A larger project, to occupy part of his time for the next several years, is *The Papers of John Charles Frémont,* which will be produced under the guidance and endorsement of the National Historical Publications Commission. Jackson's work on the documents of the Lewis and Clark Expedition received the first regional literature award of the Missouri Historical Society in April, 1965, for "not only an exciting accomplishment in editing the correspondence relating to that famous journey, but a performance which should serve as a standard in research methodology for the future."

John Francis McDermott, since 1963 Research Professor of Humanities at Southern Illinois University, Edwardsville, has long been interested in the exploration, early settlement, and cultural history of the Mississippi valley. Author or editor of articles, notes, and documents in a wide assortment of historical journals, he has edited a number of travel books and has published studies as widely varied as *Private Libraries in Creole Saint Louis* (Baltimore, 1938) and *George Caleb Bingham, River Portraitist* (University of Oklahoma Press, 1959). Among reports of early western life he is now engaged on an edition of the original diary of the Swiss artist, R. F. Kurz, which he discovered several years ago in Berne, Switzerland, and one of the diary of Charles Joseph Latrobe, whose portfolio of 125 sketches of the United States in 1832-34 he has just located.

Merrill J. Mattes is now Historian for the Office of Resource Planning, National Park Service, San Francisco. From 1950 to 1966 he was Regional Historian for the Midwest Region, National Park Service, Omaha. He was named Nebraska Civil Servant of the Year in 1958 and received the U.S. Department of the Interior Distinguished Service Award the following year. One of our most active historians of the plains and the Rockies in the nineteenth century, he has published at least fifty articles in *Nebraska History, Mississippi Valley Historical Review,* the *Annals of Wyoming,* and other journals of western history, as well as two books: *Indians, Infants and Infantry* (Denver, 1960), and *Colter's Hell and Jackson's Hole* (Yellowstone Park, 1962).

Ralph E. Morrow, Ph.D. Indiana University 1954, Professor of History at Washington University, Chairman of his department 1960-65, has from the beginning made the history of religion in America the subject of his investigations as a social historian. Since his *Northern Methodism and Reconstruction* was published in 1956, he has contributed a number of articles to the *Mississippi Valley Historical Review,* the *Journal of Southern*

History, and other professional publications. He has in progress studies of *The Rise of the Methodist Movement in America, Providence and the Peculiar Institution,* and *From Church to Denomination: Organized Religion in America, 1775-1850.* In 1954 he won the Baruch Award for Southern History, in 1959 a Guggenheim Memorial Fellowship, and he has received several research grants from the American Philosophical Society.

Richard E. Oglesby, Ph.D. Northwestern University 1962, has taught at Eastern Illinois University and is now Assistant Professor of History at the University of California at Santa Barbara. A contributor to the *Missouri Historical Society Bulletin* and other historical quarterlies, he is the author of *Manuel Lisa and the Opening of the Missouri Fur Trade* (University of Oklahoma Press, 1963). He is now engaged in editing Christian Schultz's account of his private explorations on the Ohio and Mississippi rivers in 1807-08, *Travels on an Inland Voyage,* for a new series of reprints of "Travels on the Western Waters" being inaugurated by the Southern Illinois University Press.

Oscar O. Winther, University Professor of History at Indiana University, has just finished serving as Managing Editor of the *Journal of American History* (the official organ of the Organization of American Historians and formerly entitled the *Mississippi Valley Historical Review*). He has been a Guggenheim Memorial Fellow, a Senior Research Associate at the Henry E. Huntington Library, and a Fulbright Lecturer in England. A leading student of the history of transportation beyond the Mississippi, Dr. Winther has published among other books *The Old Oregon Country, The Great Northwest, Via Western Express and Stagecoach,* and, most recently, *The Transportation Frontier.* He is currently interested in the English in the American West.

Jules Zanger, Associate Professor of American Literature at Southern Illinois University, Edwardsville, received his Ph.D. at Washington University in 1954. Among his books are editions of Frederick Marryatt's *Diary in America* (1960) and *The Beauchamp Tragedy* (1963). Critical articles by him have appeared in *The New England Quarterly, Nineteenth Century Fiction, Papers on Language and Literature,* and the *William and Mary Quarterly.* He has been a Newberry Library Research Fellow and has contributed to its quarterly. At the time this volume appears he will be finishing a year as Fulbright Lecturer at the University of São Paulo, Brazil, and he has been invited to stay for a second year.

Index